PUCCINI AMONG FRIENDS

PUCCINI AT HIS PIANO IN MILAN
(1906)

PUCCINI
AMONG FRIENDS

BY

VINCENT SELIGMAN

New York
THE MACMILLAN COMPANY
1938

TO THE MEMORY

OF

SYBIL

ACKNOWLEDGMENTS

I WISH to express my grateful thanks to my friend Antonio Puccini for allowing me to make free use of his father's letters to my mother. My thanks are similarly due to Lady Tosti, Mrs. H. V. Higgins, Mrs. Charles Adams Holder, Signor Carlo Zangarini, Commendatore Giovacchino Forzano, and Signora Fosca Leonardi for other material which has been used in this memoir.

I should also like to thank Baron Frederic d'Erlanger and Mr. Eric Gillett for their kind assistance and advice, and finally my dear friend, Signora Maria Angeli, who has helped to translate certain obscure phrases in Puccini's letters—mostly allusive, or in Tuscan dialect—which would otherwise have eluded me.

CONTENTS

CONTENTS

CONTENTS

PART V : WAR-TIME (1914–1918)

PART VI : LAST YEARS (1919–1924)

LIST OF ILLUSTRATIONS

INTRODUCTION

I

NEARLY all Puccini's biographers remark on his distaste for writing letters. Nevertheless when my mother died nearly two years ago I found amongst her papers more than seven hundred letters from him, all written during the last twenty years of his life. Nor can this have been the full tale ; many, I know, have disappeared, and others have found their way into the hands of ' collectors ' ; for it was my mother's way to give freely to all who asked.

From what remained I have selected, in whole or in part, some three hundred letters to form the basis of this memoir. In no sense of the word can it be considered a formal biography ; for one thing, it lacks the correct proportions, since it deals mainly with those years during which my mother knew him. Still less is it a critical appreciation of his work—a task for which I do not possess the necessary qualifications ; but rather the portrait, largely self-drawn, of a very lovable character, and the record of a singularly beautiful friendship.

The letters of a famous man (unless he happens also to be a man of letters—and not always even then) are not necessarily in themselves interesting. The life of a statesman can often be read more clearly in the public services that he has rendered to his country ; that of a composer, in his music. But these letters of Puccini seem to me to be of more than personal interest for the light that they throw not only on the methods of the musician but also on the character of the man. They possess no great literary distinction, nor are they particularly profound but if, as is sometimes said, the art of good letter-writing consists in the ability of the writer faithfully to reproduce his own individuality, then they must rank high ; for every line bears the imprint of Giacomo Puccini as unmistakably as does a page of his music.

2

What strikes one most, I think, about them is the extraordinary modesty of the writer. On few other men, and on no other musician, had Fortune bestowed her favours so early, so lavishly, and so uninterruptedly ; at the date when these letters begin, although barely forty-six, Puccini was beyond dispute the most popular living composer ; the memory of his solitary reverse—the fiasco of *Madama Butterfly* at Milan—had already been obliterated by that opera's subsequent triumph at Brescia, and thenceforth until the day of his death honours, wealth and fame continued ever-increasingly to be showered upon him. And yet he remained utterly unspoilt—one might almost say untouched—by his prodigious success. I search in vain through all these letters, and nowhere do I find any consciousness of this extraordinary repute in which the world held him. On the contrary, he continually laments his own insufficiency, and although he duly records his successes, it is, one feels, not in any spirit of vainglory, but chiefly in order to give his reader pleasure.[1] On one occasion only— that of his quarrel with Toscanini—the proud assertion is wrung from him that his operas " have sufficiently strong legs to walk by themselves ", and need no assistance from the Gods ; and in one of the very last letters he ever wrote,

[1] Cf. p. 146. " Just this moment had a telegram from Prague about the complete and ' absolutely thundering ' success of *Butterfly*.

" To you, dear friend of mine and of my Butterfly, I send the news the very second I have received it, in the confident knowledge that it will give you pleasure."

only a few months before his death, he asks half jokingly whether he has not as good a right as, say, a coal-merchant to invoke Doctor Voronoff's assistance in prolonging his life ; but it is typical of him that even then he promptly reproaches himself for his presumption.

In his habits, too, and in his manner of living he maintained a corresponding standard of simplicity. He had no taste for luxury or display ; and despite his ever-increasing wealth he continued to live as simply as before, practically his only real extravagance arising from his passion for motoring. Nothing is more pathetic than that rather shamefaced announcement of his purchase of an eight-cylinder Lancia—the "Roll Roice of Italy", as he proudly calls it ; "I came to the conclusion", he excuses himself, "that one only lives one's life once." A year later he was dead.

3

PARIS

December 12th, 1906

"DEAREST DAVID,

"With the approach of the first performance of *Butterfly* I am writing to ask you, as a favour, to allow Signora Sybil to come over to Paris.

The presence of devoted friends is the greatest comfort to us artists of the theatre ; after the reception—enthusiastic, or not so enthusiastic—and the excessive nervousness of a *première*, it does one so much good to find oneself *en petit comité* with the persons one loves. And why don't you take a run over to Paris too? It would give me so much pleasure to see you.

With most friendly regards, etc."

Custom ordains that an operatic composer shall not conceal himself from his public. It is not sufficient that he

INTRODUCTION

should make music for them ; he must also appear before them in person " to receive ", as *The Times* majestically phrases it, " the personal tribute of thanks " [1] —and even, on occasion, the no less personal tribute of hisses. Few of those vast audiences that welcomed Puccini in the various capitals of the world when a new work of his was making its first appearance or an old one was being revived can have realized what agonies he was passing through ; the shy retiring figure that appeared before the curtain or, on rarer and even more excruciating occasions, the speaker who rose to mumble a few words at a banquet in his honour, demanded only to be allowed to go home quietly and enjoy himself in the company of a few chosen friends whom he loved.

So too, just as public demonstrations left him unmoved when they did not actively terrify him, it was not in the roaring stream of his world-wide popularity that he took most pleasure, but in its quiet back-waters. The Genoese book-keeper who, after the *première* in Milan, insisted on branding his child with the memory of a failure by christening it ' Butterfly ' ; the ' curious and interesting ' Englishman who waited patiently outside Covent Garden for twenty-four hours in the heart of winter to hear a performance of the thirty-year-old *Bohème* ; the story, repeated to him, of the far distant inhabitants of the Polar regions who kept themselves warm by humming excerpts from his operas ; the letter (somehow preserved by my mother) of a young English boy, written long before the days of ' fanmails ', beginning : " Wonderful Maestro " ; the young soldier at the hospital in San Remo who suddenly recovered his power of speech whilst he was strumming the third act of *Bohème*—it was from such insignificant but affecting reflections of his popularity that he derived the most

[1] See p. 306.

genuine pleasure. I think that his fondness for me dated from one early morning in his villa at Chiatri when, at the age of ten and with little or no knowledge of Italian, I crept into his study and laboriously wrote out on his blotting-pad my own phonetic conception of *Un bel di vedremo*, of which I was passionately fond. It says much for the diction of that incomparable Butterfly, Emmy Destinn, that my version was instantly recognizable by the composer, who, so far from resenting the desecration of his blotting-paper, was delighted by my youthful tribute to his favourite opera.

4

And yet perhaps the most surprising thing about these letters of his is that, although they are the record of an unparalleled series of triumphs, they are most emphatically not the letters of a happy, nor even of a moderately contented, man. It is not merely the excessive sensibility of an artist inclined unduly to magnify the petty worries and anxieties of everyday life ; even less, I am convinced, is it the conscious exaggeration of a *poseur* seeking to make himself interesting and enlist sympathy by parading imaginary woes ; it is something far deeper and more fundamental, something for which he himself was unable to account—a kind of spiritual melancholy which enveloped his whole being and of which, except during the comparatively rare periods when he was at work, he could never for long rid himself. I do not mean that his letters are uniformly gloomy ; on the contrary, the characteristic note is what might be termed one of ' humorous despair '. Grand Opera and humour (except of the unintentional variety) are not generally associated together ; but Puccini could not only laugh at others ; better still, he could laugh at himself. To me the peculiar fascination of these letters lies in their air of youthful freshness which persists long after the writer has begun to lament the oncoming of old age ; for, like all great men, he never quite grew up.

I have called this memoir *Puccini among Friends* ; and I am proud to think that we were all, in a greater or a lesser degree, numbered amongst those loved ones with whom, in his own words, " it does one so much good to find oneself *en petit comité* ". But it would be idle for me to pretend that this book is not also, in a sense, a memorial to the special friend to whom the letters are addressed : my mother. What she meant to my father and to me I shall not attempt to put into words ; our loss is far too recent and far too grievous. What she meant to Puccini appears in every single one of these letters ; she had indeed a singular gift for friendship, but quite apart from the sympathy and understanding which she extended freely to him as she did to all those who were fortunate enough to win her confidence, she gave him something which perhaps nobody else could have given him—the corrective which her nature brought to his. Puccini was an Italian and a musician, highly strung, temperamental, diffident and easily discouraged, changing quickly from exaltation to despair ; and so it was not only for her vivacity, her beauty and her intelligence that he esteemed her, but for something steadfast and unshakable in her character, on which he knew that he could always rely.

But I need say no more. Just as the only photograph of her in the book is that which can be seen on Puccini's piano in the frontispiece, so too I am content that she herself should be seen indirectly through the eyes of those who loved her.

London,
October 1937

PART I

THE ROAD TO SUCCESS

(1858–1904)

CHAPTER I

' LE VILLI ' AND ' EDGAR '
(1858–1889)

" —OPERA by Giacomo Puccini (Born 1858—)." So ran the rather tactless legend on the Covent Garden programme which, with its unspoken but none the less insistent ' Memento mori ', at once amused and exasperated its subject ; for the ' dash ' indicated only too clearly the compositor's eagerness to restore orderliness to the page by filling in his brackets at the earliest possible moment.

It is a popular tradition that genius, at any rate in its early stages, can only be made to thrive on something approaching a starvation diet. The boy who first saw the light of day in the small Tuscan township of Lucca on December 22nd, 1858, conformed strictly to the requirements of tradition ; for his parents, Michele and Albina Puccini, although of gentle birth, were as poor as any of the mice that dwelt in the church of San Martino, of which Michele was choir-master and organist. Nor were the slender emoluments of this impressive-sounding but poorly endowed post to be his much longer ; for he died when Giacomo was only five, leaving to his widow the care of seven children—and little else besides.

But at least the fatherless boy started with one great advantage : he had not to toil away for years at some uncongenial task before discovering in which direction his talents really lay. Never in his own mind, nor in his mother's, does there seem to have been an instant's doubt as to the profession which he would ultimately adopt ; for he descended in direct succession from a long line of musicians ; if to nothing else, at least the heir to a great tradition. No one was ever prouder of his ancestors than Giacomo ; one of my earliest recollections is of being taken round the quiet church in Lucca, where he showed us their graves—and the grave which was already prepared for him, although he was never destined to occupy it.

The founder of this musical dynasty was his great-great-grandfather (also a Giacomo Puccini), who was born in Lucca in 1712. At an early age he attracted local attention to himself through the composition of some admirable church music, as a reward for which he was appointed Musician to the Most Serene Republic of Lucca, and received the same salary as the gentleman on whom the Republic (presumably in its less serene moments) had conferred the post of Public Executioner. Thereafter the Puccinis succeeded each other from father to son as organists at Lucca and, with one exception, as composers of ecclesiastical music. That exception was Giacomo's grandfather, Domenico, the first, but happily not the last, of the family to show a talent for profane, as opposed to sacred, music. At the age of forty-four he had written five successful operas when, in the year of Napoleon's downfall, he died suddenly ; so suddenly indeed as to arouse the suspicion that he had been poisoned by a rival and less successful composer—certainly a surer and more conclusive method of silencing competition than the effete modern practice of hiring a hostile *claque*.

His son Michele returned to the family tradition ; although perhaps better known as a teacher of music who numbered amongst his pupils the future composer of *Germania*,[1] he had, in addition to other compositions,

---

1 Alberto Franchetti.

written two Masses marked by great beauty and originality. At his death, therefore, the young Giacomo took his seat at the organ at Lucca as naturally and inevitably as the eldest son of a Peer takes his father's seat in the House of Lords. He did not even have to wait until he had attained his majority ; for the good Lucchese were justly proud of their Puccinis ; not only did the municipality honour the dead Michele with a public funeral and make his widow an allowance, but they also reserved his post of choir-master and organist for the five-year-old boy, in the meanwhile giving the office to a relative, who acted as locum tenens until such time as Giacomo should be ready to take over the duties—which he did surprisingly soon, and at a time when most boys of his age are still choristers themselves or blowers of bellows.

We have further cause to be grateful to the Lucchese ; that not one of them ever came forward later, with what Americans call 'hind-sight', to assert that the youthful organist had given early (and, to them, unmistakable) proof of that remarkable talent which was later to make him famous throughout the world. On the contrary, so far from being an infant phenomenon, Giacomo appears to have been a very ordinary boy ; not particularly studious, not particularly brilliant, not particularly devout ; indeed the only memorable incident of his youth seems to have been the occasion when he allowed his extemporization of an organ 'voluntary' to stray—much to the dismay of the congregation—from religious into secular paths.[1] At the age of nineteen he proved that he inherited the traditional Puccini bent by composing a Motet, and but for a chance occurrence it is possible that he might have begun and ended his days as choir-master and organist of San Martino, a composer, in his spare time, of Masses, Motets, and other

[1] See Fraccaroli, p. 11.

ecclesiastical music which would doubtless have confirmed
the Lucchese in their adherence to the reigning musical
dynasty, but at which those outside the ranks of Tuscany
could easily have forborne to cheer ; for, if we may judge
from his one 'religious' opera (*Suor Angelica*) he had no
special aptitude in that direction.[1]

That chance occurrence—or perhaps 'occasion' would
be the better word, since it is clear from what followed that
the call of the music of the theatre must have been in his
blood, inherited from his grandfather—was a performance
of Verdi's *Aïda* in the neighbouring town of Pisa, to which
Giacomo, with barely sufficient money to pay for the
cheapest seat in the theatre, gaily sallied forth on foot.
He walked, he listened—and he was conquered. Never till
the end of his days could he forget that wonderful night ;
the glamour of the theatre and the enchantment of the
music together proved irresistible, and thenceforth it was
apparent to one person at least that the family tradition
was at an end, and that the Lucchese would have to look
out for another organist.

And so, at the age of twenty-two, partly through the
self-sacrifice of his mother, partly through the generosity of
Queen Margherita, who had been prevailed upon to take
an interest in the boy, and partly through the financial
assistance of a rich uncle (which 'assistance' later became
mysteriously transformed into a loan to be discharged with
difficulty and compound interest by the not particularly
affluent composer of *Le Villi* and *Edgar*), Giacomo was
enabled to find his way to the Conservatorio of Milan—
the Mecca of all Italian musicians.

The town to which the rest of the world are wont to

---

[1] " The atmosphere of the cloisters ", remarks Julius Korngold, '' is
not particularly suited to our good Maestro, whose talent lies rather in
expressing worldly feelings " (*Die Romanische Oper der Gegenwart*, p. 93).

refer contemptuously and insultingly as ' the Manchester
of Italy ' must have loomed very large in the eyes of the
young man who now saw it for the first time, and whose
experience and training had hitherto been confined to the
Institute of Lucca ; nor, as his letters to my mother show,
was he ever quite able to shake off his first impressions.
To him it was not merely a big, rather drab industrial town
in the north of Italy, famous for its Duomo and its
Galleries ; it also contained, or was contained by, La Scala
Theatre, which was—and remained ever after, even when
his horizon had widened and he had become familiar with
the Metropolitan, the Opéra, Covent Garden and all the
other great Opera Houses of the world—the one, indeed
the only, centre of the operatic world. Like Verdi before
him, he never really liked Milan ; ' odious ', ' wearisome ',
' soul-destroying ', ' horrible ' are some of the adjectives
which he heaps upon it ; yet it was here that he spent a
large part of his life, returning year after year to his flat in
the Via Verdi, with increasing reluctance, but under the
compulsion of some mysterious necessity. He was, I
think, more than a little afraid of it ; but he attached an
immense—one might say an altogether disproportionate—
importance to the good opinion of its inhabitants. That is
why the reception given by the Milanese to the first performance of *Butterfly* in 1904 remained the most horrible
memory of his life—and why, after the banquet given to
him at Cova's on the occasion of the thirtieth anniversary
of *Manon Lescaut* in 1923, he was able to write with the
nearest approach to complacency that can be found in all
his letters : " At last Milan has honoured me ".[1]
 It followed naturally that as La Scala was the centre of
the operatic world and as the Milanese were the best—
though not always the kindest—judges of operatic music,

[1] See p. 345.

1 city - Milan   1 opera house - La S
and 1 newspaper - Corriere della
14   THE ROAD TO SUCCESS   P.
ONLY THESE MATTERED

so too there was only one newspaper whose opinion matte
in the least : the *Corriere della Sera.* Nothing is more astonis,
ing in his letters than the enormous importance he attached
to the verdict of Milan's leading—but essentially provincial
—journal ; he who turned impatiently aside from the
columns of praise which appeared in the foreign Press,
rarely bothering to read them or to listen while they were
being translated, was prepared to pull strings, to demean
himself, to go to almost any lengths, in order to win a
mention, however small and insignificant, in the pages of
the *Corriere.* To my mother he wrote regularly every
summer, urging her to use her influence with succeeding
London correspondents of the paper in order to obtain an
article on the Opera Season which should include, if not a
' write-up ', at least a bare mention of the increasing extent
to which the Covent Garden Opera Syndicate relied on his
operas to fill their repertoire and—it might fairly be added
—their theatre. Signor Adami touchingly relates how,
towards the end, the composer having expressed a desire
that some mention of his world-wide popularity should be
made, he had sought to give him this small satisfaction by
arranging a luncheon with Sacchi of the *Corriere.* The
luncheon took place, and although the Master's shyness
nearly prevented him from putting forward his request, the
article was duly written—only to be curtly rejected by the
editor on the grounds that some ' event ' or ' occasion '
was necessary to justify its publication. A few months later
that ' event ' occurred ; but Puccini was never destined to
read the article which would have given him so much
pleasure ; for the ' event ' was his own death.[1]

feature in Corriere finally came because g Puccini died

Not that Milan was unkind to him at first. Those three
years during which he studied at the Conservatorio were,
on the whole, happy ones. It is true that, as his letters to

[1] Adami's *Puccini,* p. 187.

his mother show, he suffered a certain amount of real hardship ; the bounty of the Queen, supplemented by his rich relative's 'assistance', were not on a scale to permit of riotous living, and, if he never actually starved in the approved manner of budding genius, it is certain that he frequently went to bed hungry. But he was young, and his privations and anxieties do not appear to have weighed upon him unduly ; and although he was not particularly studious, those years in Milan were to lead indirectly to his first outstanding success ; for the echoes of his happy-go-lucky student days can be heard unmistakably in those joyously fresh passages in *Bohème* which are the nearest that his music ever came to autobiography.

He had the singular good fortune, too, to study under Ponchielli, from whose opera *La Gioconda*, now rarely heard, his early work far more clearly derives than from Verdi. But curiously enough it was from a symphonic *Capriccio* which he wrote as a musical essay for his final examinations at the Conservatorio that he first attracted the attention of the musical world. So great an impression did it create at its first hearing that it was afterwards repeated at a concert given by the orchestra of La Scala ; and the fulsome praise bestowed upon it by the musical critics was in marked contrast with the coldness with which they subsequently reviewed those operas which captured the whole world.

Meanwhile Ponchielli had more accurately discerned the true bent of his young pupil's talent. A prize for a one-act opera having been offered by Sonsogno, the publisher, it was he who prevailed upon his friend Ferdinando Fontana to write a libretto for Puccini. The result was *Le Villi*—which duly conformed to tradition by not even securing an honourable mention. In fairness to the judges, however, it must be admitted that the deplorable script, which was subsequently to be the despair of Puccini's copyists,[1] made the work difficult, if not impossible, to decipher; after all, they were judges, not hieroglyphists. In any case neither the teacher nor the composer nor the librettist despaired; the hat was handed round the circle of Bohemian friends, and eventually the sum of £17 was collected—sufficient to pay for the printing of the score and for its performance in public.

And so, on May 31st, 1884, at the Teatro del Verme in Milan, the first Puccini opera made its bow—and was given a rapturous reception. It was the first (and perhaps the sweetest) of his many triumphs. Only one thing—or one person—was lacking to complete his happiness; his mother had been taken seriously ill and was unable to be present. To her he sent, regardless of expense, his first telegram: "Tumultuous success, all hopes exceeded, eighteen curtain-calls, first finale encored three times." A few weeks later Albina Puccini died in her son's arms, happy in the knowledge that a brilliant future was now assured for him.

But for Giacomo the period that followed was one of the blackest of his life. "I think of her continually", he writes to his eldest sister, "and last night I also dreamed of her. So to-day I am even sadder than usual. Whatever triumphs art may bring me, I shall never be very happy without my darling mother. Be comforted as much as you can and take courage—the courage which so far I have not been able to find myself."[2]

But Fortune chose this very moment to smile on him. The opera that had failed to win the Sonsogno prize had attracted the attention of Sonsogno's yet more powerful rival, Signor Giulio Ricordi, the friend and publisher of

[1] Specht (p. 35) points out amusingly how, whenever a page of music was in even a worse mess than usual, Puccini would throw in a *Scusi!* by way of apology to the wretched man who had to decipher it.
[2] See *Letters*, p. 31.

Publishing! like relation w/ publisher

father/son

Verdi. Not only did he print *Le Villi* free of cost, but he promptly secured its rights and commissioned the young composer to write another opera, advancing him in the meantime a monthly allowance which, if not princely, was quite sufficient to relieve his more pressing necessities. Thus began a relationship which far more closely resembled that of father and son than the more prosaic one of publisher and musician, and which was to continue, unbroken and unclouded, until the elder man's death in 1912.

Giulio Ricordi was one of the most remarkable, and one of the most versatile, men of his age; for he was a musician, a business man, a philanthropist and a diplomat all rolled into one. The musician in him (whose solitary recorded error in judgment was on the occasion when Puccini submitted to him with a warm recommendation a work by his friend Mascagni entitled *Cavalleria Rusticana*—only to provoke the infelicitous verdict: "I don't *believe* in the opera") was quick to recognize the merits of *Le Villi*; the philanthropist (or was it the business man?) clung steadfastly to his protégé even after the palpable failure of his next opera; and the diplomat not only planned the happy association between Puccini and his two most successful librettists, Illica and Giacosa, but later successfully prevented its disruption on at least a dozen different occasions. But if the young musician had gained a father, Signor Giulio had gained not only a son, but a gold-mine, whose riches were only determinable by the laws of copyright. Nor could any discovery have been more timely; for Puccini's first success, *Manon Lescaut*, appeared in the same year as Verdi's last opera, *Falstaff*. Happy indeed the prospector who can strike a new vein at the very moment when the old one has petered out!

At first, however, the new discovery showed little promise of yielding any very startling results. For the task of writing the book of the new opera was, from a mistaken sense of gratitude, entrusted to the author of *Le Villi* ; and whatever his merits as a man or his services as a friend, of Fontana the librettist there can be no two opinions. It is true that he afforded Puccini his first opportunity of writing music for the theatre, and for this we should be duly grateful ; but as operatic books go—not a particularly high standard, by the way—*Le Villi*, with its legendary absurdities, its sirens and its witch-dancers, was about as bad as a libretto could be ; it says much for the discernment of the Milanese public that they could perceive the glimmer of genius which was able to pierce through, and even illumine, the monstrous darkness in which it was enveloped.

But this preposterous fable of the Willis (one is tempted to call them the Willies) had at least the merit of being short. With his next attempt, *Edgar*—an opera in three acts, each worse than the one before—Fontana proved that hitherto he had not really been trying ; like the Italian General who was defeated by the Austrians, he could claim that he had achieved the impossible and had actually outdone himself. To anyone who wants a good laugh I can unhesitatingly recommend the libretto ; for it must surely hold the record in the long and richly humorous annals of operatic absurdity.

With such material Puccini could do little or nothing. For five whole years he struggled on despairingly ; he could not go back because of his contract with Ricordi's ; he could only go forward with extreme difficulty because of the mass of nonsensical encumbrances in his path. It was, I believe, the only time in his life when he found no joy, nor even solace, in composition. To make matters worse, his own infallible instinct for the theatre remained untapped, perhaps even unsuspected ; for the librettist clung tenaci-

every line of his script, defending it word by word,
though the slightest alteration might bring the
whole majestic edifice toppling to the ground—a consum-
mation which, however devoutly to be wished, was never
achieved.

It was, one suspects, mainly out of deference to the
memory of *Le Villi* that *Edgar* was not hissed off the stage
when it made its first appearance before the critical La
Scala audience on April 21st, 1889. The libretto was
rightly condemned on all sides; even Ricordi in his
Journal had to admit that the situations were 'daring'
and that the third act especially was 'dangerous'.[1]
But although a few kind words and a certain sympathy
were reserved for the composer, *Edgar* never enjoyed any considerable success in Italy, and soon disappeared altogether
from the boards. In 1905 it suffered a brief resurrection at
Buenos Aires in a slightly revised form; but the indifference
of the Argentines, despite the presence of the composer,
administered the death-blow—and since then it has been
allowed to sink into merciful and well-deserved oblivion.

It is noteworthy that the composer himself, who, like
a good father, felt a special tenderness for his less fortunate
children, and was later to fight stubbornly against the
'ostracism' of his beloved nun, Suor Angelica, and the
universal indifference of managers to the merits of his
Rondine, never once attempted to defend *Edgar*. If I were
not familiar with his hand-writing, I should be inclined to
suspect that the humorous annotations to the score which
he gave my mother had been written by one of his bitterest
critics. The title itself has been defaced by additions into:

"E   Dio ti Gu   A   Rdi da quest' opera!"
("And may God preserve you from this opera!")

---

[1] See *Letters*, p. 45.

Of the end of the second act he declares : " This ' finale ' is the most horrible thing that has ever been written." In the third act, Edgar, for no conceivable reason, elects to return from the wars disguised as a monk accompanying his own catafalque, on which reposes (apparently) a knight in armour ; but when, to the manifest disappointment of his fellow-soldiers, the knight in armour is found to include no knight, and an explanation seems obviously called for, Edgar dramatically lowers his cowl and cries : " Yes, for Edgar lives ! " Puccini's laconic annotation—*Mensogna !* (" It's a lie ! ") shows that he failed to share his hero's belief in his immortality. Only two passages in the whole opera are marked " this is good " ; Fidelia's *Addio mio dolce amor* and her lament beginning *Nel villagio d' Edgar* ; and as the drama moves forward to its unnecessarily bloody climax and the crowd are reduced to repeated and rather naïve exclamations of the word " Horror ! " Puccini is content to add : " How right they are ! " And there can be little doubt that Puccini, too, was right.

Puccini's notes on a score of Edgar given to a friend. Hilarious.

CHAPTER TWO

' MANON LESCAUT '
(1890–1893)

THE failure of *Edgar* was perhaps necessary to convince
Puccini—and, doubtless, Signor Giulio Ricordi too, now
hard-pressed by his shareholders, who failed to share their
chairman's confidence in his latest ' find ', and had some
pertinent comments to make on the folly of throwing good
money after bad—of one undoubted truth : that, whether
or not in these days of scientific substitutes it is possible to
make bricks without straw, it is quite impossible to make
an opera without a libretto. If that rich ore, which both
confidently believed to exist beneath the surface, was to be
successfully extracted, the elimination of Fontana was an
indispensable preliminary, and a subject had to be found
to which the composer could give himself whole-heartedly.

But here fortunately there was no difficulty ; for Puccini
had lately discovered the Abbé Prévost's famous novel, and
had found himself irresistibly attracted by its heroine. It is
true that neither in the literal nor the operatic sense of the
word could the irresponsible, luxury-loving Manon be
described as a *virgo intacta* ; Massenet's successful opera had
already been in existence for seven years. Nevertheless
Puccini, who was fascinated by the queer mixture of fri-
volity and passion in her character, decided, not for the only
time in his career, that too much importance could be
attached to originality ; the knowledge that he had not been
the first to enjoy Manon's favours not only acted as an

incentive but created an encouraging precedent ; it proved
that the thing could be done, and done successfully—
which certainly could not have been said of his first two
subjects.

He had at last found a central figure of flesh and blood
in whom he could believe. But although, or perhaps because,
Prévost's novel was so rich in romance, its very richness
proved something of an embarrassment ; for before it could
be transferred to the new medium of the stage, it was not
only necessary to adapt but also to select—and it was here
that the difficulties began. Released from the fontanesque
strait-jacket, the composer showed a turn for movement
and an agility which proved—to say the least—disconcert-
ing to his collaborators. He at once made it clear that he
had ideas of his own ; and, seeing that selecting was the
order of the day, he began by placing himself at the head
of the Selection Committee. Thus began the first of those
many tussles between composer and librettists which were
to enliven—and embitter—the remaining years of his life.
For he was always finding himself back in the unhappy
position of a gourmet who knows precisely how he wishes
his meal prepared, and who resolutely refuses to sit down
to table unless, and until, it is exactly to his liking. His
chefs might perhaps have overlooked his fastidiousness, had
it not been for another and even more glaring defect in
their master—that he appeared to know considerably more
about the culinary art than they. Later I shall give some
examples of how his uncanny sense of the theatre enabled
him to avoid the absurdities of which even the best of his
librettists were sometimes guilty. His supreme tragedy was
that, despite his infallible good taste, he was unable to cook
for himself ; how much valuable time would have been
saved, how much misery avoided, if only, like Wagner, he
had been able to write his own librettos !

[handwritten marginal note: now involved in selecting a Librettist + had "ideas" but unable to write his own librettos]

At least he had a hand in the making of Manon Lescaut. The title-page is unique amongst Puccini scores in that it acknowledges no authorship, and this for a very good reason : the Selection Committee had grown so large that there would not have been room to include them all on one page. The original draft was sketched out by Marco Praga with the assistance of the poet, Domenico Oliva, and was, at first, approved by Puccini ; but later, alterations, suggestions, deletions and additions—many of them of a radical nature—were made by Illica, Giacosa, Giulio Ricordi, and the composer himself—not to mention half a dozen other friends, including Tosti. With so many aspirants to the honour, the prize, by general consent, went finally unawarded, and the Abbé Prévost remained officially the only begetter of a work which he would certainly have failed to recognize, had he lived to read it. It is related of that unfortunate priest that he suffered the gruesome fate of being dissected whilst he was still alive, which makes it all the more ironical that in death he should have been no less divided—by the librettists.

As might have been expected, the book of the opera bears unmistakable evidence of its conglomerate parentage ; except for the first act, which follows Massenet's closely, the Italian is in every respect inferior to the French version. Nevertheless Manon Lescaut was not only the first of Puccini's great successes ; it was, in the opinion of many good judges, the best opera that he ever wrote. Some critics find the fourth act, with Manon's death from thirst and fever outside New Orleans, a bad anticlimax after the dramatic scene of her deportation at Havre ; just as Napoleon would have done better to perish with the Old Guard at Waterloo instead of lingering on for five years at St. Helena, so Manon too timed her exit badly—she died, in fact, exactly one act too late. Doctor Neisser, on

the other hand, ascribes the comparative unpopularity of
the last act to Italian impatience with what in Germany are
appreciatively called 'heavenly lengths'.[1] However that
may be, the youthful freshness of the music, its dainty
grace, and the lovely stream of melody which pours forth
with a generous profusion never again equalled by the
composer, combine to make the opera a work of irresistible
charm. I know that Puccini himself regarded it with special
tenderness ; long after he had grown bored to tears by the
established favourites—his *Bohèmes* and *Tosche*, as he contemptuously calls them—a revival of his earliest success
still gave him genuine pleasure, and it was only fitting that
its thirtieth anniversary should have been selected as the
occasion for Milan to honour him.

His partiality for Manon is not difficult to explain ; she
was his first love, and her tragic story, in the moulding of
which he himself had had a part, stirred him deeply.
" Only once in his life ", says a hostile critic,[2] " did Puccini
arrange his own text, and in this one case he was at last
overcome by genuine feeling. He fell in love with his own
Manon, so that, instead of being a theatrical figure, she
became part of his own life." Although it contains an
element of truth, this verdict is rather misleading ; for he
fell in love with every one of his heroines in turn ; the tears
which he shed at the death of Mimi were just as genuine
as the tears which Dickens shed for Little Nell or Paul
Dombey ; for the English novelist and the Italian musician
were alike in being unable to create unless, and until, they
could bring themselves to believe with passionate sincerity
in their creations.

Manon Lescaut was produced at the Teatro Regio, Turin,
on February 1st, 1893. Its success was immediate and
unqualified ; for the last time the voice of the

---

[1] Neisser, p. 19.   [2] Weissmann, p.

Alla Signora Sybil Seligman
con forte amicizia
4 I 05.   Tito Ricordi

"THAT QUEER CAPRICIOUS FELLOW, *SAVOIA*"
TITO RICORDI

the voice of the critics were united in praise. It was, as Puccini was fond of declaring, the only opera which brought no bitterness with it ; it was also, thanks largely to the initiative of the youthful Tito Ricordi, the first of his works to travel beyond the frontiers of Italy. We shall hear a great deal more later about *Savoia*—by which princely title Signor Giulio's son is generally referred to in the letters ; but whatever differences subsequently arose between these two men so utterly dissimilar in character and in temperament, the composer always acknowledged generously the important part which the other had played in extending his firm's activities abroad, and thereby in contributing to the world-wide popularity which the name of Puccini was to enjoy. On this occasion it was Tito, already on the look-out for foreign markets, who prevailed upon Sir Augustus Harris to present *Manon Lescaut* at Covent Garden only a year after its *première* in Turin. It received a cordial welcome both from the Press and the public, and the composer, who was visiting London for the first time, was warmly cheered when he appeared before the curtain. Those who are unaware that the collected works of Mr. Bernard Shaw include three fat volumes of musical criticism may be interested to know that the latter, with his deplorable habit of being right on any number of subjects of which one might confidently expect him to be ignorant, was almost alone in preferring *Manon Lescaut* to those already firmly established and infinitely more popular ' twins ', *Pagliacci* and *Cavalleria Rusticana*. After dilating at length on the merits of the new opera, he concludes : " On that and other accounts, Puccini looks to me more like the heir of Verdi than any of his rivals ".[1] To us to-day who can contrast Puccini's subsequent record of almost unbroken success with the repeated failure both of Leoncavallo and

[1] *Music in London* (vol. iii, p. 232).

marginalia (left margin): " The only opera which brought no bitterness with it."

marginalia (bottom left): "... heir of Verdi ..."

Mascagni to add to their original reputation, this may seem something of a truism ; in 1894, the year in which it was written, it was a bold—one might say a characteristically Shavian—prophecy.

The British public, at any rate—as so often happened— failed at the time to share Mr. Shaw's view, though they were later to endorse it with a great show of originality. The opera was given only one more performance that Season, and then (together with its author) was completely lost sight of until some years later when the astounding success of *Bohème* brought the existence of the earlier work back to the mind of some musical antiquarian, and thence back to the stage of Covent Garden. In the meantime, however, it had slowly but successfully made its way all over the Continent and had even crossed the Atlantic—although it was not until 1907 that the audience of the Metropolitan were given their first opportunity of hearing it.

I do not think that *Manon Lescaut* ever quite attained the same phenomenal popularity as the three operas that followed it ; but its success was sufficient to prove that there was plenty of room in the operatic world for two Manons. Even in France, despite that spirit of Chauvinism so much deplored by Caruso,[1] which made its inhabitants peculiarly reluctant to import from abroad an article which could already be enjoyed in the ' home-made ' variety, the Italian girl was to become a dangerous rival to her French elder sister. Her first appearance, indeed, was so successful that Massenet's publisher was seen to leave the theatre at the end of the first act.[2] Even publishers have their feelings.

Another consequence of this first success was that Puccini's financial embarrassments were at last at an end ; henceforth, metaphorically no less than in the ledger-books

[1] See p. 191.   [2] *Letters*, p. 79.

of Ricordi's, it is the publisher who is—and becomes ever-increasingly—in debit to the composer. I do not of course mean that he suddenly found himself rich overnight ; the large fortune which he left at his death represented the gradual accumulation of the next thirty years. Moreover, with the increase in wealth, came also an increase in responsibilities ; for it was at about this time that Elvira Bonturi, with her tiny little daughter, Fosca, finally decided to leave her husband, and throw in her lot with the man she loved and to whom she was shortly to bear a son. Thenceforth Giacomo and Elvira became, in everything but name, man and wife, although it was not until many years later, on the death of her husband, that it was possible to legitimize their union.

With the joys and cares of a wife and family, came also the joys and cares of a home—or homes. A lucky chance directed the young couple's footsteps to Torre del Lago, not far from their native town of Lucca ; here, in this little village which he came to prefer to all the great cities of the world, Giacomo found, in his own words, " Supreme delight, Paradise, Eden, the Empyrean, ' turris eburnea ', ' vas spirituale ', a kingdom . . . inhabitants, a hundred and twenty ; houses, twelve".[1] Although he was naturally inclined to be restless and, as his letters show, never cared to remain long in the same place ; although, like Horace, he loved the thought of the country when he was in town, and sighed for urban delights when he was rusticating ; like Horace, he too had his Sabine farm, and " the one corner of the earth that smiled upon him above all others " was Torre del Lago. At first he rented a little house there ; but later he built himself a simple but picturesque one-storied villa, stretching along the edge of the lake of Massaciucoli, where he could freely—and sometimes

In margin: Entre Elvira Bonturi

In margin: Torre del Lago

---

[1] Fraccaroli, p. 191.

feloniously[1]—indulge his passion for shooting wild-fowl. It was here, in this refuge from the noisy outside world, that he spent the happiest years of his life and that he wrote his best music; it is here that he now lies, surrounded by all those mementos of his past life which his son Tonio, with tender dutifulness, has brought together to form a perfect setting for his father's last resting-place.

There were to be many other Puccini residences, built or acquired in a moment of enthusiasm. In addition to his comfortable flat in Milan, to which he returned every winter, there was his villa at Abetone, a little mountain-side village on the lower slopes of Monte Cimone, the highest peak in the Northern Apennines. Here, as boys, my brother and I spent two very happy summers with our parents at the neighbouring hotel, only a few hundred yards distant from the Puccini villa. The hotel itself scarcely lived up to its impressive name, which suggested, as far as I can remember, not only the Grand but the Palatial, and the 'vast balcony' which our rooms boasted—or rather, of which the proprietor boasted—consisted of a narrow and extremely perilous ledge which, to our great disappointment, we were never allowed to use; but there was the magnificent view of the mountains, the lovely woods of Boscolungo, carpeted with wild strawberries of which we took uncounted toll—and a performing bear which we fed with the surplus of our depredations. There were also the rather more dubious joys of touring the neighbourhood in Puccini's car; the trouble was that one never quite knew when—and how—one would get back. In those days motoring was more or less in its infancy, and a special element of danger, or uncertainty, attached to

[1] See *Giacomo Puccini* by his friends Marotti and Pagni, which contains in chapter 2 an amusing account of how he was arrested for 'poaching'—and how he was triumphantly acquitted.

driving in the mountains ; moreover, the very appearance of the car, in spite of the fact that it was the latest 1904 model, would have genuinely shocked Harry Tate. Puccini had been one of the pioneers of motoring in Italy, and it was a pastime of which he never wearied : I do not know exactly how many cars he owned at one time or another in between the museum-piece in which we explored the Apennines and the eight-cylinder limousine Lancia purchased only a few months before his death ; but if photographs of them all have been preserved, they would form an interesting commentary on the progress of the mechanically propelled vehicle. In those days pride only too often came before a fall, or, at the very least, a stoppage ; we would sally forth triumphantly, but sooner or later the first signs would become apparent of some mysterious engine trouble—destined to remain a mystery both to Puccini and his chauffeur ; and when at last, with one indignant, expiring grunt, the car came to a standstill by the roadside, his humiliation and despair knew no bounds. It was, I genuinely believe, the repeated indignity of those return journeys over the steep mountain passes in a one-horse carriage, or even a farmer's cart, which made him begin to dislike Abetone, and finally led to his rejoicing over the sale of the villa.

Then there was the villa at Chiatri, perched thirteen hundred feet up on the mountainside above Torre del Lago. His idea had been to retire there in the summer when the heat at Torre del Lago became intolerable ; but as late as 1906, many years after he had bought it, he was able to describe it as " the famous villa in which I have never, or hardly ever, lived ".[1] It commanded a magnificent view of the surrounding country, but it was, as he admitted himself, rather a wild spot ; the road ended some way short

[1] See p. 82.

of the villa, and the last part of the journey, as far as I can remember, had to be accomplished on foot. Nevertheless I have particularly tender memories of Chiatri ; for my mother accepted his invitation, one summer, to stay there, and it was here that the scene of the desecration of his blotting-paper took place, thus forging the first link in our friendship.

His love of the inaccessible—or the only just accessible —also led to the acquisition of the Torre della Tagliata in the Maremma, with its excellent shooting but impossible and impassable roads. But sooner or later in every case his passion waned in the face of practical difficulties, just as his enthusiasm for a new libretto had a way of dying down as quickly and as inexplicably as it had arisen ; Abetone became 'deadly boring', and the mountain air suddenly and surprisingly failed to agree with him ; Chiatri became uninhabitable because of the difficulty in getting letters and telegrams quickly enough ; and the Torre della Tagliata had to be sold owing to the insurmountable obstacles in the way of obtaining food supplies and other necessities. Only to Torre del Lago did he remain consistently faithful—though, alas ! in the end Torre del Lago did not remain faithful to him. But that was far away in the distant future, and belongs to a later part of the story ; he was to enjoy his Paradise for more than a quarter of a century before he was at last driven out by the encroachments of modern Civilization.

Many homes.

Torre del Lago - he remained faithful to.

TO THE YOUTHFUL DEFILER OF HIS BLOTTING-PAD

CHAPTER THREE

' LA BOHÈME '
(1894–1896)

THERE never was a more elusive country than Bohemia. Those rather muddle-headed gentlemen who evolved the late (and every day becoming later) Treaty of Versailles, decided that it was in Czecho-Slovakia ; the English intelligentzia unhesitatingly locate it in Bloomsbury, or Chelsea, or wherever else their particular coterie happens at the time to be congregated ; Shakespeare, to the dismay of cartographers, endowed it with a sea-coast : Henri Murger (as was only to be expected of a Frenchman) placed it in Paris—and Puccini (not to mention Leoncavallo) found it in Milan. From all of which one is driven to conclude that Bohemia exists in no particular country, but only in the hearts of young men and elderly statesmen.

It is true that the opera on which Puccini's claim to immortality most securely rests is avowedly based on Murger's *Vie de Bohème* ; that the characters, in spite of their Italianized names, are supposed to be French, and that the action takes place in Paris ; but just as Bizet composed his immortal *Carmen* without ever having taken the trouble to cross the Pyrenees, so Puccini, who was later to devote so much time to acquiring the right ' local colour ', wrote *La Bohème* before he had crossed the Alps. Nor was the journey necessary ; for the inspiration, if not the story, is derived first-hand from his days as a student at the Conservatorio in Milan.

Not to mention Leoncavallo. I have always had a weakness for the story of the man who, stopped in the street by a stranger asking his way, replied with great difficulty, " Th-th-there are s-s-six m-m-million inhabitants of L-L-London—so w-w-why the h-h-hell did you p-p-pick on me ? " Similarly, when one contrasts the very limited number of operatic composers with literature's boundless wealth of novels, poems, plays, short stories and legends on which (together with their own imagination) they are free to draw, one is led to enquire why they should have such a singular way of ' picking on ' the one subject which has just been selected by a rival composer. This Pirandellian theme of ' Two composers in search of the same libretto ' is one that is constantly recurring in Puccini's career ; we have already noted the two *Manons*, and later, as we shall see, the duplication of *Tosca* was only avoided by some rather questionable sleight-of-hand on the part of Giulio Ricordi ; later still, no less than four ' little wooden shoes ' seemed likely at one time to emerge from the lasts of rival cobblers ; and in the meanwhile there were—and although few people are probably aware of it, there are still—the two *Bohèmes*.

There was no question of bad faith on Puccini's part, although later there was to be bad blood on the part of Leoncavallo. Without ever being intimate friends, the two musicians had known each other a long time ; and when Puccini was still at work on *Manon Lescaut*, the composer of *Pagliacci*, who (lucky man !) was not only self-sufficient in the matter of operatic texts but often possessed an exportable surplus, had submitted to the other a script based on Murger's romance, which he did not propose to set to music himself. Puccini, who had scarcely taken the trouble to glance through it, declined it with thanks ; one surmises that, on the principle of *Timeo Leoncavallos et dona ferentes*, it may have occurred to him that a gift which was of such little use to the donor would be of little more use to him.[1] When, therefore, some years later, the two men happened to be comparing notes at a café in Milan, and Puccini innocently mentioned that he had at last found a perfect subject in a libretto which Illica and Giacosa were adapting from the *Vie de Bohème*, he was astonished to see the portly Leoncavallo bounce up from his chair, as though he had been stung by a scorpion. " But you *can't* do it ! " ejaculated the latter. " It was my idea, and, what is more, I'm setting it to music myself." " Very well ", replied Puccini composedly, " then there will be two *Bohèmes* instead of one " ; and on the following day the bewildered Milanese public, having been apprised by the morning edition of the *Secolo* that Maestro Leoncavallo was at present at work on an opera entitled *La Bohème*, rubbed their eyes with astonishment when they read in the midday edition of the *Corriere* that Maestro Puccini was engaged on a precisely similar task.[2] Leoncavallo was first in the field ; but the very modest success of his work was soon completely eclipsed by his rival's triumph, and although two *Bohèmes* were born, only one survived.

Bohème is the first of the three operas on the title-page of which the names of Illica and Giacosa appear together with that of the composer. The combination, which had been brought about by Giulio Ricordi, was an ideal one ; at last Sullivan had been provided with his two Gilberts. Nevertheless the work of collaboration did not, at first, progress smoothly ; on innumerable occasions it would have broken down altogether, but for the timely intervention of the fourth, but by no means silent or ' sleeping ',

[1] Specht, p. 130.
[2] Fraccaroli (pp. 83-4) gives a most amusing account of the famous meeting between the two composers.

partner, whose infinite tact and patience were to be severely
taxed during the coming years. Fortunately Signor Giulio
had been trained in a good school of diplomacy ; the man
who had succeeded in reconciling that irascible old gentleman, Verdi, with the brilliant but hated Boito, and to
whom in consequence, equally with Shakespeare, we are
indebted for the glorious Indian summer of *Otello* and
Falstaff, found it a relatively simple matter to arbitrate
between these three rather difficult, but eminently lovable,
young men. Yet it seems a trifle unfair that his name
should only appear in his professional capacity as Publisher
on the title-pages of the operas to which he contributed so
much.

For ' difficult ' these young men certainly were. Illica,
despite his wonderful powers of improvisation, was no less
impetuous in temper than in thought ; having flung out
idea after idea, he would fling himself out of the room in a
rage ; Giacosa, although more even-tempered and methodi-
cal, was given to poetic moods of extreme despondency
when he would begin to doubt, not indeed the ability of
those with whom he was called upon to work, but his own
capacity to carry out what was required of him—with the
result that both librettists, either from excess, or lack, of
temper, were continually threatening to throw in their
hands. Meanwhile Puccini remained quite inexorable in his
demands ; he knew exactly what he wanted, and he was
determined to get it at no matter what cost in time and
trouble to his weary librettists. " I hope that Illica will
cool down ", he writes on one occasion to Giulio Ricordi,[1]
" and that we shall get to work. But I too want to have my
say when the occasion arises "—perhaps the most perfect
example extant of that figure of speech known to school-
boys as ' litotes or meiosis ' It is impossible not to admire

(although it must have been excessively irritating to his fellow-workers) the bland and imperturbable manner in which he sets out to submit the latest version of the last act to the usual minute and relentless scrutiny—just as though it were a rough draft, and had not already been completely rewritten from beginning to end no less than four times. But at least, if he did not spare others, he did not spare himself either ; for there never was a more conscientious artist.

At length his perseverance was rewarded, and he had succeeded in extracting (though by no means painlessly) a really well-balanced libretto from his collaborators, and one to which he could give himself whole-heartedly. " And now ", as he was to write nearly thirty years later of *Turandot*, " the libretto is not only complete, but very beautiful. It is up to me to write the music ! "[1] It had taken two years to prepare the libretto ; eight months later the opera was finished.

The *première* was given, under Toscanini's bâton, on February 1st, 1896, at the Teatro Regio in Turin ; it was the third anniversary of *Manon's* début at the same theatre. But on this occasion Turin was more grudging of its approval ; the reception on the opening night was little more than cordial, and the Press were almost unanimously hostile. It is surely a waste of time to go on belabouring, as most of Puccini's biographers delight in doing, the ineffable fatuity of the musical critics ; but what does really appear surprising in retrospect is the extreme slowness with which the public themselves grew aware of the merits of the new opera. Here is no Grand Opera, no epic tale, here are no subtleties that require constant hearing before they can be properly appreciated ; but a simple, unaffected tale of everyday life and death ; what one might call the

[1] See p. 347.

sublimation of those ' little things ' which were so dear to
the heart of the composer, and in which his true strength
lay. Surely, one would have thought, of all his operas
Bohème, with its high spirits, its air of youthful gallantry,
its mixture of laughter and tears, should, by the very simplicity of its approach and of its idiom, be the quickest to
find its way into the hearts of its listeners.

And yet the very reverse was the case ; at each repetition in Turin it was noticeable that the reception grew
warmer and the applause louder ; but it was not until some
months later at Palermo, after having in the meanwhile
been received with cold indifference by the Romans, that
the opera can at last be said to have come into its own. The
evening had begun inauspiciously enough ; not only was it
the thirteenth of the month, but it was a Friday ; and the
conductor, Leopoldo Mugnone, who had a superstitious
dread of *iettatura* (the evil eye), hesitated to go on—a
catastrophe, he predicted, was bound to occur. Puccini
was in reality no less superstitious—his letters to my mother
abound with the sign of the first and fourth finger raised to
ward off ' accidents '—but on this occasion he was for once
determined to show a brave front against the powers of
evil, and was feverishly urging the conductor to take his
place, when it was discovered that the first of the predicted
disasters had already occurred : the oboist, on whom much
depended, was absent from his oboe. Eventually the delin-
quent appeared, Mugnone reluctantly raised his bâton, and
the curtain went up, an hour late, to the accompaniment of
murmurings from an impatient audience. . . . A few hours
later one of the most extraordinary scenes ever witnessed
even on the exuberant stage of Italy was being enacted ;
such had been the delirium of the audience that they flatly
refused to leave the theatre until they had had their final
encore, and eventually Mugnone gathered together a hand-

ful of the orchestra (for the remainder, doubtless including
the oboist, had long ago retired to their beds) and once
again raised his bâton whilst on the stage a Mimi in
ordinary clothes expired afresh in the arms of a wigless
Rodolfo.[1] But the Sicilians had just cause to be proud of
that particular Vesper ; they had set a fashion which even
to-day, forty years later, shows no signs of having become
out-moded.

Encouraged by this reception, Mimi set forth with a
lighter heart on her travels abroad ; to their credit it must
be said that foreigners generally, and the English in particular, gave her a far warmer welcome than she had at
first known in Italy. Once again it was Tito Ricordi who
acted as her *courrier* across the Channel ; but on this occasion
he adopted the bold strategic experiment of varying not
only the method, but the point, of attack. Damped by
London's comparative indifference to, and subsequent
neglect of, Manon, he decided to look elsewhere for a
starting-point for her successor ; perhaps because he had
heard that what Lancashire thinks to-day London is sure
to think to-morrow, or possibly because he had been
misled by the definition of Milan as ' the Manchester of
Italy', it was the northern city that was selected for Mimi's
début on April 22nd, 1897. The opera in which she
appeared, however, was not *La Bohème*, but *The Bohemians* ;
it was too much to ask of the Carl Rosa Company—or,
for that matter, of the Mancunians—that they should know
Italian.

It does not appear that Puccini's first (or later) impressions of Manchester were very favourable. In a letter to
a friend, describing the great cities that he had visited, he
defines it as " the land of smoke, drunkenness, cold, rain,
cotton (but God help anyone who doesn't wear wool

[1] Fraccaroli, pp. 102-3.

there ! . . .) and fog. A regular Inferno."[1] Moreover, when
he and Tito arrived to attend the rehearsals, they were
horrified to find the orchestra disposed after a fashion
which they had never seen outside a circus ; the bass brass
and the drum peeped coyly out from the two boxes on
either side of the stage, and gave forth detached blares and
pops which nearly frightened the composer out of his
wits.[2]

In his *Golden Age of Opera*, Mr. Herman Klein, who had
travelled to Manchester on behalf of *The Sunday Times* to
write a review of the new opera, gives an amusing account
of the utterly woebegone and dejected appearance of the
two young men on the eve of the first night, which they
were convinced would end in a most ghastly failure. Their
fears, however, were unfounded ; and on the following day
they all returned together in a special saloon carriage to
Euston, Puccini all smiles at his success and " radiant with
the recollection of genuine Lancashire cheering ".[3] It was
perhaps as well that he knew no English ; otherwise, if we
may judge from a few choice specimens of the translation
given by *The Times* critic, his radiance might have been
somewhat clouded over. " 'T'was an Englishman, then—
Lord or milord as may be " ; " Her food most pre-
dilected is the heart " ; " And I, Marcel, I will not hide
you "—the latter, as is apparent from the original, being
an assurance of frankness, and not an undertaking to
refrain from inflicting chastisement—an immunity of which
the translator might have been thankful to avail himself.
Granted the difficulty of having to shape the line to the
rhythm of the music, one is nevertheless tempted to
wonder what manner of men these translators of operatic
librettos can be ; sturdy patriots, one imagines, of one or

[1] Fraccaroli, p. 190.   [2] Wakeling Dry, p. 72.
[3] *The Golden Age of Opera*, p. 223.

other country, with a profound ignorance of foreign
languages and a no less profound contempt for all music
and poetry, who have undertaken their distasteful task
solely out of enmity to the composer ; almost certainly
humorists, too, and conscious humorists at that—for I
refuse to believe that it would be possible so repeatedly to
attain the same ludicrous effects, unless they were deliberately intended. To take but one simple and well-known
example, nobody but a conscious humorist with a strong
anti-Puccinian bias could have possibly translated ' *Un bel di
vedremo* ' into 'One fine day we'll see him ' ; the very air
of guilelessness about the adjective betrays its wicked
intent—and how perfectly it succeeds in wrecking the
original !

Nevertheless *Bohème* survived the worst that the translator could do, and continued to appear with ever-growing
success in (more or less) English guise, until the memorable
Summer Season of 1899 at Covent Garden, when it was
heard for the first time in this country in Italian, with
Melba in the rôle of Mimi. Nobody could deny that her
singing of the part, which suited her voice admirably, added
enormously to the popularity of the opera ; but even her
greatest admirers must have regretted that she should continue to cling to it with ever-increasing obstinacy and in-
appropriateness right down till the night, nearly thirty
years later, when she gave positively the last of her many
Farewell performances. It is one of the major tragedies of
opera (for audiences no less than for prima donnas) that
there are no nice elderly, white-haired ' leads ', as there
are on the stage, for singers past their prime ; how much
we should have been spared if only Shakespeare—and
Gounod—had thought of providing an alternative version
of *Romeo and Juliet* in which Romeo falls in love with the
Nurse !

The opera itself can no longer be said to be in its prime ; but in the forty years that have passed since its first rather shy appearance in Turin, it has shown the most remarkable powers of endurance. When one looks down the long line of screeching Musettas, grandmotherly Mimis and heavy-weight Rodolfos who at one time or another have raised what was left of their voices in song, one is amazed that it should have survived the many indignities to which it has been subjected ; and yet, with the possible exception of *Butterfly*, it is still given more often than any other opera. It appears to be not only time-proof but very nearly fool-proof ; when, for instance, a couple of years ago at Covent Garden, it was found at the last moment impossible to give the much-advertised *Cenerentola* owing to the sudden illness of the tenor, *Bohème* was substituted literally at an hour's notice, by a ' scratch ' cast hastily gathered together without rehearsal—and its success was such that many of the audience were glad that Cinderella had been prevented from attending the Covent Garden Ball.[1] Even the most virulent critics of Puccini's music—those who condemn equally the crude violence of *Tosca* and the saccharine senti-mentality of *Butterfly*, the cinematography of the *Fanciulla* and the ' pseudo-chinoiserie ' of *Turandot*—generally spare a kind word for *Bohème* ; it is significant that in Germany, where any music which is not dull, long-winded and unin-telligible, is *ipso facto* regarded as suspect, it is the one opera which seriously vies in popularity with Wagner. " I have heard *La Bohème* perhaps a hundred times ", says Herr Specht,[2] " and know every bar of it—yet not a single one has lost its freshness for me." It would seem that, unlike some of her interpreters, Mimi has the secret of perennial youth.

[1] See *Among the Covent Garden Stars*, by Josephine O'Donnell, pp. 101-3.   [2] Specht, p. 135.

CHAPTER FOUR

' LA TOSCA '
(1897–1900)

SHORTLY after he had completed *Edgar*, Puccini was taken by some friends to hear a performance of Victorien Sardou's powerful melodrama, *Tosca*, then being given at the Filodrammatico in Milan, with Sarah Bernhardt in the title-part. What had impressed him most about the performance was that, despite his comparative ignorance of French, he was able to follow the action of the play without the slightest difficulty. We may note in passing that he applied exactly the same test to the next two plays which he set to music : *Madame Butterfly* and *The Girl of the Golden West*, both of which he heard in English—a language of which he was even more ignorant than he was of French. For, quite apart from any other qualities which he might look for in a play, one thing was absolutely essential ; that it should be simple, straightforward, dramatic—and that its action should be intelligible to a deaf-mute.

The impression created on his mind, however, by this particular performance cannot have been more than transitory ; he went so far as to discuss the possibilities with Signor Giulio and with Illica—after which the matter was quietly allowed to drop. Perhaps one day in the distant future it might be reconsidered . . . but in the meantime there was *Manon Lescaut* . . . and, immediately after *Manon Lescaut*, there was *Bohème* . . . and so it was not until nearly ten years later, when the disquieting news reached his ears

41

that his father's pupil, <u>Franchetti</u>, had designs on the lady,
that Floria Tosca suddenly became infinitely desirable in his
eyes ; his ardour still further increased when Verdi let it
be known that only his extreme old age prevented him
from running away with her himself. This was more than
enough ; thereupon a conspiracy was set on foot which
would have appealed to Machiavelli no less than to
Maskelyne. By a judicious mixture of Florentine cunning
and the legerdemain of the ' disappearance trickster ',
Giulio Ricordi, who was Franchetti's publisher, and Illica,
who had already drafted the libretto for him, so played on
that unfortunate composer's feelings that they were soon
able to persuade him that *Tosca* was utterly unsuited to be
set to music ; that, in any case, the libretto was vile ; and
that in fact the sooner he began to look elsewhere for a
subject the better. And so, with a flourish and a hey
presto ! the trick was done ; on the same day that Franchetti cancelled his contract, a fresh one was signed with
Puccini. In fairness to the conspirators, however, it might
be added that the world, no less than they, was to gain by
Franchetti's loss.

Once again those three rather difficult young men set to
work under the benign presidency of Signor Giulio to draw
up an effective libretto. On this occasion, when in doubt,
they had the advantage of direct recourse to the Oracle
himself ; for Sardou took the greatest interest in the pro-
ceedings, and, though full of years, proved no less full of
advice. Rather to their embarrassment, he showed himself
indefatigable in devising fresh horrors to add to an already
sufficiently horrible story ; nothing could daunt him and,
with a fine disregard of topography, he insisted on Tosca
hurling herself from the platform of the Castel Sant' Angelo
into the Tiber : a feat which would certainly have created
a record for the long jump from a standing position, since

[handwritten marginal note: tricked Franchetti out of Tosca]

the river flowed more than fifty feet away. One is surprised that the enterprising old gentleman did not think of employing a catapult for the occasion.

But apart from the awkward question of disposing of the body with reasonable accuracy, Tosca's death was not attended by any of those heart-burnings and recriminations which had cast such a shadow over Mimi's last days on earth. There continued to be differences of opinion, of course ; but Illica was learning to control his temper, Giacosa his dejection ; only Puccini remained immutable in his demands—and in his superior judgment. Herr Specht, who has made a special study of the different drafts of the libretto, confesses his amazement at the composer's rare insight into the essentials of musical drama and unerring instinct for the theatre, which he contrasts with the librettists' frequent lapses of taste and obstinate adherence to antiquated conventions.[1] Incredible as it may seem, in the first version of the torture-scene (which afterwards became one of the grimmest and most striking passages in the whole of the opera) the hero, whilst in the process of being tortured, is actually allowed to sing a regular aria, which is swelled to a quartet by the voices of the heroine, the judge and the little rat of a police-agent.

From this and other absurdities Puccini saved himself by his own infallible sense of the theatre. In addition he had to face opposition from an unexpected quarter, for he found himself one day called upon to defend himself against his hitherto staunch supporter, Signor Giulio, who had taken a violent and unaccountable dislike to the entire third act. This he did quite unanswerably in a long letter, memorable for its calm reasoning no less than for its proud confidence.[2] Yet one final obstacle stood in his path : with unpardonable fatuity the librettists had allowed Cavaradossi to take

[1] See Specht, pp. 155-6.   [2] See *Letters*, pp. 130-32.

farewell of the world in an excessively tedious and pedantic 'Latin Hymn', embracing amongst a number of other topics, the whole range of politics and the Arts. Puccini was in despair ; he could do absolutely nothing with the task that had been set him ; for his instinct told him that, 'with one hour to live',[1] it was inconceivable that the painter should have either the time or the inclination for such lofty, academic musings. No : the farewell to Art must be changed into a farewell to the woman he had loved . . . and so the most famous passage in the opera was born with no words but the "*Muoio disperato*"[2] for which the composer himself was responsible. I remember hearing him say that admirers of "*È lucevan le stelle*" had treble cause to be grateful to him : for composing the music ; for causing the words to be written—and for declining expert advice to throw the result into the waste-paper basket.

Eventually the work was completed to everybody's satisfaction, and Monsieur Sardou, with rather surprising modesty, graciously admitted that the new book was in many ways an improvement on the original play ; it is only fair to add, however, that he regarded the libretto as his own handiwork, and that later he came very near to believing that he was also the composer of the music. And yet, when one examines the text even in its final and much improved form, it is not difficult to understand why Puccini had hesitated so long before deciding to put it to music ; for it was not in the least in his genre. Hitherto his music had been distinguished by its delicacy and its refinement ; his surest effects had come from the recording of the 'little things', to which he lent a peculiar beauty and significance all his own ; the light of a candle that goes out

1 Tosca, Act 3 : " *Vi resta un' ora* ".
2 " I die in despair."

and is rekindled, the touch of a hand, the quarrels of lovers and the renewal of love ; even Death, when he comes, appears in gentle guise, not as the Destroyer but as the merciful dispenser of Euthanasia to poor weary mortals. But now he found himself in the position of a vegetarian, at once tempted and disgusted by the sight of a large, juicy steak ; for *Tosca* was strong meat indeed ; here, in the course of three short acts, one is called upon to witness one ' grilling ' by third-degree methods ; one torture-scene ; one attempted rape ; one assassination with the knife ; one execution by shooting ; and one leap to suicide if not actually into the Tiber. Even those who are not averse from a little blood and thunder might be pardoned for complaining that Sardou had rather overdone it ; in the case of blood and thunder, as in the case of other commodities, there is such a thing as over-production. The same stricture might be applied to the villain whose sinister presence directly dominates the first two acts, and whose evil spirit indirectly dominates the third ; that mixture of ' bigot and satyr ', Baron Scarpia, with his rather unhappy gift for gloating ' asides ' ("My design is succeeding ! " "Ha ! the poison is working well!" etc.), seems to have stepped straight out of a Lyceum melodrama ; it is not until we have before our eyes the tangible evidence of Tosca's sanguinary knife that we can bring ourselves to believe that he is—or was—a creature of flesh and blood.

And yet the astonishing thing is that Puccini actually brought it off, and by the brilliance of his musical effects no less than by the sureness of his theatrical instincts succeeded in purging the story of most, if not all, of its theatricality and extravagance. From the crash of the three opening chords, with their sinister threat of Scarpia's all-pervasive presence, right down to Tosca's despairing leap into eternity, there is scarcely a moment when one does not

feel oneself carried breathlessly away by the music. The
music succeeds, where even the genius of Sarah Bernhardt
must surely have failed, in making us believe not only that
such things can happen, but that they are actually happening
before our eyes. Medea may not slaughter her children
before the public gaze ; but Scarpia can torture Cavaradossi and indulge in any number of other unpleasant
habits without provoking from us a word of protest or a
smile of disbelief. "*Questo è luogo di lacrime!*" [1] as he warns
his victim, and the audience feels equally disinclined to
laughter. If *Tosca,* from a purely musical point of view, is
not Puccini's greatest opera, it is surely unrivalled as a
tour de force.

Appropriately enough, it was in Rome, where, exactly
a century before, Scarpia had expiated his last infamy, that
the first performance was given at the Costanzi Theatre on
January 14th, 1900. Once again the evening began badly ;
rumours had been circulating from mouth to mouth that
certain mysterious ' enemies ' of the Maestro had determined
to seize this occasion to make him pay dearly for his two
previous successes, and, less than a quarter of an hour
before the performance was due to begin, Mugnone, whose
nerves had never been his strong point, was calmly informed
by an official that if anybody threw a bomb during the performance he was immediately to play the National
Anthem. Since a similar outrage had recently occurred at
Barcelona while he was conducting, causing several deaths
in the audience, it can readily be imagined that the
wretched man was even less in a condition to do justice to
Puccini's music than he had been on that famous night of
Friday the thirteenth at Palermo. No sooner had the curtain gone up than alarming noises were heard from the
audience ; they were only protesting against the late arrival

[1] *Tosca,* Act 2 : " This is the place for tears."

of newcomers, but the Management took fright, and a few minutes later the curtain was lowered. After this false start the curtain went up again and the rest of the performance proceeded without incident ; but, possibly because everyone was nervous and neither the singers nor the conductor were at their best, or possibly because Puccini's ' enemies ' were really present in large numbers, the reception, although quite friendly, was not marked by any scenes of great enthusiasm.

Nevertheless *Tosca* survived its indifferent start as easily as it surmounted the snarlings of the critics, now in full cry against a composer who had dared to add success to success in their despite. Like its predecessor, it triumphed abroad even more rapidly than it had in Italy. As far as England was concerned, it no longer required *Savoia's* insidious campaign of penetration to gain admission ; from an unknown and neglected ' outsider ', Puccini had become a hot favourite, and it was taken almost as a matter of course that his new opera should be given in the Summer Season at Covent Garden less than six months after its *première* in Rome. The performance was noteworthy not only for the magnificent singing and acting of Ternina in the title-part, but also for Antonio Scotti's first appearance as Scarpia—a rôle which he was to continue to play to perfection until his retirement from the stage of the Metropolitan Opera House thirty-three years later. There have been several other outstanding Scarpias ; Vanni Marcoux, who thrilled his audience by imparting to the attempted rape a greater air of purpose and verisimilitude than is customary on the operatic stage, and who made it perfectly clear why the Head of the Roman police kept a sofa in his dining-room, was one ; Mario Sammarco, although his appearance suggested a retired butler of unimpeachable morals rather than a lascivious aristocrat, was another ;

Stats from 1935.

but it may be doubted whether there has ever been a more consistently satisfying interpretation of the part, both from the point of view of singing and acting, than that of Caruso's much loved friend, whose recent death in extreme penury was one of the many unhappy consequences of the Wall Street slump.

If one may judge from available statistics, *Tosca* ranks third, if not second, amongst Puccini's successes. At the Metropolitan, for instance, *Bohème* heads the list with 202 performances, *Tosca* is second with 166, and *Butterfly* third with 163.[1] At Covent Garden, on the other hand, although *Bohème* still heads the list with 128 performances, *Butterfly* is second with 101, and *Tosca* third with only 65.[2] In both cases, *Manon Lescaut* lags a long way behind, with only 57 and 21 performances respectively to its credit. But whereas no Season of any length appears to be complete if it does not include *Bohème* and *Butterfly*, the record of *Tosca* is more intermittent—and this for a reason which is obvious : it is the only Puccini opera which demands not only good singing but also first-class acting. From time to time a really great artiste, like Madame Jeritza, identifies herself with it and gives a new and powerful fillip to its popularity ; but it can barely survive a mediocre performance. I ventured earlier to express the opinion that the brilliance of the music and the composer's remarkable sense of the theatre had done much to remove—or perhaps it would be better to say, disguise—the inherent absurdities of the plot and of the characterization ; this assertion, however, needs one important qualification. I do not believe that even the most irreverent opera-goer could find much to

[1] See *The Metropolitan Opera, 1883–1935,* by Irving Kolodin, Appendix II. These figures cover the period from the original performances until 1935.

[2] See *Records of the Royal Opera, Covent Garden,* by Richard Northcott. In this case the record does not go beyond the year 1921.

Tosca - only opera to require both great singing & great acting.

laugh at in a good performance of *Tosca*; but in a bad one—well, when it is funny, it is very, very funny. The second act is particularly vulnerable in this respect ; no audience can be fairly expected to maintain its gravity at the spectacle so frequently offered at Covent Garden (and elsewhere) of a Scarpia, doubly handicapped by shortness of breath and embonpoint, chasing an elderly and no less voluminous Tosca round the stage in an effort to extract from her that ' price which it is as patently a physical impossibility for her to pay as it is for him to receive ; and when, at the close of the act, we are entertained with the lady's unavailing efforts to balance the crucifix on the still heaving expanse of the ' late ' villain's chest, one feels that the only thing lacking to complete one's enjoyment is the appearance of Mr. George Robey from the ' wings ', pleading with us with raised eye-brows to ' desist ' from our unseemly merriment. Puccini himself had few illusions on the subject ; the cruellest thing that he could find to say about Ducas' *Ariadne and Blue-beard*, was that he would nearly—or very nearly—prefer to attend a performance of *Tosca* at Covent Garden.[1] No wonder he had such a horror of being present at his own ' executions ', as he called them !

[1] See p. 135.

CHAPTER FIVE

' MADAMA BUTTERFLY '
(1901–1904)

WITH *Tosca* successfully launched, Puccini started at once to look for a successor. It was not that he could not, and did not, enjoy life ; he loved his shooting and his motoring, and had recently, through the acquisition of a motor-boat (the first of many), found a new method of combining his two favourite sports. He loved, too, to surround himself with a few chosen friends in whose company he could unburden himself and banish for a while that spiritual loneliness and melancholy which so constantly oppressed his spirits ; he had even begun to lose his dread of big cities, and now derived a certain furtive enjoyment from his enforced visits to London, Paris, and the other capitals of Europe—provided always that he did not have to stay too long, and was not called upon to show himself off to strangers. Above all, he loved to return from his journeys abroad to Torre del Lago and the warm Italian sun ; for he was, to a singular degree, influenced by climatic conditions. Extremes of cold, or of heat, affected him profoundly ; it is a peculiarity of his letters to my mother that there is scarcely a single one, except the briefest of notes, which does not contain some reference, approving or the reverse, to the weather. But all his joys—even the joys of a temperate Italian sun—turned to bitterness if they had not work, or the more or less immediate prospect of work, as a background.

Other men in his place might well have been glad to
rest awhile and enjoy the fruits of their success and popularity. The ' glittering prizes ' of the world—as the world
understands them—were his for the taking. Fortunately for
him, his incurable shyness effectively dispelled the fear
that he might allow himself to degenerate into a popular
idol, at whose feet countless admirers would doubtless
have been only too happy to fall down and worship.
Quite apart from his shyness, his keen sense of the ridiculous would have made him a most unsatisfactory object of
adulation ; as history shows clearly, the deification of
mortals is only possible when both the deifiers and the
deified are guiltless of humour. And this sturdy Tuscan
was a man, not a manikin ; a man too, who, for all his
delicate sensibilities, was far more at home in the countryside, with a gun slung over his shoulder, than in the exotic
atmosphere of a drawing-room.

There was yet another reason why the prospect of in-
activity was hateful to him. He was now forty-two and at
the very height of his powers ; but already a feeling of
urgency was upon him, and the growing dread of oncoming
old age had begun to haunt his dreams. If he was still to
make music for the world, there was not too much time to
lose, and his spirits chafed at the very thought of delay.
Hitherto he had never been at a loss for a suitable subject ;
no sooner had he been off with the old, than he was on
with the new, opera. But now, for nearly a whole year, he
found himself becalmed in the first of those ' interim '
periods which were to grow longer and longer as time went
on, and which lend to so many of his letters a touch of
wistful plaintiveness, if not of downright despair.

Not that there was, either then or later, any lack of
suggestions and ideas ; a popular composer in search of a
subject finds himself literally overwhelmed with well-

meaning, but for the most part futile, proposals. There was, for instance, Victor Hugo's tremendous novel, *Les Misérables*, which for a time he seriously considered as a successor to *Tosca*; there was Benjamin Constant's *Adolphe*, which, however, he found 'very poor material indeed'; [1] there was the inevitable *Cyrano*, and—no less inevitably—there was Gabriele D'Annunzio, now making positively his first appearance on the scene as aspirant to the rôle of collaborator—a part which that versatile poet was never destined to play, although he was constantly popping out from the 'wings', dressed up in a new costume.

The credit for bringing *Madama Butterfly* to Puccini's notice has been variously ascribed to a number of persons; actually, I believe, it was his friends Alfredo and Maria Angeli who took him, during the summer of 1900 when he was in London for the *première* of *Tosca* at Covent Garden, to see Belasco's adaptation of John Luther Long's short story, then running successfully at the Duke of York's Theatre. Once again, as in the case of *Tosca*, he was able to follow every single detail of the plot despite his utter ignorance of the language; in addition he found in the pathetic little story of the geisha girl something which appealed profoundly to him not only as a musician but as a man. If he may be said to have fallen in love with each of his heroines in turn, his love for Butterfly was of a purer and more ethereal nature, since it was mingled with the divine spirit of compassion. Manon suffered for her own follies, Tosca for her jealousy, and even the gentle little Mimi had deserted her Rodolfo for a rich nobleman; only Cio Cio San was without sin, and her tragedy stirred him even more deeply than had the fate of her more culpable sisters.

On this occasion there were no doubts, no hesitations in

[1] See *Letters*, p. 140.

his mind ; the only delay—and it seemed much too long to the impatient composer—was due to the necessity for securing Belasco's consent. " The more I think of *Butterfly* ", he writes to Signor Giulio, " the more irresistibly am I attracted. Oh, if only I had it here that I might set to work on it ! " [1] It was not long before he was in a position to do so ; and once again those three rather difficult young men—a little less young now, and infinitely less difficult— set to work with a will to produce their masterpiece. It was their third work of collaboration ; it was their best ; but alas ! it was also to be their last. Shortly after the opera had been completed, the untimely death of the gentle Giacosa broke up for ever the partnership which had yielded such wonderful results. His loss was irreparable ; and if it was a tragedy for Puccini, it was scarcely less of a tragedy for his fellow-librettist. Bereft of Giacosa's assistance—moral as well as material—Illica found himself utterly unable to satisfy the composer's exacting standards, although, as we shall see later, it was not for want of trying. He survived until 1919 ; but his name never appeared again on the front page of a Puccini opera.

It was little short of a miracle that Death had not inter- vened even earlier to break up the partnership. Shortly after he had completed the first act, Puccini was involved in a serious motor accident ; he was found lying unconscious beneath his overturned car, nearly asphyxiated by the petrol fumes, and it was only thanks to the presence of a doctor, who was at hand to administer first aid, that he escaped with a broken leg, several months in bed, and a permanent limp. But the creative frenzy was upon him, and long before his leg was healed he had resumed work ; less than a year after his accident, he had written the last notes of *Butterfly*.

[1] See *Letters*, p. 141.

Although the composer carried the marks of his accident with him to the grave, no such injury is to be found in the work which it interrupted and so nearly terminated ; not even the most fanciful nor the most censorious could pretend to discover in it any traces of the sick-bed. It is, in fact, the quintessence of Puccini ; the most typical and characteristic of all his operas. It is also a touchstone ; for those who like his music it is his best opera, for those who dislike it, his worst. His qualities—or, if you prefer it, his defects—appear here as through a magnifying-glass, and tendencies, already hinted at in his earlier work, stand out for the first time in bold relief, enlarged if not actually exaggerated. In a word, the listener will either be enchanted with its exquisite pathos, or dismiss it off-hand as senti- mental trash. Take, for instance, the central theme ; it has been alleged against him by his detractors that he wrote exclusively for, and about, women, and although there was nothing in the least feminine about him, it is certainly true that his strongest inspiration derives from female loves and female suffering. It is in the delineation of his heroines that his musical touch is surest ; by contrast his male characters, although given excellent vocal opportunities, appear curi- ously shadowy and unreal. This tendency, already apparent in his earlier work, is even more strongly emphasized in *Butterfly*. The whole opera revolves round the character of Cio Cio San ; her virginal innocence and childlike love for her handsome American lieutenant ; her tenacious faith, which refuses to accept the patent fact of his desertion ; her brief moment of joy at his return, followed by her fathomless misery when she learns the truth ; and then her supreme act of renunciation—in this pathetic little figure Puccini found that touch of true poetry which is so perfectly mirrored in his music. Just as Butterfly is the most lovable of all his heroines, so Pinkerton is the most un-

lovable of his ' heroes '—if such a term can be applied
to that cold-blooded and thoughtless seducer, in many
respects a more repulsive character than even the wicked
Scarpia. It is significant that during the whole of the all-
important second act he is absent from the stage, and appears
only for a brief moment in the last to express shame-faced
regret for the tragedy which he has brought about. Even
the well-meaning but ineffective Sharpless, who shakes his
head dolefully throughout the three acts, suggests a nodding
mandarin rather than an American Consul, and merely
serves as a foil for the central figure. Of all the male characters, only the Bonze, with his dramatic denunciation of his
renegade niece, leaps into life for one brief instant. From
first to last one figure stands out alone : Butterfly herself,
" rejected yet happy ".[1]

Rejected she certainly was—and very nearly for ever.
A curious graph might be made by comparing the various
receptions accorded to the first hearings of Puccini's operas
with their subsequent estimation in the eyes of the world.
Beginning with *Manon Lescaut*, which was unanimously
acclaimed as a masterpiece, we find that *Bohème* was first
heard with complete indifference, *Tosca* with only the most
tepid approbation, whilst *Butterfly* was scarcely heard at all.
His later operas, on the other hand, none of which as yet
have shown any sign of rivalling their predecessors in
popularity, were greeted with an enthusiasm tempered only
by a spirit almost akin to veneration.

A dozen different explanations, none of them entirely
satisfactory, have been given to account for the behaviour
of the audience that assembled at La Scala on the night of
February 17th, 1904. Some, at least, of those present
appear not only to have been endowed with the gift of
divination, but to have had the additional advantage of a

[1] *Butterfly*, Act I : " *Rinnegata e felice* ".

most efficient organization. Commenting on the Milanese *première* (which was also the *dernière*) in his musical Review, the hitherto urbane Signor Giulio remarks, with an unwonted touch of acidity, that " the performance given in the pit seems to have been as well organized as that on the stage, since it too began punctually with the beginning of the opera ".[1] There could have been no question, of course, of any personal hostility to the composer, for I do not believe that he ever made an enemy in his life ; but it would seem probable that those mysterious ' enemies ' of his music—or perhaps ' rivals ' would be the truer word—whose existence had already been suspected on the first night of *Tosca*, were on this occasion present in greater numbers—and better drilled. The grandson of Domenico Puccini was to be silenced by a hostile *claque* ; other times, other weapons.

A plausible explanation, this ; yet one which does not square with all the facts. Like a too violently prosecuting Counsel, or an obviously biassed summing-up from the Bench, the clamour of a minority, however vocal, often has precisely the reverse effect from that which was intended. By themselves, the wrecking tactics of the pit could not have prevailed ; the rest of the audience too had to have some cause for dissatisfaction. Causes there were undoubtedly, though to-day most of them seem rather trivial ; a few bars, for instance, at the opening of Butterfly's entrance vaguely recalled a passage from *Bohème*—a form of reminiscence which has always proved peculiarly abhorrent to the Milanese, who see in it an attempt to deprive them of their money's worth by fobbing them off with second-hand goods. In addition it must be borne in mind that the opera, as we now know it, differed in certain small but not unimportant respects from that which received its baptism

[1] See *Letters*, p. 138.

of fire at La Scala. The first act was longer by a rather
wearisome and irrelevant passage (now wholly eliminated)
in which one of the relatives invited to the wedding-feast
gets drunk ; further, the composer had made what was
almost his solitary error in theatrical judgment by insisting
that the two parts of the second act, now separated by an
interval and an intermezzo, added later, should be played
continuously—and an hour and a half's consecutive music
is more than a Milanese audience has been schooled to
endure.

But, whatever the real causes, the fiasco was complete.
For the first and only time in his life, Puccini had to listen
to that sound of whistling which, to an Italian musician,
is so much more terrifying than the screaming of a shell or
the bursting of a bomb. One curious, but by no means
unusual, phenomenon may be noted, as of interest to
students of mob psychology : that whether the audience
had made up their minds in advance to condemn the opera,
or whether something in the performance had aroused their
disapproval, they left the theatre thoroughly pleased with
themselves, as though they had done a splendid evening's
work. " Never ", records Signor Giulio laconically, " were
so many cheerful and satisfied faces to be seen—as of those
who have taken part in a collective triumph." [1]

The shock to Puccini was all the greater since he had
been looking forward to the evening with serene, and almost
unexampled, confidence. At the rehearsals it had been
noticed that of the vast army of labourers, most of them
unseen and many even unsuspected, who assist at the birth
of a new opera, every single one—down to the stage-
carpenters and the unskilled workmen—had tiptoed silently
about his business, his eyes filled with tears, and had
returned day after day to listen to the music, whether it

[1] See *Letters*, p. 138.

present for 1st failure

was his duty to be present or not. So sure was the composer of success that, for the first time in his career, he had invited those nearest and dearest to him to be present, so that they might share with him in his triumph.

Let us hope at least that they helped to alleviate his sorrow ; for he suffered, on that night, a hurt far deeper than that which he had experienced a year previously in his motor accident. It was in the summer of the same year that my mother first met him in London ; at the time the memory of that terrible night was still painfully vivid to him, and could only with the greatest difficulty be exorcised ; indeed I believe that it remained with him till his dying day. I know that in my youthful mind it became somehow confused with stories of the French Revolution with which I had just become acquainted ; for many months after I first met him, my particular nightmare was of a sea of upturned faces, all jeering and whistling and shaking their fists at a solitary female figure, who sometimes wore the stately appearance of Marie Antoinette, and sometimes the humble guise of a little geisha girl. . . .

To the outer world Puccini gave no sign of what he had suffered ; he immediately withdrew the opera after its solitary performance, at the same time refunding the large sum which he had received from the management of La Scala by way of royalties. He then retired to Torre del Lago—that ' other Eden ' where he was always able to heal him of his grievous wounds—and set to work calmly and with unimpaired confidence to make the few trifling alterations in the score which, in the light of recent experience, he deemed necessary. On May 28th—scarcely three months after the original fiasco—his confidence was magnificently vindicated at the Teatro Grande, Brescia, where Butterfly, ' rejected yet happy ', made her second appearance, and was received with an enthusiasm which must have caused the

Butterfly pulled after 1 performance. Revised

3 mo later. 2nd appearance a success.

Milanese to reflect uneasily over their recent ' collective
triumph '. Thence the opera travelled to London in the
following year : a marvellous cast, including Caruso, Scotti
and Destinn, made it the most memorable event of the
Covent Garden Season ; its further journeyings to Paris,
Vienna, Prague, Berlin, Brussels and the United States we
shall be able to follow through Puccini's own eyes.
Writing thirty years later, Signor Adami remarks that to-day
Madama Butterfly is the most popular opera in the world.[1]

[1] See *Puccini* by Adami, p. 50.

PART II

OUT OF WORK

(1904–1907)

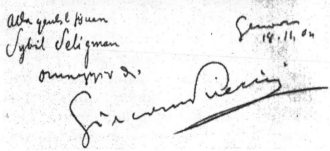

THE BEGINNING OF A TWENTY-YEAR FRIENDSHIP

(1904)

Quote -P...
London -...
"The kind caterer"...
to my caprices
Presents of every kind!

CHAPTER ONE

RESEARCHES AND REHEARSALS
(October 1904–April 1906)

Enter Sybil

PUCCINI's letters to my mother, on which the remainder of this book is based, were all written in Italian, interspersed (especially when he was in Paris) with an occasional French phrase, and—more rarely still—with a word or two of English, almost invariably misspelt.

Many of them, of course, are not of any general interest ; even from those that I have finally selected, numerous omissions have been necessary. London represented, for Puccini, the world's emporium, and " the kind caterer to his caprices ", as he calls her, was bombarded with commissions of every sort and variety. For himself, rough tweeds, gloves, socks and ties (" my special weakness ") ; for Elvira, stockings, furs and materials for dresses ; for his friends, presents of every kind (" The clock has arrived —Praised be the name of Sybil—and Vickery ") ; furniture for Torre del Lago, varnish for the villa at Abetone, a Dutch carpet for the new house at Viareggio ; a special kind of match for use in a fast motor-boat ; a supply of insulin (never used) ; a grand piano (I prefer not to specify the make, as it had subsequently to be returned because, after delusively auspicious beginnings, it developed into " a regular charabanc ") ; Abdulla cigarettes by the thousand ; an Irish setter, *bonne pour la chasse* and trained to bring back dead birds to its master—" it must not be too old, but it need not be a prize dog " ; an elixir to restore the moral—

63

these are some of the examples selected at random from my mother's ' shopping list ', most of which I have omitted from the letters.

In addition, as I have already mentioned, nearly every letter contains some allusion to the weather, to whose influence he was extraordinarily susceptible ; in the summer, the *caldo Pisano* (Pisan heat) " which you adore and I abominate ", and in the winter, the cold damp climate of Milan, figure with unfailing regularity. There are, too, innumerable references to the state of his health and that of Elvira, to minor ailments which pass as quickly as they have arisen, as well as enquiries about my mother's health, most of which I have left out. In order to avoid wearisome repetition, I have also severely topped and tailed his letters ; for he was particularly lavish in postscripts, and nearly every letter concludes with affectionate messages not only to my mother, but to my father, my brother and myself—not to mention his greatest friends in London, the Tostis and the Angelis.

I have also endeavoured to suppress as far as possible any personal expression of opinion that might give pain to the living or injure the memory of the dead. From the very nature of the correspondence it is inevitable that such troubles and disputes as he had should figure prominently in it. " You are the person who has come nearest to understanding my nature—and you are so far away from me ! " he cries despondingly. But the mere fact that he could, and did, unburden himself on paper often helped to dissipate his troubles and drive away his melancholy. On such occasions he might, on the spur of an angry moment, commit some hasty judgment to paper, which he would have been the first to recall as soon as the fit of irritation had passed.

A word of caution, however, is necessary on tl use of the word ' Pig '. In the first place it was few English words that he knew and, as such, was to cover a lot of ground ; in the second, the English, or Italian, variety of animal is utterly different from the French *cochon* or the German *schweinhund*. Used frequently in self-accusation (" I am a *pig*—but a *good pig* ") it is in the same benevolent Pickwickian sense that it is frequently applied to others—notably to his dear friend Tosti, whose own assembly of china pigs at 12 Mandeville Place was scarcely less remarkable in number and variety than Puccini's metaphorical collection. It would be amusing to make a list of all those whom at one time or another Puccini includes in this category, if only because they appear to have so little else in common : Sir Thomas Beecham, house decorators, various members of the Staff of the *Corriere della Sera*, Mr. Henry Higgins, the manager of the Fiat works, *Signor Pig* Toscanini, a number of French composers and journalists, Tito Ricordi—and every librettist with whom he was called upon to collaborate. If one had to paraphrase the word, one would say : the gentleman and/or friend, conductor, tradesman, journalist, impresario with whom I find myself in temporary disagreement. To read more into the word would be to fail utterly to understand Puccini.

The earliest letter to my mother that I have been able to find—an acceptance of an invitation to dinner—is written from the Savoy Hotel, where he always stayed when he was in London, and is dated October 22nd, 1904. It was, I believe, some time earlier in the same year—shortly after *Butterfly's* triumph at Brescia—that they first made each other's acquaintance at the house of their mutual friends, the Tostis.

Through the freakish instrumentality of the barrel-organ the name of Tosti has become finally and uniquely associated with one, and that one by no means the best, of the many songs which he wrote ; so that Tosti's

P's use of "pig" described

They meet

Good-bye, with Hobson's choice and Shanks' mare, has definitely passed into our language. In those far-off Victorian days when the art of singing was regarded as an enviable social accomplishment, and a young lady 'brought' her music with her to a dinner-party as inevitably as to-day she would bring her lip-stick (though convention demanded that it should be absent-mindedly smuggled in, only to be 'discovered' later, when called for, with cries of surprise) it could truthfully have been said that no music-case was complete without one or more of those delightful songs which earned for their composer a knighthood—an honour all the more remarkable since Tosti, although he had lived the greater part of his life in this country, obstinately refused to give up his Italian nationality. With no less obstinacy, for that matter, he had refused to learn English, and after living forty years in London could proudly boast that his vocabulary was smaller than the number of years of his residence. But many things were permitted to *Ciccio* which would have been denied to others ; for he, together with his charming Belgian wife—who, happily, still lives, and must be accounted one of the youngest and most active octogenarians in the world—occupied a unique and privileged position in English Society. Early in the eighties he had been appointed teacher of singing to the Royal Family, and even in those august circles, where humour is notoriously a tender growth, only too easily nipped in the bud by the icy breath of disapproval, he could venture with impunity on jests which, coming from any other source, would infallibly have drawn the deadly rebuke : "We are not amused".[1] There can, in fact, have been

[1] When the Music-Teacher of the Royal Family was first asked to bring his wife to Court he introduced her as "my wife—the happiest woman in the world."

"But why do you call her that ?"

A mon premier petit ami

"TELL 'CICCIO' THAT I LOVE HIM"—SIR PAOLO TOSTI

few people who were not amused by him—and fewer still
who did not love him.

In bringing Puccini and my mother together, Tosti was
introducing to each other two of his dearest friends. He had
known the composer of *Edgar* and *Le Villi* from his early
days in Milan when he was still a struggling, and more or
less obscure, musician ; as we have already seen, he had
been one of the many cooks who had helped to stir the
broth of *Manon Lescaut*. He had also been, for many years,
on terms of the most intimate friendship with my parents ;
my mother had a contralto voice of exceptional quality,
and Tosti, who was no less famous as a teacher of singing
than as a writer of songs, regarded her not only as his
favourite, but also his best, pupil. Although she never
appeared professionally, my mother frequently sang, generally accompanied by her teacher, at charity concerts in the
South of France, at Villa d'Este and St. Moritz—or
wherever else we happened to be spending the holidays ;
everywhere the beauty of her voice together with the charm
of her manner on the platform gained for her golden
opinions. As she was also passionately fond of opera, it
was only natural that her friendship with Puccini should
ripen quickly—indeed, the only thing that surprises me is
that they should not have met before.

It was not until the autumn of the following year,
1905, that Puccini returned to London ; for he had, with
some reluctance, accepted a very lucrative offer to be present
in the spring at the opening performance of *Butterfly* in
Buenos Aires. In consequence of this, his first trip across
the Atlantic, he was not able to return in time for the

" Because, Ma'am, she *is* my wife."
A look of doubt, almost of disapproval, crossed the Royal features—
only to be cleared away by a slowly dawning smile. " *Mais vous n'êtes pas
modeste, vous !* " remarked Queen Victoria.

continued from pg. 66

première of *Butterfly* at Covent Garden on July 10th to share with Destinn, Caruso and Scotti the enthusiastic applause with which it was greeted. Owing to its enormous success, however, the opera was given again in the Autumn Season, with Rina Giachetti, Zenatello and Sammarco in the principal parts, and on this occasion the composer was able to superintend the rehearsals himself. How seriously he took his duties, and how anxious he was to find another subject, appear from the following note, written from the Savoy:

" You are so very kind! Thank you ever so much for taking such a prompt interest in my affairs. I shall be only too delighted to hear from you the plot of Kipling's play.[1] The only thing is that I don't know at what hour I could come and call on you ; I can't get away from the rehearsals before six o'clock. Would you be at home any day except Saturday at that time ? The three books you mentioned —*Mérimée*, *Anna Karenina*, and *The Last Days of Pompeii*—I know, but they don't suit me."

Largely owing to the composer's untiring efforts at rehearsals, the success of *Butterfly* was even greater than in the summer; during the short Autumn Season it was given no less than eleven times, which must very nearly have constituted a record. We may note in passing that it was perhaps a blessing in disguise that Puccini's time should have been so fully occupied with the successful launching of his latest opera, since it prevented him brooding too much over his inability to find a successor. As soon as he had satisfied himself that *Butterfly* was firmly established in London, he left for Bologna on a similar errand ; from the

---

[1] Kipling's novel, *The Light that Failed*, had recently been adapted to the stage, and, with Sir Johnston Forbes-Robertson in the leading part, had had a big success in London.

two letters that follow it is clear that he retained very pleasant memories of his stay in London, and that his hatred of big cities, so vehemently expressed in some of his earlier letters to his friends, was rapidly beginning to disappear.

MILAN
October 30th, 1905

" I had to fight like anything at Bologna, but it was a real success ; I've written to Tosti too, giving him the details. One of the audience fainted at the end of the second act, and absolutely ruined the effect. Toscanini conducted marvellously ; the rest were good—but not more than good.

Thank you for your kind letter and for the newspaper-cuttings. I am very well, but I certainly miss London and the friends I left behind me there! Elvira sends you her fondest love ; the stole was a terrific success—thanks to the good taste of the charming person who chose it."

MILAN
November 4th, 1905

" I'm leaving to-night for Torre del Lago, after having stayed a few days here and in Bologna—they certainly haven't been as happy as the days that I passed in London —days which for me will always be unforgettable! How I remember everything—the sweetness of your character, the walks in the Park, the melodiousness of your voice and your radiant beauty. Believe me when I say that I am plunged into the depths of despair and that my surroundings are oppressive to me—how often I think of my all too short stay in London !

I send you all my affectionate thoughts, and do please write to me—a really nice letter to console me for the loss of your charming and delightful company."

TORRE DEL LAGO
December 16th, 1905

" Thank you for the magnificent pen which works beautifully. I have read Tennyson's *Enoch Arden*, which I quite liked, but the material is too slender for an opera— at least for a strong opera of the kind that I really need now. . . . The characters and the emotions portrayed are vivid and true to life, though—the choice is a good one and does honour to the exquisite taste of the kind lady who made it ! "

MILAN
January 2nd, 1906

" Elvira and I heartily reciprocate your kind wishes. Your beautiful pen remains unemployed! I only wish I could use it . . . but up till now I've had nothing to do . . . it really is a very sad state of affairs!! You who were so kind as to suggest for me *Enoch Arden* (which has been set to music by Maestro Coronaro of Milan ¹)—don't grow tired and discouraged, but continue to search and . . . find that which neither my poets nor my publishers nor I have been able to find. You read so much, and you are so clever and intelligent that I have hopes—then again English literature is not so well known as ours or the French—so who knows that you may not make this lucky find for me!"

MILAN
January 11th, 1906

" Thank you for taking an interest in me. I made

---

¹ I have been unable to find any trace of an *Enoch Arden* by Maestro Coronaro—presumably the Gallio Coronaro whose *Festa e Marina* is described as " a slavish imitation of *Cavalleria Rusticana* " (*A Thousand and One Nights of Opera*, by F. H. Martens, p. 312). It is possible that his version of Tennyson's poem was an even more unblushing plagiarism, and has in consequence perished utterly. The only operatic version of *Enoch Arden* recorded is one by Rudolf Raimann, given for the first time in Leipzig, curiously enough, in this very year.

immediate enquiries about Kipling's novel [1] and have managed to find a French translation ; if I am favourably impressed by it, I'll get hold of the dramatized version from the publishers. God grant that you have been able to hit the mark! I have given up the idea of Marie Antoinette altogether."

The story of Marie Antoinette exercised an extraordinary fascination over Puccini; he was always " giving up the idea altogether "—only to return to it later, as though it were an entirely novel suggestion. We have by no means heard the last of that luckless Queen, though in the end he decided that, just because she had lost her head, there was no reason why he should lose his. In the meanwhile Kipling's (operatic) ' Light ' was to ' fail ' before it had been properly kindled.

MILAN
January 13*th*, 1906

" *Kipling's no good !* I've read the novel, and there are certain passages which I love, but taking it altogether it's too small and too much in one key—then that wretched blindness is not only at the end of the work, but is the very *kernel* of the story—besides, the end of the novel with the death of the blind man on a camel in Africa isn't possible on the stage—at least, not on our Italian stage. Heaven only knows what kind of *mise-en-scène* they had in London —real live camels and a battle, etc. Perhaps you could let me know roughly—now that I am acquainted with the book—how it was adapted to the stage. If you saw the play yourself, you could easily remember into what scenes it was divided—and if you haven't seen it, it would be easy to find out from someone who has. This idea has just occurred to me whilst I am writing to you and is a sort of

[1] *The Light that Failed.*

last despairing hope . . . I am so utterly depressed by this feverish and disheartening period of searching ; not only I, but those who are near me, my publishers and many others, are losing heart . . . so forgive me if I take advantage of your goodness."

Early in February we went, as usual, to Nice. Puccini was expecting to go there too to superintend the rehearsals of *Manon Lescaut*, but the exact, or even the approximate, date of the first night seems—rather surprisingly—to have been kept a secret from him. As time goes on, the tone of his letters becomes more and more plaintive : " About Nice and *Manon*", he writes, " I haven't heard a word, and Ricordi too in Milan doesn't tell me a thing. If it isn't too much trouble, do you think you could possibly find out for me when this blessed opera is coming on ? "

At last the first night of the ' blessed opera ' arrived, and—with it—the Puccinis. From the evidence of a diary of mine preserved by my mother, which had just been presented to me on my tenth birthday and which was the only one that I ever kept, it becomes clear—through a spate of consonants—that the two families saw a great deal of each other. " Dined at the Caffé de Paris with Mamma, Pappa, and the Puccinnis " ; " Went with Mamma, Pappa and the Puccinni's to Tosca, an oppera by Puccinni " ; " Lunched with Mamma, Giacomo and Elvira "—and so on. It is from this stay at Nice that my first clear-cut recollections of Giacomo date. I can see him now, strolling up and down the Promenade des Anglais in that leisurely manner which was so characteristic of him ; indeed so slow was his progress that it could hardly be called walking at all, and every few yards he would come to a complete standstill, pausing to light one of his eternal cigarettes, or to think over some point in the conversation that interested or amused him. I remember, too, a curious trick which he had, when searching for a word or an idea that eluded him, of clicking his fingers with a gesture of comical despair and a rueful smile—rather like someone trying unsuccessfully to catch a fly. He took considerable care of his personal appearance and was invariably well-dressed, although—unlike many other musicians—he avoided sartorial eccentricities or exaggerations ; for some reason I always picture him at that time dressed in a dark blue suit with white stripes, with light gloves and a walking-stick—a reminder of his automobile accident—in his hand, and his soft hat, which he often wore even indoors, cocked at a slightly jaunty angle. But more clearly than anything else do I remember the look of indulgent affection in his large brown eyes, and the rare sweetness of his frank smile—and yet, even when he was in his happiest and jolliest mood, there always seemed to lurk at the corners of his mouth a hint of melancholy, if not of actual suffering—the look that one sometimes sees on the faces of the blind.

Of course I worshipped Giacomo. Until I was sent to a private school later that year, my mother had taken me with her everywhere, and my opera-going dated back to a memorable afternoon three years earlier at the Costanzi Theatre in Rome when—my mother having been suddenly taken ill—I attended a performance of *Germania*, seated in solitary splendour in the Royal box, and trying to conceal my embarrassment behind an enormous box of chocolates presented to me by an over-generous Management. I just succeeded in sitting through the opera—after which I was extremely sick. Since then I had been taken repeatedly to the opera and, having inherited my mother's musical taste

t, however, any of her musical abilities, it was

o's operas that I always loved best and that—I am

Character: "The type of man to whom children and dogs take instinctively"

not in the least ashamed to confess it—I still love best.
And now that I had come to know my hero, I used to gaze
at him in rapt adoration, wondering where all this lovely
music issued from—privately I thought that there must be a
tap somewhere, if one could only find it, which he could
turn on and off at will. But, quite apart from his music,
there was something extraordinarily lovable about Giacomo himself ; he was, if I may be permitted a well-worn
cliché, the type of man to whom children and dogs take
instinctively.

About Elvira, of whom, of course, I also saw a great
deal, I was—frankly—not so certain. She was at that time
still a very handsome woman, though built on rather
generous lines with, in particular, very large hands and
feet, which may perhaps have partly accounted for the fact
that Giacomo was apt to refer to her jokingly as his
'policeman'. Her temper always appeared to be a trifle
uncertain, and her voice, which she was apt to raise over even
the most trifling matter, quickly became harsh and discordant. The fact was that I was more than a little afraid of
her, and it was only after a severe internal struggle that I
could bring myself to raise my face to hers to be kissed ;
the fear of ' having one's nose bitten off ' had assumed for
me a literal rather than a metaphorical meaning. I hasten
to add, however, that my nervousness was entirely unjustified, and that during all the years that I knew her I
never experienced anything but the greatest kindness at her
hands, and, if I may judge from her letters to my mother,
she always looked upon me with the utmost affection.

Towards the end of March we returned to London, and
the Puccinis to Torre del Lago.

TORRE DEL LAGO
March 24th, 1906

" From your wire I can picture to myself the horrible

Elvira - his "policeman"

crossing you must have had ; we fully expected it, seeing what filthy weather we've had—here too we've returned to the wind and rain of winter. How we miss Nice, and above all our beloved and unforgettable Sybil ! Not a minute goes by that we don't talk of you !

Tosti writes that *if* and *when* he comes to Milan he'll send me a telegram—and I'm not going to budge from here until I hear from him. Tell him that, and give him my love. Your flowers had already arrived, and are here on the dining-room table to comfort our eyes and to remind us of the kind sweet lady who gave them to us.

A kiss for my dear Vicent." [1]

TORRE DEL LAGO
March 28th, 1906

" We're leaving at ten o'clock for Milan, decided to do so by your telegram about Tosti who—the *Pig*—never wired to me. I'll go to the *Figlia* [2] and let you have my impressions at once. Elvira had your letter yesterday ; but your kindness passes all bounds ! Thanks on behalf of Elvira, and thanks also for the present which you say you are sending me—I remain in a state of stupefaction, my head bowed like that of a slave who doesn't know how to rebel."

With the arrival of the Tostis in Milan, one more determined effort was made to find Puccini a suitable subject for an opera—and a suitable collaborator. " We have been all the time ", writes Lady Tosti to my mother, " with Elvira and Giacomo, the Ricordis and D'Annunzio"

[1] To save confusion, I had better mention that Puccini never seemed able to make up his mind about my name ; Vicent, Vincent, Vini, Winnie, Vinnie, Wincent and the Italianized Vincenzo and Vincenzino are some of the variations which appear in the letters.
[2] *La Figlia di Jorio.*

—and it soon becomes apparent that this was not a mere chance gathering of friends, but yet another endeavour to bring together Italy's leading composer and her greatest man of letters.

The omens were not altogether propitious; for the great event of the Season at La Scala, Franchetti's adaptation of D'Annunzio's powerful peasant drama of his own wild home in the Abruzzi, *La Figlia di Jorio*, had ended in dismal failure. "A semi-fiasco", Puccini calls it charitably; but Lady Tosti, who had been present at the *première* with the Puccinis, is more explicit in apportioning the blame for this 'half-failure'. "The drama is fine, but the music! . . . The greatest bore you can imagine, and the woman who sang has a bad voice and is a real monster!"

It may be that, privately, Puccini shared Lady Tosti's view that the fault lay with the composer whom he had, as we have seen, indirectly dispossessed of *Tosca*; at any rate he asked for nothing better than to collaborate with the author of the 'semi-fiasco'. As a poet and dramatist, D'Annunzio was now at the very height of his fame, though the many other leading rôles which he was subsequently to fill in the course of his remarkable career must at that time have been unsuspected even by himself; the discredited and penniless exile who returned from Arcachon to lead his country into the War on the side of the Allies; the super-Geddes who served successively in the cavalry, the infantry and the navy, and topped it all by leading a squadron over Vienna, dropping—characteristically—not bombs but pamphlets; the self-appointed Governor of Fiume who, for the space of fifteen months, defied not only the Italian Government but the whole of Europe —and lastly the Prince of Monte Nevoso to whose home at Gardone Mussolini himself deemed it an honour to be invited.

MILAN
March 31st 1906

" Tosti is very well, but he says that the life here tires him ; to-morrow he and I are going alone together to Monza in order to be able to breathe a little more freely ; after that he is going to spend a few days in the Abruzzi.

La Figlia was really a semi-fiasco ; we're now hard at work negotiating with D'Annunzio over the libretto ; I think a decision will be reached to-day.

I've talked such a lot about you to *Ciccio*,[1] and you can imagine in what terms. I'm very proud of my magnificent letter-case and that very original purse—so many thanks again. Lots of kisses for Vincenzo from me, and from Elvira too."

MILAN
April 6th, 1906

" Tosti has gone off to the Abruzzi. . . . Nothing has yet been decided, and I'm having a wretched time ; I think that even Signor Giulio's feelings towards me have changed ! I'll write you another letter in greater detail ; as you know, I make the great mistake of being too sensitive, and I suffer too when people don't understand me and misjudge me. Even my friends don't know what sort of man I am— it's a punishment that has been visited on me since the day of my birth. It seems to me that you are the person who have come nearest to understanding my nature—and you are so far away from me ! !

I am sending you a little photograph to remember me by—a thousand affectionate thoughts for that exquisite and beautiful creature who is the *best friend* I have."

MILAN
April 10th, 1906

Not a word has been heard of Tosti since he went off.

[1] Tosti.

He and Berthe [1] ought to be back to-morrow ; but I'm absolutely in the dark about everything. Tito has left for Monte Carlo and then he is going on to Brussels for *The Resurrection* ; [2] since he left, the negotiations with D'Annunzio for the libretto have been completely abandoned. I am in a state of utter apathy ; Signor Giulio is no longer easy to deal with and won't pay attention to anything—he seems to me to have altered towards me too. . . ."

Needless to say, Giulio Ricordi's feelings had not altered in the least ; but the slightest suspicion that his affection towards him showed signs of cooling was sufficient to plunge Puccini into the depths of despair. The simple truth was that Signor Giulio was beginning to suffer from that disability from which not even the greatest publishers are exempt : he was growing old.

Meanwhile, with the return of Tosti, another cloud was dispelled. The negotiations with D'Annunzio were actively renewed, and a few days later Tosti was able to write in triumph to my mother : " I shall be back at the latest on Sunday—what a joy it will be to see you again, and *how* many things I shall have to tell you—*all good!* I end up by giving you the great news : the contract for a Puccini-D'Annunzio opera has been *signed !* "

[1] Lady Tosti.
[2] Opera by Francesco Alfano, first performed in Turin in 1904. Thirty years later Alfano, for whose work Puccini had a special regard, was entrusted with the delicate task of putting the final touches to his unfinished opera, *Turandot*.

CHAPTER TWO

D'ANNUNZIO, 'CONCHITA' AND OTHERS
(June 1906–January 1907)

EARLY in May Puccini paid a flying visit to London ; the following letter, written after his return, is typical of dozens of others written upon leaving England. Although, of course, it was my mother's company that he missed most, there was something, I think, in the tranquil atmosphere of our home and of our surroundings which he missed too—something which he could not always find in his own home ; for there never was a happier family than ours, nor one more completely devoted to each other. It would perhaps be not altogether fanciful to see, too, in these regrets a reflection of his admiration for certain qualities which he discerned in England and the English nation. "You have so much poise", he writes elsewhere, "and something essentially English about you, too." [1] It was precisely this attribute of ' poise ', so alien to the Latin temperament, which he admired and envied all the more because he found his fellow-countrymen—and himself—lacking in it.

MILAN
June 7th, 1906

"I had your nice card this morning. Thanks for the stick, and a million thanks for all the kind attentions which you and your husband showered upon me during my stay in London—a delightful visit which I shall always

[1] See p. 188.

look back on with a heart full of gladness and of gratitude.

Elvira thanks you for the magnificent cushion and apologises for not having written ; she's still with Fosca [1] and the children from morning till night. How I hated having to leave you, when the moment came for getting on to the boat at Folkestone ! It made me absolutely miserable to think of all I was going to miss—your charming and delightful company—and all your friends—and your dear sister—I felt as though my heart were being torn asunder. But we shall soon be seeing each other again at Abetone, and if there is anything you want me to do or to arrange, please command me—nothing could give me greater pleasure than to attend to your wishes.

There is no news here ; D'Annunzio is ill, but I don't believe he has anything ready for me. I haven't seen Tito yet ; he is President of the Congress of Publishers, and all his time is taken up. . . ."

MILAN
June 14th, 1906

" To think that there is a World Exhibition in Milan. . . . ! But there's absolutely nothing to do and one doesn't know how to pass the evenings—and even if there *were* any entertainments on, they wouldn't be of any use to me—*I amuse myself in my own way, I do*—Oh God ! I'd quite forgotten ! I've had the luncheon-basket ; it's beautiful and most commodious—we'll give it its first outing together in the cool shady woods at Abetone.

Good-bye, dearest friend—I must stop because they're calling to me."

TORRE DEL LAGO
June 22nd, 1906

" I have signed an agreement for *La Femme* [2]—and

---

1 Signora Fosca Leonardi, Elvira's daughter by her first husband.
2 *La Femme et le pantin.* See later.

D'Annunzio has telegraphed that he has recovered, and that he is coming to a villa quite close here, in order to get to work with me and for me until such time as his labours shall have been crowned with glory. We'll see.

I'm as lazy as a bear—Elvira and I are both well—the only thing I want is to see you soon again.

Yours very affectionately,

THE SUCCESSOR (Naughty !) "

This unusual signature, and the playful reproach which accompanies it, need a word of explanation. For some reason (most certainly not that of vanity) Puccini never very much relished being called " The Successor of Verdi "—a designation which, in view of his growing popularity, came tripping only too readily from the pen of every journalist who was acquainted with the names of both composers— and little else about them. I question indeed whether a great musician, however many imitators he may have, can ever be said to have a legitimate successor ; genius is no old-clothes store from which second-hand garments may be obtained ; the mantle of the dead is buried with them, and those who follow after must fashion their own. One thing only Puccini owed to the elder man, and that was his choice of a career ; it was, as we have seen, that performance of *Aïda* at Pisa, which had first filled him with a humble yet determined spirit of emulation.

Comparisons, when they are not odious, are merely silly ; and nothing could well be sillier than a comparison between Verdi and Puccini. Except for their nationality and their inveterate shyness, the two men had absolutely nothing in common ; Verdi was born an Italian peasant and throughout his long life retained the essential characteristics, both good and bad, of his class—simplicity, directness, fecundity, and that grand, elemental quality which, together with a certain coarseness inseparable from such glorious profusion, he succeeded in communicating to his music. Puccini, despite the poverty of his parents, was of gentle birth, and every line of his music, so utterly removed from the broad, passionate notes of the elder man, reveals the fastidious delicacy of the patrician. From *Le Villi* until his death forty years later, despite the fact that he was never for one moment deliberately idle, he composed in all only seven more or less full-length operas, one operetta, and four one-act works, whereas Verdi, in the first sixteen years of his career, had already written nineteen full-length operas (two of them twice over) and had, moreover, indignantly rejected a very lucrative contract because it would have confined him to writing only one opera a year. One might as sensibly compare the writings of Dickens and Mr. Max Beerbohm.

CHIATRI
July 1st, 1906

"I haven't had any letters from you ; you know how much we like to get them ! This place is cool with a beautiful view and comfortable to live in—it's the famous villa in which I've never, or hardly ever, lived ; it's about four hundred metres up, overlooking the sea and the lake. There's a splendid view ; I'll bring you here in September to see it, and if you like to stay here with the boys you can be its mistress. All the same there are no amusements here ; it's a really wild spot, and it can also be boring—and for me it *is* a bit boring—the more so as I have no work to do ! No news yet from D'Annunzio ! "

CHIATRI
July 4th, 1906

"It's some time since I've heard from you—what has happened ? Has your time been so much taken up lately that you have almost forgotten those who are so fond of you? We're still exiled in this villa, but I've got to go back, because letters here are only received after a long delay, and then telegrams aren't delivered at all ; and just at present I'm continually exchanging letters with Tito first in Paris and now in Berlin on the subject of *Butterfly*. It's going to be given at the Opéra Comique in November, but Carré [1] wants me to make certain alterations, to which Giulio Ricordi thinks it would be against my dignity to consent. I don't yet know what it's all about, and what changes or cuts are being proposed ; but Tito keeps urging me on to leave for Paris so as to get down to work. I'm completely undecided—and, as I said, it's difficult to communicate from here.

Vaucaire [2] is enthusiastic over *La Femme et le pantin* ; he writes to me that in a week or so he will send me a draft of the first two acts."

We spent the month of August at Abetone, where the Puccinis were already comfortably installed in their villa, and early in September my mother and I spent a few days with them at Chiatri, and afterwards at Torre del Lago. I have many happy recollections of that holiday, which, at the time, I imagined to be a holiday for Puccini too. I remember motoring with him in the mountains, and watching him shoot *beccafici*, [3] and I remember several enchanting picnics in the lovely woods of Boscolungo ; what, however, I was too young to appreciate was that it was also a very busy month for him, with many comings and goings.

Most important of all, there was the arrival, and subsequent departure, of D'Annunzio, true—at any rate in

---

[1] Albert Carré, Director of the Opéra Comique from 1898 until 1914, and again from 1918 until 1925.

[2] Maurice Vaucaire, the French writer.

[3] A form of diminutive snipe.

the earlier stages—to his promise to work with and for the Maestro, " until such time as his labours should have been crowned with glory ". My mother had already met him in Rome ; in addition to the photograph that appears in this book, I found numerous others of him, generally on horseback and engaged in surmounting improbable obstacles, together with a number of letters addressed to the " Sybil of the North " (*Sibilla Nordica*) lauding her singing to the skies—although he is not, I believe, particularly musical. But this was the first—indeed, I believe the only—occasion on which I set eyes on him. It is disappointing to have to admit that I have only the dimmest recollections of the great poet ; I suspect that at the time I was more interested in the tame bears and the wild strawberries for which Abetone was famous.

No writer alive can have been more gifted with imagination than D'Annunzio. He would unfold his ideas to Puccini, and the latter would listen, spell-bound ; at last—at last his patience was rewarded, and he had found that for which he had been waiting so long ! But the trouble always seems to have been that directly the poet put his ideas on paper they had an unaccountable way of changing shape, and what eventually emerged was something utterly different from the original conception.

So it was now with *The Rose of Cyprus*. The poet had declaimed, and the musician had listened, enraptured ; what a poet—and what a poem ! Decidedly everything in the garden was lovely—and not least lovely the Cypriot rose. My mother's pen, so long unemployed, was taken out of its case and filled expectantly . . . and then D'Annunzio arrived at Abetone with the manuscript. The original blend of legend and fairy-tale which had so captivated the composer had completely vanished ; in its place had sprung another rose, which might conceivably smell as sweet, but

Alla Sibilla nordica .   Gabriele d'Annunzio

16 marzo 1908

Roma .

A COLLABORATOR MANQUÉ—GABRIELE D'ANNUNZIO .

was most emphatically not the bloom which had originally commended itself to Puccini.

There was really nothing to be done about it. D'Annunzio had not been inured in the hard school through which Illica and Giacosa had (somewhat reluctantly, it is true) passed ; besides, the future Prince of Monte Nevoso could scarcely be expected to chop and change, to write and rewrite, as though he were still in a classroom. He had written his libretto ; his labours—in his own eyes, at least—had been duly crowned with glory, and it was for the composer to take it or leave it. Puccini left it. To be precise, he voiced his ' doubts ', to which the poet responded with his ' regrets '—and so, with these and other mutual expressions of good-will and of esteem, the two men parted, promising to resume their work of collaboration at some future date. Six years later they were to do so, but, as we shall see in due course, with equally negative results. In the meanwhile the famous contract, the signing of which had brought so much joy to Tosti's heart, had, in Puccini's own words, " petered out ". [1]

However, there are always compensations. In the words of a later creation of Puccini, that profound philosopher—and rogue—Gianni Schicchi : " In this world, if you lose one thing, you may find another ". [2] Shortly after D'Annunzio had left, Maurice Vaucaire, the French writer (sometimes referred to in Puccini's letters as " The Vicar ") arrived, bringing with him the libretto of *La Femme et le pantin.*

I do not know precisely how, or under what circumstances, the idea of putting Pierre Louÿs' novel to music

[1] See *Letters,* pp. 232-3, in which Puccini imparts the " by no means joyful " news to Signor Giulio.

[2] " *In questo mondo*
    una cosa si perde . . .
    una si trova ".

new libretto arrived . . .

La Femme et le pantin

first occurred to Puccini ; it is certain, however, that he had already signed the contract in June.[1] The book, which was first published in 1898, had enjoyed an enormous vogue (though I think that its success was, at least in part, a *succès de scandale*) and it had already been dramatized in French and in German ; but it certainly does not appear, at first sight, a subject which would lend itself naturally to Puccini's music. It may be described as a story of low life in Seville, and the central figure—for it would be giving the word an unusual connotation to describe Conchita as ' the heroine '—works in a cigar factory ; in her leisure hours she proves to be one of those singularly unpleasant women, known vulgarly as ' teasers ' (though no doubt Mr. Freud has a word for it) who delight to lure men on deliberately, only to disappoint them, but through no motives of chastity, at, or just before, the crucial moment. It is not until the man whose death she has endeavoured to bring about, firstly by the weapon of ridicule (Act 3) and subsequently by the more direct method of the knife (Act 4), has beaten her to within an inch of her life that she recognizes that true love has at last come into her life, and, regardless of bruises, throws herself with the happy sigh of a tired child into his arms (Curtain). At the time it was all regarded as very devilish ; to-day we should merely call it Dell-ish.

Obviously the torture-chamber had no horrors for the composer of *Tosca*—though, having on that occasion supped full with them, he might have been pardoned for hesitating to return to the same dish. Nor did he shrink from that particular form of mental torture which underlies Pierre Louÿs' theme ; on the contrary we find many years later in *Turandot* a curious echo of this queer, sadistic hate which eventually turns into love—though the motives of the

[1] See p. 80.

P's nickname by locals in Torre del Lago was

Chinese Princess were infinitely purer (if scarcely more intelligible) than those of the Spanish slut. Where, however, the story seems definitely unsuited to his particular genre is in the complete absence of any moderately agreeable, or even human, traits in the leading characters. His heroines in particular, although they were not required to be spotless—for did he not delight to be known by the villagers of Torre del Lago as the *Maestro cuccumeggiante* ? [1]—had at least to be lovable—or whatever word approximates nearest to the untranslatable Italian *simpatico*. And this Conchita was certainly not.

He realized the truth of this himself—but it was already too late. In the meanwhile Vaucaire's French libretto had been passed on to a Giacosa-less Illica (whose version, incidentally, satisfied neither Puccini, nor Vaucaire, nor Pierre Louÿs) and the Press were full of accounts of the forthcoming Puccini opera, *Conchita.* Worse still, Signor Giulio Ricordi developed a violent enthusiasm for the libretto, and used all his powerful influence to persuade a now disillusioned composer to reconsider his decision. It took Puccini, as we shall see, the best part of a year to disentangle himself from the knot into which he had unwittingly tied himself. But the curious thing about the whole business is the apparent absence of any initial enthusiasm on his part. There had been in the past, just as there were to be again in the future, other subjects which momentarily attracted his fancy only to be discarded later ; but, however short the love-affair, it had always at least begun in raptures. Only in the case of *Conchita* do we get a curt announcement that the contract has been signed—and nothing more. His later references to the lady in question are uniformly unenthusiastic, until she finally becomes " the cursed Spanish slut ".

[1] " The composer of harlots' music ".

'Conchita' signed/contracted, then dumped.

TORRE DEL LAGO
Sept. 19th, 1906

" You have left a big void in our hearts! The days come and go as God wills, and I go and lose myself in the woods.

I have heard from Tito, who is in Paris; I've got to be there towards the end of next week—oh! if only I could find my dear Sybil still there! But you're sure to be in Folkestone; however, I hope you'll come for the *Première*—you promised me you would!

And the tragic story of your luggage! It's strange, because you certainly registered it to Paris, and it's impossible that it could have got lost. So Sybil is left with one solitary dress—what a shame! It really is a misfortune; and now you certainly won't say, 'Who cares a fig'![1]

I send a thousand sincere and affectionate thoughts to you who are so kind, so wise, so sympathetic and—let's say it openly—so beautiful."

TORRE DEL LAGO
September 25th, 1906

" I'm rather preoccupied about *Conchita*—or rather, I am feeling weaker on the subject!—What frightens me is *her* character, and the plot of the play—and then all the characters seem to me unlovable, and that is a very bad thing on the stage.

At this very moment *Savoia* is being rocked in the cradle of the deep; he wrote me too a most loving letter.[2] Thanks for the really charming present which you sent to Elvira—we are for ever thinking of our dear Sybil—I'll write again."

[1] The original is a somewhat stronger expression. It was the refrain of a good many of those poems, not always marked by great delicacy, which Puccini and Tosti loved to exchange with each other.

[2] Tito Ricordi was on his way to America for the tour of *Butterfly*, of which more will be heard later.

The next letter is of special interest since it contains the first reference to Oscar Wilde's plays. Through the courtesy of Mr. Robert Ross, his literary executor, my mother had had access to two of Wilde's hitherto unpublished plays—*The Duchess of Padua* (which Puccini here mistakenly calls 'Mantua') and the unfinished *Florentine Tragedy*. My mother appears to have read them to him earlier—probably during the summer at Abetone—and now that his 'fears' for *Conchita* had begun to take concrete shape, it was only natural that he should revert in his mind to Oscar Wilde. It should also be borne in mind that in the previous year Richard Strauss had created an immense sensation with his *Salome*, which was based on Wilde's play. Who knew but what it might not be worth while to take another dip into the same lucky bag?

MILAN
October 1st, 1906

" Just arrived, and I'm still black from the smoke of the tunnel—but I'm writing to you at once. Do try to get hold of Wilde's Plays—*Conchita* is still weak, but she may recover her strength in Paris. All the same it's a good thing that I should read 'Mantua'; thank you for taking the trouble.

I'm going to see *Papa Savoia*[1] to-day about the *Conchita* contract—I shan't tell him about my doubts!"

TORRE DEL LAGO
October 5th, 1906

" *Conchita* is coming back to life; I've come to terms with Illica as the other poet made a bad job of it. I don't know what to think of the delay in putting on *Butterfly* in Paris; I wonder if it is some intrigue of Messager?[2]

[1] Giulio Ricordi.
[2] André Messager—composer of *Véronique*, etc.

Meanwhile I have returned to Torre del Lago where the weather is magnificent—I spend my time wandering through the woods—how I miss your delightful companionship! But I hope to see you again in Paris.

We are well ; Elvira sends you all sorts of messages. And what is Tosti doing; is he all right ? Give him my love. And now in London the Autumn Season will be starting at Covent Garden ; I advise you to put wax in your ears for the executions ! Poor Butterfly ! Please tell me how she went to her death ! "

TORRE DEL LAGO
October 12th, 1906

" Have you still got Wilde's *Florentine Tragedy* ? Oh, how I should like to read it again ! I would have it translated and discuss it with Illica—will you send it back to me ? I give my *oath* not to publish it, nor to give it to anybody to read except Illica—send it to me, send it to me !

Just this moment had a telegram from Paris not to be there before the 22nd ! What a long time to wait ! Oh, how I should like to come to London ! You don't know what joy it would give me to see you again—and I can't ! Dear Sybil, if you knew how often I think of you ! "

Puccini had intended to pay only a brief visit to Paris in order to superintend the rehearsals of *Butterfly* ; but a series of unfortunate delays ensued after his arrival, and the *première* did not finally take place until the very end of the year.

Throughout these two months he was compelled to remain on in Paris, kicking his heels and protesting more or less vigorously against his fate. These continual postponements were all the more vexatious to him since, in a weak moment which he afterwards bitterly regretted, he had accepted an offer of Heinrich Conried, the Impresario of

The Met offer

the Metropolitan, to assist at the productions of *Butterfly* and of *Manon Lescaut*, the latter now receiving the distinctly belated honour of a *première* at New York's leading opera house.

The impatience which he expresses in the following letters is therefore easy to understand ; what, at first sight, appears less comprehensible is the importance which he attached to securing an unqualified success in Paris. *Butterfly*, it might be argued, had already 'arrived' ; in every important city in Italy, with the exception of Milan, its triumph had been complete ; it had found its way as far as Budapest, and it had been one of the greatest successes ever known at Covent Garden. It must be borne in mind, however, that he was still haunted by the memory of that terrible fiasco in Milan, and was therefore all the more determined that his latest—and, as he believed it to be, his best—opera should be given every possible chance elsewhere. Also the Opéra Comique was, in his eyes, the most important Opera house in the world after La Scala, since it had been largely owing to M. Carré's initiative and enthusiasm that *Bohème* had attained its prodigious success on the Continent. Yet another reason for his great attention to detail in the production was the highly critical attitude of the French Press (quite possibly inspired, as he hints, by some of the less successful native composers) towards any foreign musician whose works were in danger of occupying too much space on the national boards. As the composer of *Manon Lescaut*, *Bohème*, *Tosca* and now *Butterfly*, he had become a marked man ; from the French nationalist point of view, there was altogether too much of him. It behoved him, therefore, to cut the ground, as far as possible, from under his watchful critics' feet, and to allow them no occasion for complaint other than his success. Lest, however, we should complacently contrast

English tolerance with French chauvinism, it is as well to add that a similar slogan of " English Opera Houses for English Composers ! " would not have evoked a responsive echo in the heart of the most sturdy British patriot—not even a contemporary Colonel Blimp could have been prevailed upon to stir from the vapours of his Turkish bath in order to join in the hue and cry.

In the intervals of rehearsing, Puccini found himself increasingly preoccupied over *Conchita*. By coming to Paris he had, as it were, put his head into the lion's mouth, and his presence was seized upon by all those who were interested in strengthening him in his half-hearted resolve. Firstly there was, of course, ' the Vicar ', whom he liked very much—though I fancy that he preferred inspecting motorcars in his company to discussing the merits (and demerits) of the libretto. Then there was the author of the novel itself, Pierre Louys—generally referred to as *Inouï*, either from rhythmic analogy, or possibly because it was a favourite adjective of the novelist. Finally there was the ' terrible ' and mysterious Mr. Spiridon, whom I have been unable to identify ; from his continued ' insistence ', however, I suspect that he too was in some way interested in *Conchita*.

PARIS
[Undated]

" Wednesday morning—I'm writing to you in bed ; I feel so wretched—for the past two or three days my spirits have been black, black. I'm not feeling too well and I'm depressed ; what an impossible character I have—nothing is able to make me cheerful, and I see everything through dark-coloured spectacles. I'm tired to death of everything—including Opera.

Rehearsals have started, but they go slowly enough to drive one to despair. They're cutting the opera too much ;

Madame Carré [1] will do fairly well, but she wants too many cuts—the reason being that she feels that the strain would otherwise be too much for her strength. But there's no other way out ; because if she doesn't sing the part, they're sure to put the opera on one side, and that will be the end of it—and that's another reason for my low spirits. Oh ! how I would like you to be by my side—you always inspire me with so much courage !

I've had a letter from Conried asking me to leave on December 15th ! This is another source of annoyance—I don't want to go ! Tell me—have you got, or do you know of, some medicine that raises the moral and is good for someone who, like myself, is rather run down ? Such a medicine must exist in London, and you who know everything will find it for me—for your faithful friend who cares for you so much—you will, won't you ? The thought of seeing you again for a few days in Paris cheers me up—and why doesn't Tosti make this sacrifice for me ?—I should so love to see him here ! "

GRAND HOTEL DE LONDRES
Friday

" I had a telegram from Tosti yesterday in Czech. [2] Thank him very much for it, and tell him that when I feel in the mood I will write him a secular song in leaping verse.

It appears that *Butterfly* will only be coming on at the end of the month ! As for Madame Carré . . . as an artiste, she's not up to very much, but I hope she'll end up by doing it well. She certainly doesn't move one, except by those insincere mannerisms which, as they are never tired

[1] Marguerite Girod. She made her début at the Opéra Comique in 1901 as Mimi.

[2] It is scarcely necessary to add that Tosti who, after living nearly all his life in England, could not speak English, was no less ignorant of Czech. The language in which he and Puccini corresponded was a language of their own.

of telling you, are characteristic of a Parisienne.

Excuse all these outbursts of mine, dear Sybil ; but I have such absolute confidence in you—you are so good and so devoted to me, as I am to you. I shall be so happy when I see you again—are you coming here soon ? I hoped to give you a surprise by coming to London, but I see that it can't be done. I have to be there every day to try to prevent them from straying from the path which I have laid down.

This morning at eleven I am going out with Vaucaire to look at a *voiturette*—the thought of this cheers me up and distracts me. He's nice, Vaucaire, and we talk about you a lot together."

PARIS
[Undated]

" The rehearsals went better to-day—but Madame *pomme de terre* is not up to it. The *mise-en-scène* is lovely, and the orchestra is beginning to warm up. Overjoyed at the thought of seeing you again."

PARIS
October 31st, 1906

" Thank you for your letter—I'm ever so much better. Since yesterday I've been taking the elixir which you sent me, and for which ever so many thanks. Would you very kindly get them to send me the book on *moi-même.*[1]

You can't imagine how much pleasure it will give me if you come here soon ; certainly this hotel hasn't got that *chic* to which you are accustomed, but we shall have the pleasure of having you near us. For the last two or three days there have been no rehearsals—perhaps that's why I feel better !

Let's hope for the best, but I'm afraid for Madame Carré ; she's weak and has little intelligence, but I've got to put up with her if I want *Butterfly* to be given, and I can't

---

[1] *Giacomo Puccini*, by Wakeling Dry, which had just been published.

make a change in the cast—so I have to make a terrific effort to pay her compliments and see if I can get some good out of her by dint of encouraging her."

PARIS
November 8th, 1906

" I have had Wilde's Plays.

I saw De Lara,[1] who was most awfully nice, with Giordano [2] at a dress rehearsal at the Opéra Comique, and he told me how poor the performances had been at Covent Garden. What a pity ! But with such an orchestra, etc., etc., it was only to be expected—but this *entre nous.*

I'm in the worst of tempers to-day—and you write that you will be coming on the 24th—you keep on putting it off ! And when is *Butterfly* coming on—I haven't the vaguest idea ! We're starting rehearsals again to-morrow ; I'm tired to death of Paris—I should like to be in London or Torre del Lago—or in a wood where the foliage is thick."

The impression created on Puccini's mind on re-reading Wilde's *Florentine Tragedy* was evidently a favourable one ; for a few days later he wrote to Signor Giulio : " Oscar Wilde's manuscript, *A Florentine Tragedy*, which pleases me very much, has arrived. . . . It is only one act, but beautiful, inspired, strong and tragic : three principal char-

[1] Isidore De Lara, the composer of *Messaline, Les Trois Mousquetaires, Naïl*, etc., who died quite recently. Although he was an Englishman and lived for the greater part of his life at Claridge's Hotel, his work was more appreciated in Monaco and elsewhere on the Continent than in his native land, where his untiring efforts to found a National Opera House met with little response. He was a man of considerable personal charm and had a wide circle of friends ; what endeared him especially to Puccini was that, unlike most composers of the second rank, he never grudged others their success.

[2] Umberto Giordano, the composer of *Andrea Chenier, Fedora*, etc.

Interested in Oscar Wilde's The Florentine Tragedy, Then shelved.

acters, three first-class rôles ".[1] But the wily Signor Giulio
had already set his heart on *Conchita*, and he was not going
to allow her to be ousted by any Florentine rival. We do not
possess his reply, but it must have served its purpose most
effectively in damping Puccini's enthusiasm ; for, less than
a month later, he confesses sadly to my mother that Wilde's
play is not 'suitable'. The idea was in consequence shelved
—though several years later it was to be taken up again.

Meanwhile the rehearsals dragged on with maddening
deliberation. On November 14th he writes despondently :
" *Butterfly* won't come on till the beginning of December " !
He is, however, to some extent consoled by a cable from
New York reporting that *Butterfly's* triumphant progress
through America continues unchecked : " After Washington, Baltimore, and Boston, now New York—good ". The
tour, organized by the American impresario, Mr. Savage,
and superintended in its earlier stages by the enterprising
Savoia, was an event quite unprecedented in operatic history;
for six months an enormous company—for not only understudies for all the principal rôles, but understudies to the
understudies had to be brought along in case of accident,
illness or fatigue—visited all the important cities of the
United States in turn, giving eight performances a week—
not from a selected repertoire, but of one opera only :
Butterfly, in an English version. More than two hundred performances in all had been given when the tour concluded.
It was a truly remarkable feat of organization and fully
deserved the success with which it met ; it was, too, an
amazing tribute to the popularity of Puccini's music.

PARIS
[*November 20th,* 1906]
" Six o'clock—just back from the rehearsals. I'm in a

[1] *Letters*, p. 236.

terrible state of panic about Mme. Carré ; I'm afraid she hasn't the force necessary to go through with the opera. But that's enough—we must hope for the best. All the same I'm very anxious—and I'm so tired of being in Paris ! I'm leading such a dull, silly existence.

Did you read in the papers about Caruso ? It's my belief that the whole thing was a put-up job by some hostile impresario. [1]

Your rooms are reserved for Friday ; I'm waiting for you with the greatest eagerness—you will bring, with your smile, a little joy into my life. My health has been better these last two or three days ; I feel less run down—but I find this country so oppressive. In spite of the fog and in spite of the climate London never tires me—oh, I adore London !

[1] On November 14th a terrific sensation had been caused in New York by the arrest of Caruso in the monkey-house in Central Park on the charge of annoying a certain Mrs. Hannah Stanhope. Although the lady in question did not appear in court, the complaint of the arresting officer was accepted as sufficient testimony, and he was convicted. Caruso at the time staunchly maintained that he had been victimized, and I believe that I am right in saying that his innocence was subsequently established. In the meanwhile, however, he was an easy prey for every dull-witted buffoon unable otherwise to raise a laugh ; for many years to come, 'monkey-house' jokes vied in popularity with mothers-in-law, kippers, landladies and the rest of the stock-in-trade of the music-hall comedian.

The audience of the Metropolitan, at any rate, were not slow to give their verdict, as the following rather pathetic little note of Caruso, written to my mother two days after the opening of his season, clearly shows :

HOTEL SAVOY
NEW YORK
November 30th, 1906

" DEAR FRIEND,

" You can't imagine how welcome your letter was to me. It did me so much good, and I needed it—because with all that has happened, my spirits were very depressed.

I've already made my début with *Bohème*, and I received a demonstration of sympathy the like of which has never been seen."

I saw in the *Figaro* that Melba and Zenatello have been singing some of my music at Court [1]—thank Tosti so much, and give my love to Berthe.

Au revoir soon."

My mother's eagerly awaited visit to Paris was abruptly terminated a couple of days after her arrival by a telegram from my father, informing her that I had had a serious accident at my preparatory school. I had somehow managed to fall off the horizontal bar in the gymnasium clear of the mattresses, and it was thought at first that I was suffering from internal injuries and that an operation would be necessary. It proved to be a false alarm; but my mother stayed by my bedside day and night until I had quite recovered.

PARIS
[Undated]

"We are in a state of continuous anxiety; yesterday evening's telegram made us very unhappy, but to-day we live again—how glad I am of the improvement! Poor Vini —and poor mother of his! You can't imagine how wretched we felt during your sad journey. I think of how much you suffered and of the promised telegrams which you didn't receive—did you get one of mine at Dover? Anyhow, let's hope that everything turns out all right—and soon too. You know, boys recover very quickly—give him all sorts of fond messages from me and lots of kisses—don't forget to go on giving me news of him. I received the medicine

---

[1] Both King Edward the Seventh and Queen Alexandra were very fond of opera, and during the Season Tosti would often be called upon to arrange a private concert at Buckingham Palace or elsewhere, when operatic excerpts would be given by the leading singers, accompanied by Tosti. I have no doubt that the music to which Puccini refers must have been that of *Bohème*, which was King Edward's favourite opera—a predilection which, curiously enough, was inherited by his son, George V.

and the letter from Carignani [1]—fancy your thinking of that too ! Oh, you really are wonderful—all my thanks.

That Spiridon is coming to see me now ! Alas ! It's half past ten and it's raining— the weather is miserable, just as I am miserable now that you have gone. Elvira sends you a host of messages, and I more still than she."

PARIS
December 4th, 1906
[9.30 A.M.]

" I'm just getting up—had your letter this very moment. Oh, how glad I am at the good news of Vini !

I'm not at all well—since the moment you left I've had nothing but days of discouragement, filled with the usual unhappiness. All I ask is to be allowed to retire into my shell—if only I could get out of going to America, or put it off ! Heaven only knows when I shall see you again— that too adds to my unhappiness, because when I see your smile I feel myself revived, as though I were born again.

I'll write a line to dear Vini—give him lots of kisses from us. Tonio [2] is coming here in a few days' time ; Vaucaire has left for Nice—but the terrible Spiridon is still here ! The second séance takes place to-morrow ! "

PARIS
December 10th, 1906

" As I wrote to you, the rehearsals are going ever so much better. . . . It appears that the [*Florentine*] *Tragedy* is no good ; all things considered, there isn't very much

---

[1] One of Puccini's very oldest friends, and a member of the famous ' Bohème Club ' at Torre del Lago, which met almost nightly whilst the opera was being composed. Nearly all the pianoforte scores of Puccini's operas were arranged by Carignani.

[2] This is the first mention of his dearly loved son, on whom he was to rely more and more in after years. Although Tonio was some years older than I, he was at this time still at school.

to it, and besides it's only in one act, which isn't suitable. *Conchita* too is growing weaker in my mind ! I am as usual —with no work to look forward to ! It's a sad state of affairs—but I feel better to-day—my face is less black ! Spiridon is ill !

I'm so glad about Vini—let us thank God that everything has turned out all right."

The end—or rather, the beginning—now seemed in sight, and Puccini wrote to my father the letter which I have quoted in the Introduction, asking that the *Signora Sybil* might be allowed to come over for the *première*. The permission was of course readily granted—but in the meantime Mme. Carré had been taken ill.

PARIS
December 14th, 1906

" How simply maddening—I'm absolutely furious ! I got David's telegram this morning and I was counting on seeing you again—and now Mme. Carré has a sore throat and fever, and *Butterfly* has been put off till after Christmas— and I expect it will be later still before it comes on ! So as I have to go to New York soon I've decided to *quitter la place* and go to Milan to refurnish my wardrobe and then on to Torre for a few days to recover—I'm absolutely fed up with Paris ! I shall come back for the *première* and then I shall sail for New York. I haven't even decided when I shall sail ; there's a boat on the 5th and another on the 9th—but I think the 9th may be too late as they are in a hurry to put on *Manon* and *Butterfly*. *Savoia* says the tour is a huge triumph and that they're going to give two hundred performances.

Does David's permission hold good for after Christmas too ? Like that I could see you before I sail. Please thank him for his great kindness."

AFTER THE *PREMIÈRE* OF " BUTTERFLY " IN PARIS
(1906)

There were to be no further delays. At long last, on December 28th, *Butterfly* made her first appearance in Paris, and the composer's untiring and—on the whole—patient efforts were rewarded with a brilliant success. My mother paid a flying visit to Paris and had the satisfaction of witnessing his triumph.

PARIS
January 2nd, 1907

"Just had your telegram—how was the crossing ? I still see the *drapeau* in the Place Vendôme fluttering, and I have thought of you so much ; now that I know you to be at rest in your own home, received with all the honours and fêted, I'm glad.

We are like lost people without you—we are always talking about dear Sybil, and in the morning we thought we heard you coming in to pay us a little visit, but the room was all too quiet—without you. Last night, like wandering beggars, we went and dined at an Italian inn, and afterwards we *went for a walk* in the mud through the little streets of Paris, and then, worn out, we were in bed by eleven. To-day a boring lunch (for the libretto ! ! !) at Mme. X—we're counting the hours until we leave—if it were only to-morrow : Paris bores me as much now as it does you ; as for Mme. Carré, with all her vain attempts she seems to me like a woman who wants to be sick and can't—poor Butterfly !

I don't feel I want to see anybody ; give my love to David, the boys, Tosti, Berthe and Angeli [1]—but you are the most 'angelic' of them all. Elvira and Tonio send you all sorts of affectionate messages—and I all the nicest things I can think of."

[1] The late Signor Alfredo Angeli, one of his greatest friends in London.

PARIS
[Undated]

" It's half-past seven ; I've stayed indoors all day in pyjamas—I'm getting up to go to the third night (of *Butterfly*) this evening. I wasn't able to get a box as they are all taken. At ten o'clock I've got to go to that horrible Madame X—she is going to make me listen to a tenor who will sing some of my music ! ! ! ! How jolly ! ! ! Elvira is going to bed at eight ; she's lucky. We're dining in our sitting-room ; *Inouï* called this evening, very *épatant* ; he returned to the subject of *Conchita* for a change ; he won't let me alone—not a bit of it ! He's a sticker, that fellow !

I've secured accommodation on the boat—a cabin amidships and a vomitorium for Elvira. What is that *pig* of a Tosti doing—has he ceased to compose poetry ? Give Berthe all sorts of affectionate messages and say that I'll write to her before I leave. I went to the Duchess of Camastra last night and dined before with Capriello—they talked about you such a lot and with the greatest affection. We are always remembering you and saying how much we miss our dear Sybil ! !

Midnight. Tonio has returned from the opera, I from Madame X—the house was so full that Tonio couldn't find a seat ! It's a magnificent success ; Mme Carré is *toujours faible* and disagreeable—she scarcely bows to me ! And who cares a—fig ! "

PARIS
[*Saturday*]

" I'm longing to be at sea ; in my present state of mind I look on the prospect as a relief—there's a pessimist for you ! But I've got nothing more to do here and it seems a waste of time remaining on—I'm already thinking with joy of the pleasure of coming home, when I hope to see again my dear Sybil who is such a consolation to me—

when you were in Paris, it was quite another story ! I'm
bored to tears with *épatant, inouï, Opéra Comique, Ritz, Rue
de la Paix, Faubourg St. Honoré, Champs Élysées—c'est assais* [*sic*].
Good-bye, dear Sybil of Cumae."

PARIS
January 8th, 1907

" We're on the move—the greatest confusion reigns in
our room. The waiter whose button you pulled off is
unhappy. Poor buttonless boy—he's really to be pitied ! I
wrote a beautiful letter to Carré—I'm wearing a pair of
shoes that hurt me—It's raining—Everything is sold out
for to-morrow's performance at the Opéra Comique.
Yesterday's *New York Herald* had another article attacking
Butterfly ! Thank you for *L'Art et la mode*.

By the time you get this letter, I shall be on my way to
Caruso. The painter took me to see my portrait—very
gobinghi;[1] so much so that you have to hold your nose
in order to look at it ! I look exactly like a Lord Mayor of
London."

[1] I'm afraid that I am responsible for this word ; it was part of my
brother's and my ' nursery ' vocabulary and was used to describe an
ordinary, everyday action. It was an exceedingly popular word with
Puccini, and figures rather more prominently in these letters than I have
acknowledged. It was also a favourite of Tosti's ; on one occasion, when
he was invited to a rather solemn dinner-party, he looked round as he
sat down and remarked across the table to my mother (in Italian) that
there was a very large quantity of ' gobinghi ' present. " You naughty
man ! " protested his hostess, coyly tapping him with her fan, " you
forget that I know Italian and understand every word you're saying."
" Not *every* word," replied Tosti.

CHAPTER THREE

GODS AND GODDESSES OF SONG

(AN INTERLUDE)

" PUCCINI ", remarks Herr Specht,[1] " was a peculiarly inexorable, and not always a very amiable, judge of his conductors and singers." At this juncture, whilst he is still
on the high seas " on his way to Caruso ", it might perhaps
not be inopportune to examine Specht's rather sweeping
dictum in the light of the composer's attitude towards the
famous tenor in particular, and more generally towards the
other Gods and Goddesses who deigned to appear in his
operas. I make no apology for this Olympian interlude ;
for his relations with the interpreters of his music are not
only interesting for the light that they shed on his character ; they are also of importance since, unlike many other
composers who conducted their own operas, thereby deter-
mining for all time their precise conception of their work,
Puccini, as we have seen, contented himself with super-
intending their production, and it is only from casual
remarks and hints scattered here and there in his letters
that we can gauge his musical wishes and intentions.

It cannot be denied that he was singularly fortunate in
his interpreters. From first to last Toscanini was constantly
associated with his work ; as early as 1890 he had conducted
a performance of *Le Villi* at Brescia ; thirty-six years later,
he introduced *Turandot* to the world. Of the composer's
relations with the greatest of all Italian conductors I shall

[1] Specht, p. 13.

have more to say later; but in addition a long and imposing list could be made of the famous names which came to be especially associated with one or other of his operas; Melba, Ternina, Destinn, Jeritza, Martinelli, Scotti, Sammarco and—most famous name of all—Enrico Caruso.

Although Caruso's triumphs extended over the entire field of Italian and French Opera, and even trespassed occasionally, but with more questionable propriety, on Wagnerian territory, both those who remember him with delight in *Pagliacci* and those who would like to forget him as the Knight of the Holy Grail will probably unite in associating him chiefly in their minds with the composer who furnished him with no less than five of his most famous rôles; that he should have named his two sons Rodolfo and Mimmi is as much a tribute to his love of *Bohème* as to the curious and somewhat unconventional circumstances of their begetting.

It would be hard to say which of the two, the composer or the singer, had the greater cause to be grateful for this happy association. Neither, of course, was essential to the other; if the poor organist of San Martino had never strayed from the paths of ecclesiastical music, Caruso would still have been acclaimed the greatest tenor of his age, if not indeed of all time; and if Caruso had continued till the end of his days to work in a small Neapolitan warehouse, Puccini's music would no less surely have found its way to the ends of the earth. But just as the voice lent additional lustre to the music, so too the music was the ideal medium for the voice.

Those who delight in statistics may be interested to know that during the fourteen years in which Caruso's voice was at its best—that is, from the beginning of the century until the outbreak of the War—he sang altogether in some forty different operas, and out of about a thousand appearances in all on the stage no less than three hundred were in the rôles of Des Grieux, Rodolfo, Cavaradossi, Pinkerton and Ramerrez.[1] It would be difficult to decide in which of the five Puccini operas he appeared to greatest advantage ; many will remember the magnificent singing which contributed so largely to the initial success of the *Fanciulla* in New York—although this was a privilege denied to us in Europe ; others would doubtless prefer to remember him in the more familiar *Bohème*, or his glorious rendering of *E lucevan le stelle* in the last act of *Tosca*, with that authentic sob in the voice which every Italian tenor has since striven in vain to copy ; others again may give their vote for his singing of the love duet in the first act of *Butterfly*—though the unsympathetic character and tightly fitting uniform of the naval lieutenant,[2] combined with his absence from the stage throughout the whole of the second act, prevent it, perhaps, from being the ideal Caruso part. Everyone, however who heard him in that too little known opera, *Manon Lescaut*, agrees that his singing in it was unsurpassed ; *The Times* obituary notice, indeed, singles it out as his finest performance, and adds that nothing so brilliant had been heard since Mario was at his best.[3] With this verdict Puccini himself agreed, as we shall see in the following chapter. " Caruso was amazing ", he writes of his performance as Des Grieux. " He is singing like a God "

[1] I derive these figures from Appendix C of *Enrico Caruso*, by Pierre Key and Bruno Zirato.
[2] The uniform of Lieutenant F. B. Pinkerton of the United States Navy was always causing trouble and adverse comment. In describing the *première* at Covent Garden, the musical critic of *The Times* (July 11th 1905) remarks : " Signor Caruso sang so well that his appearance was easily forgiven, but when he was not actually singing some of the audience were moved to observe that he looked like an Inspector of police." Whatever else he may or may not have looked like, he certainly did not look like a lieutenant in the United States Navy.
[3] *The Times*, August 2nd, 1921.

—though he adds slyly, " I think it will give you pleasure to hear this—which is why I am telling you."

My mother had met Caruso shortly after his first appearance at Covent Garden in the summer of 1902, when, like everybody else, she had promptly fallen in love with his voice. Thereafter he became a constant visitor at our house in Upper Grosvenor Street during the Opera Season ; when he was not rehearsing or resting his voice preparatory to singing in the evening, he would come to lunch and then—how well, as a little boy, I remember it ! —would follow the usual comedy of enticing him towards the piano. Not that my mother ever *asked* him to sing, or even suggested it ; with Society hostesses tumbling over each other and offering him fabulous sums to sing a couple of songs at their parties, not even a liberal helping of his beloved macaroni could be regarded as a fair return for the privilege which we were all secretly longing to enjoy. Fortunately his affection for his hostess, his extreme good nature and the lure of the piano nearly always proved sufficient ; my mother had only to show him some song with which he was not familiar—it was, incidentally, through her that he became acquainted with many of the numbers which he afterwards sang so successfully at concerts or for His Master's Voice—and the trick was done ; for hours on end he would continue to sing, partly to give us pleasure and partly for the sheer joy of singing.[1] Not that the pleasure was confined to my mother and the few

[1] Amongst Caruso's many letters to my mother—rather artless effusions, it must be confessed, written in a large, round, schoolboyish hand-writing and giving, for the most part, somewhat naïve accounts of his triumphs all over the world together with the invariable assurance that his ' musical-box ', as he called his voice, is better than ever—I find the following : " The musical-box is going splendidly and is my delight, because when I am singing well I give myself much pleasure without knowing that sometimes I am giving pleasure to others too. At least they say that I do ! But I don't know ! "

friends gathered together in our tiny drawing-room ; on
these occasions all work was indefinitely suspended in the
house, and the servants would congregate together on the
stairs outside ; moreover, since it was essential in such a
small space to have the windows wide open when he was
singing, passers-by in the street would stop and listen,
spell-bound by the glorious notes that issued forth through
the open windows.

Puccini had, of course, known Caruso for many years—
ever since that day when a young and more or less unknown
tenor, whose great ambition it was to sing *Bohème* at a local
theatre, had, greatly daring, made his way to Torre del
Lago to seek an audition. He had only to gain admittance,
and the rest was simple : he sang *Che gelida manina*—and
was promptly engaged. The two men had, in reality, little
in common ; there was always something a trifle exaggerated and florid, something—as it were—larger than
life-size about the great tenor ; not only his voice, but his
appearance, his clothes, his manners, his appetite and his
mode of living were all on a grand scale which accorded ill
with Puccini's modest and self-effacing habit of life.
Nevertheless they remained good friends, and they were,
together with Scotti, Angeli and a few others, members of
that ' Italian Band ' which forgathered during the London
Opera Season at Pagani's under the benign presidency of
the ' Master-bandit ', Tosti, to exchange badinage (not
always of a very refined nature) and to indulge in practical
jokes and ' leg-pulling ' at each other's expense. There was,
for instance, the famous occasion when Caruso, by means of
a faked photograph and telegram, was induced to leave the
warm restaurant on a very cold and rainy night and wait
half an hour at a draughty London terminus to keep an
assignation with a love-sick and beauteous damsel—who, of
course, turned out to be a blood-relation of Mrs. Harris.

12.MANDEVILLE PLACE,
W.

" *YOUR* TENOR "—CARUSO SEES HIMSELF

CHAP. III   GODS AND GODDESSES OF SONG   109

The spirit that had breathed life into *Bohème* was slow to die in the heart of its creator—or of its interpreters.

To say that Puccini was ' jealous ' of Caruso because of his friendship with my mother would be ridiculous ; nevertheless I fancy that I detect, behind certain of his less amiable references to ' Your tenor ', as he frequently calls him, just a suspicion of pique. The tribute to his ' god-like ' singing in *Manon Lescaut* is, as we shall see in the following chapter, swiftly followed by a denunciation of his performance in *Butterfly*—a denunciation which, however, does not extend to his voice.

About Caruso's singing there can, I imagine, be no two opinions. Even to-day the gramophone records, made more than a quarter of a century ago when the art of recording was in its indistinct but noisy infancy, still testify un-equivocally to that unique quality which Thomas Burke has so aptly described as "gold swathed in velvet". About his actual performances on the stage, however—and it was with these that Puccini was principally concerned—I con-fess that I am more doubtful ; his presence was by no means impressive, and in certain costumes he was not more than a step—and a very short step at that—removed from the ridiculous ; his acting, with one or two notable exceptions such as his Canio in *Pagliacci*, never went beyond a sketchy and only just serviceable makeshift of gesture and move-ment. So far he was not much better, and not much worse, than the average run of Italian tenors ; where, however, he definitely fell short of other, and more serious-minded, singers was in the liberties which he permitted himself to take on the stage—more especially after he had ' arrived '. It is an open secret that his failure to be re-engaged at Covent Garden between the years 1907 and 1914 was due as much to a certain increasing playfulness which he was apt at that time to display on the stage as to the higher

fees which he now commanded ; for he was not in the
least greedy for money ; moreover, as the Manager of the
Metropolitan, Gatti Casazza, truly remarked : " Any
amount you may pay Caruso, he is always the least expensive
artiste to any management". [1] It is but a short step on the
operatic stage from the sublime to the ridiculous, and it is
therefore all the more essential that the singers, at least,
shall maintain their gravity ; but Caruso at that time was
regrettably apt, when he was not singing himself, to keep
up a running fire of by no means inaudible conversation
for the benefit of his friends in front (including my mother)
interspersed with humorous or unfavourable comments on
the vocal efforts of his fellow-artistes. It was even alleged
that on more than one occasion he marked his disapproval
of the singing of a certain prima donna not merely by words
but by means of an action which is expressly forbidden in
foreign railway-carriages.

His biographers sorrowfully admit that some of his
pranks proved very embarrassing to his fellow-players, and
cite as an example a performance of Bohème at Covent
Garden, in which Marcello was unable to put on his coat
to go out and fetch the medicine for the dying Mimi
because Caruso had sewn up his sleeves, and Colline was
similarly prevented from putting on his hat because it had
been filled to the brim with water [2]—which was surely
carrying the Bohemian spirit a little too far. Nor was he
satisfied to play practical jokes on others ; his own acting
tended more and more towards buffoonery. There was, for
instance, as he proudly explained to my mother, a new
labour-saving device which he had recently come upon ; for
years, when called upon to portray on the stage those intense feelings of emotion to which operatic heroes are
notoriously prone, he had felt it his duty repeatedly to

[1] See Key and Zirato, p. 211.   [2] Ibid., p. 202.

empty and fill his lungs to the utmost limit of their capacity, at the same time emitting stertorous sounds indicative of anger, sorrow, love—or whatever other overmastering passion he was supposed at the time to be labouring under. Then one day a brilliant idea suddenly dawned upon him—exactly the same impression, with enormous saving of breath and of energy, could be conveyed by a rapid and continuous movement of the shoulders to and fro. The effect, both on and off the stage, though not quite so realistic as Caruso maintained, was at any rate irresistibly comic.

All of which may have been very humorous, but was scarcely calculated to commend itself to the luckless composer of the opera which was being ' guyed '. The fact was that, not altogether unnaturally, success at one time had rather turned Caruso's head—though I believe that later he settled down and became more serious. Even so the creator of Bohème might easily have forgiven him ; for he too, as we have seen, enjoyed pranks, and remained, in many ways, a boy till the end of his days. What he found less easy to overlook were the liberties which Caruso—and other great singers—were apt to take with his music. The public— even the decorous and unemotional audiences of Covent Garden—would be carried away on a wave of wild enthusiasm by those famous ' high C's ' on which Caruso (until his voice began to show signs of wear, and the music had to be secretly transposed half a tone lower) loved to linger at altogether inordinate lengths ; but the composer can scarcely be blamed for preferring to hear his music sung as he himself had written it, and for resenting its degradation into a vehicle for what is vulgarly known as ' stunting '. Everyone has heard of the stinging rebuke administered to Battistini by the aged Verdi at a rehearsal : " It is I who write the music : it is for you to sing what I have written ". One's imagination boggles at the thought of what that fiery old gentleman might, or might not, have said to the versatile M. Chaliapine, who has been known on occasions to treble the rôle of singer, conductor and composer ; it would certainly have been worth hearing.

Doubtless Puccini frequently sighed for that simpler, and more Draconian, age. But quite apart from the tendency of well-known singers to indulge in pyrotechnics and thereby to transform the music into a kind of non-stop Marathon endurance test, there was this further reason why he preferred a less scintillating but more level performance—that whilst, in the condominium of song, the Gods and Goddesses are reasonably indulgent towards each other and can even be brought, on special Gala occasions, to divide the worship of mortals, they both share with Dictators a marked distaste for the proximity of possible rivals to the throne—the desert air cannot be too remote a locality for the wasting of such sweetness as they may possess. Even Caruso, whose ascendancy could never for one second have been challenged, constantly hints in his letters to my mother at the machinations of mysterious ' enemies ' and rivals, and preferred to be surrounded on the stage by mediocrities. The ' Goddesses ' were even worse in this respect ; and as this idiosyncrasy chimed in perfectly with the natural parsimony of managements, who always sought to counterbalance the star's salary by engaging the rest of the cast as cheaply as possible, leaving— most improvidently—the rest to Providence, the result was nearly always a hopelessly unbalanced performance. Thus it is that one's otherwise treasured memories of Melba's earlier appearances in *Bohème*, and Destinn's lovely Cio Cio San become obscured and diluted by the recollection of a series of Musettas and Suzukis of almost unbelievable hideousness; and however succulent the dish gastronomically associated with that great prima donna, one cannot be expected to make a whole meal off *Pêche Melba*. From the composer's point of view such a result was even more deplorable; for if he wrote a quartet, it is to be presumed that he required four voices to be blended together, and not—as generally happened—a duet assisted, or hampered, by a more or less inaudible accompaniment in the background. That Puccini suffered intensely from these 'executions' at Covent Garden and elsewhere I can personally testify; indeed so quickly did he tire of his earlier works and so apprehensive was he of the treatment that might be meted out to them, that he could rarely be induced by my mother to accompany her to a performance of any of his operas except the very latest one, and he never tired of chaffing her on her amazing powers of endurance in being able to listen night after night to those 'old carcasses' of his, as he called them. He was particularly critical of the Covent Garden Management, which appeared—in his opinion—to think that it had done all that could be reasonably expected of it by engaging a 'star' or two, and to whom the words *mise-en-scène* and *ensemble* meant little or nothing. I do not think, however, that he fully appreciated the handicap under which Covent Garden laboured; of all the great cities of the world London was—and still remains—the only one that lacks a permanent home for opera, and the difficulties in the way of 'assembling' a number of singers and musicians for a short season and welding them, in the course of a few weeks or even days, into one harmonious whole are well-nigh insuperable.

On the whole, however, I do not feel that Specht's sweeping stricture of Puccini is justified—even if we base ourselves on his private correspondence, in which he naturally expresses himself with the greatest freedom. It is true that some of his references to Madame Carré in the previous chapter are the reverse of amiable, and that his attitude in general towards those Divinities who were more concerned to shape their own ends than those of the composer savours at times of irreverence. " If ", he remarks ungallantly of Destinn, " the ' Divi ' are not properly bridled, as they say of horses, they become, after a time, impossible performers." [1] But although he might laugh good-naturedly at Melba's sexagenarian (or was it septuagenarian?) Mimi,[2] and might even, under provocation, rail at Caruso himself, his criticisms of the great singers associated with his operas were by no means uniformly unfavourable. In the case of Maria Jeritza, for instance, he is almost lyrical in his praise not only of her acting and singing generally (incidentally, how he would have loved her as the cruel Princess Turandot, if he had only lived to see it !) but also of her specific performance in the second act of *Tosca*, " in which", he says, " she does certain things marvellously ". [3] When one bears in mind that she elected to sing *Vissi d'arte* (commonly miscalled ' The Prayer ') lying recumbent at full length on the boards, literally biting the dust, the composer's whole-hearted approval of her action appears rather mystifying. It may be argued that it was more natural that she should address her remarks to Heaven and to Scarpia from the position in which she happened to find herself after her recent struggle with her would-be seducer on the sofa, and that at least it was an improvement on the good old-fashioned method of coming as far forward as possible in the centre of the stage, and dividing her reproaches between the conductor and the audience. Nevertheless I find it surprising that Puccini, with his pro-

[1] See p. 241.
[2] Cf. p. 327. " I am sorry that Melba is ill, but I think that Mimi will be glad to be *unsung* by her ! "   [3] See p. 319.

nounced dislike of any form of 'stunting', should have
bestowed his blessing on this remarkable, but artistically
unjustified, *tour de force*. If Caruso had decided to sing
E lucevan le stelle suspended head downwards from the
ramparts of the Castel Sant'Angelo, Puccini might have
been astounded, but I doubt whether he would have
approved. It may be, however—if I may adapt the old
Latin ' tag '—that *Quod licet divae, non licet divo.*

Towards singers of less renown but of good-will he was
uniformly indulgent and forbearing. In Brussels, for instance, he writes of the performance of *Butterfly* : " The
ensemble and the cast are excellent—better than in Paris,
better even than in London with all its *Divi* ". [1] Again
during the rehearsals of the same opera in his small native
town of Lucca, he writes : " The singers are good, and
their voices fresh ; the *mise-en-scène* is very sweet " ; and
later : " Everything went off well and there was sufficient
poetry in the performance ; the artistes were average, but of
good-will and sincere—this is the essential for *Butterfly* "—
and, he might well have added, for all his operas. Indeed
in this one sentence, with its clearly stated preference for a
uniform level of attainment and—by implication—its dis-
trust of one-sided ' greatness ', he tells us exactly how he
conceived that his music should be rendered.

[1] See p. 186.

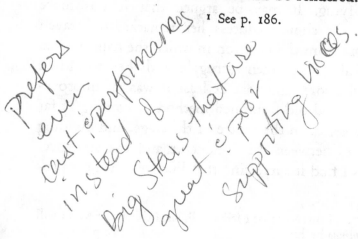

Prefers even performances cast & performances instead of big stars that are great & poor supporting voices.

CHAPTER FOUR

NEW YORK—AND AFTER
January 1907–May 1907

On board *Kaiserin Auguste Victoria*
January 15th, 1907
Tuesday evening

" WE'RE two days off from New York—crossing fair—
there were big seas to-day—I'm all right, Elvira not so good.
As far as comfort goes we're very well off on this boat, but
there are not many passengers ; no one speaks Italian and
few speak French. It's beastly not knowing the language,
and it makes me unhappy—but I hope it won't be so bad
in New York, and besides a month passes quickly. Shall I
get any letters from you? I'll write to you often and keep
you *au courant* of everything."

HOTEL ASTOR
NEW YORK
[*January 23rd, 1907*]

" The first night of *Manon* was the night we arrived—I
landed at six and by eight o'clock I was already at the
Opera. A magnificent evening and a great reception—a
really big success—Caruso was amazing, Cavalieri [1] good.
Now *Butterfly* is being rehearsed, with Farrar. [2] It's an awful
nuisance in the hotel not being able to speak the language,

[1] Lina Cavalieri, who was not only a fine singer but one of the most
beautiful women of her time.

[2] Geraldine Farrar, for many years the favourite soprano at the
Metropolitan, whose audiences had this further cause to be grateful to
her—that she retired from the stage when she was still more or less in
her prime. "*O si sic omnes*—— ! "

but bit by bit one gets used to it, and manages to make oneself understood. The time passes so quickly here that it seems as though we haven't been here one day—rather, one hour. I'll write to you again at greater length when I have time—I must stop now because it's 10.30 in the morning, and at 11 I have to be at the Opera for the rehearsal."

HOTEL ASTOR
NEW YORK
January 25th, 1907

" *Butterfly* is coming on in ten days' time—there have been some great successes here, and it's my operas that draw the biggest crowds. I'm well, but I'm badly in need of a little peace and quiet—I don't understand your sudden departure for Nice—I had thought of disembarking at Plymouth! So how am I going to see you?

I haven't seen your relations yet [1]—but I'll go there one of these days—I wonder if you have gone so early to Nice on account of Vinnie? Is he not well? And you, my dear? I am sure you are the same dear beautiful, healthy, lovable person that you always were. Much love to David and Vinnie, who is sure to be with you. Caruso is singing like a God—I think it will give you pleasure to know this, which is why I am telling you. I have heard strange news about *Savoia*—he has written saying he wishes to leave the house of Ricordi, and asking to be employed by the Impresario Savage (the man who ran the tour of *Butterfly*)—but Savage won't hear of it. There certainly must have been trouble in Milan between father and son—or has he some other reason which prevents him living quietly in Italy? Who knows ? Needless to say, this must be strictly *entre nous*—it's a secret which was told me by someone who actually read his letter.

[1] He had been given a letter of credit on the American banking firm of Messrs. J. and W. Seligman and Company.

It's terribly cold here—13° below zero! But it's dry and sunny. I'm beginning to recover from my feeling of bewilderment of the first few days—I'm going to have your medicine made up to-day, to raise my spirits a bit, which are, as usual, rather low and depressed. I see a lot of Scotti and we talk about you—I liked Cavalieri in *Manon*; she did it really well."

> HOTEL ASTOR
> NEW YORK
> *February 3rd, 1907*

" We're in the midst of rehearsing *Butterfly*, which is coming on on the 11th—rehearsals are going fairly well, but not too well, partly on account of the imbecility of the conductor, and partly on account of Butterfly's lack of *souplesse*. I'm half dead ! I'm so tired of this life ; I've had to arrange the whole of the *mise-en-scène*—all the musical side of it—and my nerves are worn to shreds ! How I long for a little calm ! Believe me, our life is not to be envied—the texture of our nerves, or at any rate of mine, can no longer stand up to this drudgery, these anxieties and fatigues.

I should like to leave as soon as my work is finished, but there's no good boat and I shall have to wait till the 26th. After the *Première* I shall go to Niagara—*if* I go ! We'll see."

> HOTEL ASTOR
> NEW YORK
> *[February 18th, 1907]*

" We're leaving on the 28th, and not on the 26th—on the *Provence*. It will be impossible to come to Nice ; I've too much need of absolute rest at Torre and then I've got to go at once to Milan, where *Conchita* is waiting to torture me—*Savoia* writes to me that he has found the translator for it—oh God ! Oh God !

I've had all I want of America—at the opera all is well,

and *Madama Butterfly* was excellent, but lacked the poetry which I put into it. The rehearsals were too hurried, and the woman was not what she ought to have been. Also as regards your *God*,[1] (*entre nous*) I make you a present of him —he won't learn anything, he's lazy and he's too pleased with himself—all the same his voice is magnificent. I've been ill for five days with influenza—I'm getting up to-day; I feel rather washed out, but it will wear off. I haven't found a single new subject; I'm wandering in the darkness as usual—It's a sad thing. I'm so tired of my old operas that it makes me positively sick to hear them torn to pieces again! I shall either have to change my profession or find a good libretto. Dear Sybil—I don't know what to do, and it's a torture to me to go back to Milan, Spain[2] and Vaucaire! Oh, why are you leaving Nice so soon? If you had stayed till the end of March, I would have come and paid you a visit—why leave so soon? And are you all right? And are you enjoying yourself? I'm sure you are!

I haven't yet been able to call on your relations—isn't it a shame! *But I'm going—to-morrow*, the 19th—it's all fixed up—they were kind enough to write me a line. . . . Perhaps I shall go to Niagara Fall—to-morrow night I'm going to China Twon [*sic*]—all booked up until we leave. I so much need—rest! Write to me to Torre del Lago, and give Elvira's love and mine to David."

It must have been at the very end of his stay in New York that Puccini was taken to see David Belasco's play, *The Girl of the Golden West*, which was one of Broadway's

---

[1] It is rather ironical that in the facsimile letter reproduced in Key and Zirato's biography (p. 208) Puccini, in apologizing to Caruso for the smallness of his part in *Butterfly*, should seek to console him with the reflection that "it will make it all the easier for you to learn". This does not appear to have been the case—at any rate in New York.

[2] I.e. *Conchita*.

biggest successes at the time, since it is clear from the foregoing letter, written only a week before his departure, that
he had still found no subject of interest. Once again he was
able to follow the story despite his ignorance of the
language ; according to most of his biographers, he was so
enchanted with the play that he determined forthwith to
set it to music. This seems scarcely borne out by the facts ;
for although he wrote a number of letters to my mother
on his return there is not a word about *The Girl* until
April 15th—nearly two months later—when he mentions
casually that " Messer Belasco " is sending him a copy.
Although he fell in love, *more suo*, with his Californian girl
later, this was not a case of ' love at first sight ' as it had
been with Cio Cio San. Minnie had first to dethrone her
royal rival, Marie Antoinette, before her place was secure ;
indeed it was not until after his visit to London in June
that—largely on my mother's advice—he finally made up
his mind.

His first concern, however, on his return from America
was the removal of the ' Spanish ulcer '—an operation all
the more delicate since it entailed opposing the cherished
wishes of the man whose opinion he valued most in the
world : Giulio Ricordi. His reluctance to offend his old
friend was increased by the fact that the dissensions in the
house of Ricordi, already hinted at in his letter from New
York, had now come to a head : Tito decided to leave his
father's firm, and accordingly asked Puccini for a written
testimonial to his abilities in matters operatic, adding that
Ricordi's would feel his loss very much. " And he is right ",
comments Puccini, who had no great love for *Savoia*, " for
one has to recognize that its development abroad is in great
part due to him." In the end, however, Tito withdrew his
resignation, and Puccini could adhere with an easier conscience to his determination to be rid of the hated ' Spanish

slut '. It turned out to be no easy matter, however, and the endless arguments and threatened law-suits took their toll of his energies—and of his temper. A minor worry—but one which he took more light-heartedly—was the disappearance of the manuscript of *The Duchess of Padua* which, together with the *Florentine Tragedy*, Robert Ross had entrusted to my mother, and she in turn had passed on to Puccini. I do not know if it was ever discovered ; but as the play was published shortly afterwards the consequences cannot have been very serious.

TORRE DEL LAGO
April 2nd, 1907

" *Inouï* [1] is furious—he has written me a letter, asking for damages ! I have written back—a good letter too.

I'll write to Tosti—tell him I love him and apologize to him for me—his letter, forwarded from New York, is on the table in front of me waiting to be answered—and I'm such a lazy pig that I've done nothing about it yet. I am longing to see you again in the summer—how can one exist so long without Sybil ? Henceforth you have become an institution for us. I have had the pens—thanks for everything—to-day I'm wearing a green tie (one of your last ones) which is a beauty. I haven't got my new car yet ; I'm signing the agreement to-day."

TORRE DEL LAGO
April 10th, 1907

" There is terrific excitement in the house of *Savoia* because I have given up the idea of *Conchita*. *Inouï* is in a rage and has written me a letter claiming moral and material damages for my refusal—I wrote him a good and serious answer—but so far I have had no reply. Tito is in Palermo putting on one of his usual failures—I am resting under doctor's orders and now I feel fairly well.

[1] Pierre Louÿs.

I wrote to Fosca and told her to look for the libretto and Oscar Wilde's play, *The Duchess of Padua*, and asked her to send them off—But Fontana [1] offered the libretto to *me*! So Franchetti's story can't be true."

Torre del Lago
April 15th, 1907

" Illustrious Lady,

" With the most profound respect and the humblest obeisances I kneel before you, beauteous among the beauteous, and bring you my news—Messer Belasco is sending me a copy of *The Girl of the Golden West*, and *Inouï* has written me another idiotic letter, claiming damages and indemnification for not having put his libretto to music! Ridiculous—*rigolo*! I haven't answered him yet, because I'm too lazy. I'm very unhappy because I haven't succeeded in finding *The Duchess of Padua*! Fosca writes from Milan that it isn't there—and I've had a good look round here, but to-morrow I'll search in every nook and corner and turn everything upside down and inside out till I find it! Tell your friend [2] to go on waiting a little longer, and prepare him, if you can, for the eventual loss of the *Duchess*. All the same I still hope to find this wretched woman who haunts my dreams with thoughts of the embarrassment to which I am putting you with your friend! I would willingly go to see him and impress upon him the saintly virtues of patience and—perhaps too—of resignation!"

---

[1] Ferdinando Fontana, who was responsible for those two masterpieces, *Le Villi* and *Edgar*; it would be interesting to know what he would have made of Wilde's play. I do not know what " Franchetti's story " can have been ; it is possible that he was trying to revenge himself for the loss of *Tosca* by wresting *The Duchess of Padua* from Puccini ; if so, he must have thought better of it, for he never put it to music.

[2] Robert Ross.

TORRE DEL LAGO
April 24th, 1907

" I'm in trouble over *Conchita,* over Colautti and the *Florentine Tragedy,* not to mention another librettist as well. As regards the former, Ricordi [the father] has written me page after page to try to persuade me to set it to music, saying that the Italian translation is most beautiful and beseeching me to change my mind. I've promised him to go to Milan and read it, and then to discuss again this subject which I do not consider suited to the stage. All this is upsetting—it's so depressing to have to go on fighting over the Spanish slut.

And then Colautti, who made a very bad first act of the *Florentine Tragedy,* asks to be paid for the *beautiful* work he has done—and another librettist in Florence threatens to bring an action against me if I don't pay him for the dirty mess he has made—they're all *gobinghis!* ''

MILAN
May 3rd, 1907

" Just arrived—I've seen Ricordi. I've already taken up a defensive position to ward off the cursed Spanish assault! How pleased I was to see you and David at Como ! But that too is now a thing of the past—I am rather sad, my dear Sybil ! How I envy you your character, and above all your physical and your moral balance—give my love to the dear, kind Tosti and ditto ditto David.

Poor Vini ! He wrote me such a sweet letter and I— lazy pig that I am—haven't even answered it, and on top of that I've lost his address. I lose everything—including *The Duchess of Padua.*''

The struggle over *Conchita* lasted for several days, but in the end the composer prevailed over the publisher—short of writing the music himself, it is difficult to see how Signor

Giulio could have had his way. He did the next best thing, however, and persuaded Riccardo Zandonai to set it to music. *Conchita* was produced in Milan in 1911, and its failure, despite the fact that the music had much to commend it, proved conclusively how right Puccini had been to set his face against such an unnatural and impossible subject.

"At last I can breathe again!" he writes thankfully, now that he is released from the hateful Spanish bondage. But he was not to enjoy his liberty for long; in the very same letter he announces that he has a wonderful new idea, and that he is commissioning Illica to write the libretto. The 'new idea' was, in fact, no novelty, but—Marie Antoinette. It is quite clear, therefore, that the impression left on his mind by *The Girl of the Golden West* cannot have been nearly as profound as his biographers suggest.

Those who have shed innumerable tears over the fate of the French Queen might well, if their quiverful is not exhausted, spare a few for her luckless librettist, Luigi Illica. According to Adami,[1] the original libretto, which had entailed a considerable amount of historical research work, and had been drawn up at Puccini's special request, was divided into no less than thirteen scenes. Perhaps Illica would have done well to pay heed to a popular superstition and start with twelve, or even fourteen; for the libretto to which he had devoted so much time and care was gradually dismembered bit by bit and scene by scene until now, when Puccini is overcome with enthusiasm for his 'new idea', there are only three scenes left: imprisonment, trial—and death.

But, as we shall see, this was not the worst; even in this truncated form, *The Austrian Woman*, as she has now become, was never destined to be reanimated by the

---

[1] See *Letters*, p. 226.

divine breath of music. Her downward path from imprisonment to trial, and from trial to the guillotine is closely paralleled by a corresponding decline in Puccini's enthusiasm as revealed in his correspondence : from certainty to doubt, from doubt to—silence. Thus one more ' might-have-been ' became a ' never-was ' ; and Illica, we are told, vented his outraged feelings on the ever-tactful Signor Giulio—who, for once, must have been hard put to it to find a suitably soothing reply.[1] The fact was that, after Giacosa's death, Illica's luck had deserted him, and he had completely lost the power to please.

MILAN
May 9th, 1907

" I have side-tracked *Conchita* and I have even convinced Ricordi. *To-day I can breathe again*—after so many days of struggle and the vilest temper. To-morrow I shall see Illica about an idea I have—which seems to me a grand one ! The last days of Marie Antoinette. A soul in torment—First act, prison ; second act, the trial ; third act, the execution—three short acts, stirring enough to take one's breath away. I'm absolutely taken up with this idea of mine—and I have found a title which seems to me fitting and appropriate because I couldn't call it *Marie Antoinette*, seeing that it only deals with the one episode of her tragic death. The title is : *The Austrian Woman*—what do you think of it ? I'll tell you when the agreement has been signed—which will be to-morrow, or shortly afterwards—Good-bye, my dear, for the present—For mercy's sake don't say that I have ceased to be fond of you—you are, and you always will be, our dearest and our staunchest friend in life and in death."

MILAN
[*May 12th*, 1907]

" At last the agreement has been signed—I am going to

[1] See *Letters*, p. 227.

do *The Austrian Woman* and I think it is an opera which will make an extraordinary impression. How happy I am at the thought that I shall soon be able to work again! I hope to be able to begin to write in the summer.

I can't come to London ; I should like to, but I can't make up my mind—Thank you and David for your kind invitation, and don't be angry with me—at any rate I am certain to see you in Italy in August."

MILAN
May 14th, 1907

" What plans have you got for the summer ? I've let it be known that Abetone is for sale, but if you and the family are coming, *I won't sell.* I've asked a stiff price for it, and that I shall stick to—and it's practically impossible even to give it away, unless some fanatical admirer of mine should come along—about which I am sceptical. I intend to go to Torre next week, and at the end of June I shall have my car—a landaulette with plenty of room for five inside—my idea is to go in it to Carlsbad for the cure. Why don't you and David come ? I should be so glad to have you as our guests for the journey—and for ever after.

I'm quite well now—my mind is calmer at the thought of the work that lies ahead of me—so you like the subject ? I warn you that it will be terrible—so much so that for two pins I would give up the idea ! But there's no tenor part—perhaps not a baritone either ; a lot of chorus—*Her*—and lots of minor parts. It's an original type of opera of its kind —and that attracts me—and above all it will be strikingly and painfully effective."

MILAN
May 17th, 1907

" I've written to Tosti to-day in prose and in poetry— The work on the libretto is progressing and is going—with God's will—excellently. So far we are only at the beginning, but I can already see the direction which it is taking ; let's hope my interest in the subject continues, and I'll put all of me into the opera. It's a very daring theme, though highly artistic—do you think such a subject would have a success at Covent Garden ? "

MILAN
[*May* 21st, 1907]

" I have written three letters to Tosti and haven't had an answer—please smack him hard from me. Antoinette has dried up for the time being ; the librettist has asked for a fortnight's grace, and I have had to concede it to him. He has some previous work to dispose of and then he'll start on it again. I'm afraid that another summer will pass without work and that puts me in a bad temper. Supposing I were to come to London ? But how can I ? No, no, it's not possible—you'll see that I shall end by staying on in this horrible, soul-destroying Milan. Dear Sybillina, how I should like to see you ! "

In spite of these protestations, Puccini was able, shortly after, to come to London. On the back of the programme of a concert given on June 11th at the Aeolian Hall by a Miss Kitty Cheatham (" The Distinguished American Discuse ") I find the following in his handwriting :

" How well this pen writes !
For two pins I would take it away with me.
[*Signature*] G. PUCCINI

But I don't dare because I haven't any courage—it's a fine thing to steal—oh, how well I understand thieves ! How happy they must be !

What a divine feeling it must give one to break open a safe, to rifle a house, to seize on a woman covered with diamonds !
[*Signature*] G. PUCCINI "

PART III

LA FANCIULLA DEL WEST

(1907–1910)

CHAPTER ONE

THE MAKINGS OF A LIBRETTO
(June–September 1907)

MY mother undoubtedly took advantage of Puccini's visit to London to press the claims of *The Girl of the Golden West* ; before he had left, the battle was more than half won. It was she who commissioned the translator (also a bit of a 'traitor', according to Puccini, who loved a play on words [1]) just as later it was she who chose the curious hybrid title by which the opera came to be known. Rightly or wrongly, she thoroughly mistrusted *Marie Antoinette* ; it was not because, as Puccini chaffingly suggests, there was no part in it for *her* tenor, nor was it merely because the subject was ' sad ' ; but she felt instinctively that the theme was stale and hackneyed, and that it contained none of those elements from which he was wont to derive his finest inspiration. It was not long, as we shall see, before he completely shared her view, and his enthusiasm for *The Girl*, so backward in manifesting itself, had reached fever-point.

But what—it may well be asked—were those precise qualities which he looked for in a libretto and which, presumably, he must have found in Belasco's play ? It is not an easy question to answer—though, to a certain extent, he answers it himself in these letters. We can begin by dismissing as unworthy even of consideration the absurd charge brought against him by certain of his biographers

[1] The Italian for translator is *traduttore*, and for traitor *traditore*.

that, encouraged by the large dividends which *Butterfly* had
recently drawn from London and New York, he deliberately chose a ' pot-boiler ' with a strong American flavour
calculated to make a special appeal to the not too refined
Anglo-Saxon palate. He was not a business man concerned
with extending the market for his goods abroad ; not only
was he too great an artist to allow himself to be influenced
by such sordid considerations, but he was also quite incapable of writing ' to order '. No one who has read his
letters thus far can doubt his transparent sincerity ; whatever his limitations, the subject which he chose had to be
one capable not only of arousing, but also of maintaining,
his whole-hearted enthusiasm. His standards may not have
been particularly lofty, but they were exacting ; indeed
they were ruled by an almost automatic prohibition, since,
from the moment that he had ceased to believe in what he
was writing, he could no longer write. This will appear
even more clearly later, when we come to examine the one
work which he was definitely commissioned to write : the
Viennese operetta, *La Rondine*.

It was not unnatural that he should turn again to the
source from which his previous opera was derived ; in
addition, he found in *The Girl of the Golden West* that for
which he looked primarily in any libretto : a dramatic,
straightforward story with plenty of incident. If anything,
this tale of life among the Californian miners in the ' Gold
Rush ' of 1848 suffers from excess of incident ; so much
so that it might appear—and did appear to many—more
suited to the screen than to the stage. Shorn of its trim-
mings—its local atmosphere of cake-walks, squaws, coon-
songs and gambling saloons—it is, like all Puccini's operas,
essentially a love-story ; but Minnie, who lives unmolested
amongst these rough, lawless, dissolute miners, attending
to their wants spirituous and spiritual and cleverly mixing

whiskies with Bible classes, is utterly different from any of his previous heroines ; was it altogether a coincidence, I wonder, that Puccini, who had himself so recently discovered the possibilities of a Platonic friendship à l'anglaise, should find himself attracted by this essentially Anglo-Saxon type? Yet Minnie, too, when love at last comes into her life, is prepared to fight for it ; despite her discovery that the man with whom she has fallen in love is none other than the hunted bandit, Ramerrez, she hides him from his pursuers in the loft, and when his presence is betrayed to the Sheriff by the blood dripping down from his wound, stakes her hand against his life over a game of poker. In the last act—that scene in the vast Californian forest which was the composer's own special contribution to the play—it is she who, when the terrible ' man-hunt ' is over and the noose is already round her lover's neck, pleads for his life with each of the miners in turn, and finally secures his release.

With four consecutive successes to his credit, Puccini was now in the position known to contract players as ' vulnerable ' ; what—the critics asked themselves—could be the reason for this depressingly uniform record? Being critics and, therefore, wiser than the generality, they were not slow to find the correct answer ; he owed his success to the fact that he copied—himself.[1] In reality he never wrote to a pattern, just as he could never write to order ; but the critics were able to derive a modicum of satisfaction from certain points of resemblance which undoubtedly existed between the story of The Girl and that of Tosca. Once again the soprano-heroine contends with the baritone-

[1] They were at least on firmer ground than Toscanini's latest biographer, Herr Paul Stefan, who solemnly informs us that parts of Turandot were ' cribbed ' from Verdi's Tosca—a work which does not exist outside Herr Stefan's imagination. (Toscanini, by Paul Stefan, p. 85.)

villain (who is, incidentally, also a representative of the police) [1] for the life of the tenor-hero ; once again the 'price' demanded for a trifling miscarriage of justice is that of the lady herself—though the Sheriff's intentions, if no less unwelcome, are at least more honourable than those of Scarpia. But there the resemblance ends, and the *dénouement* is utterly different ; for the gentle Minnie excels as a card-sharper rather than as a sharper of knives, and— as though to disprove the old saying that luck at cards and luck in love do not go together—succeeds where Tosca's more downright methods so signally failed. *The Girl* is, in- cidentally, the only Puccini opera from which death, whether natural or unnatural, sudden or lingering, individual or wholesale, is entirely banished. " *Troppo sangue, troppo sangue !* " [2] chant Ping, Pang and Pong dolefully in unison ; for once their creator agreed with them, and it was, I think, this absence of 'blood' which was one of the attractions to him of Belasco's play.

HOTEL BELLEVUE
PARIS
[*June* 1907]

" After a rather rough crossing during which Elvira was extremely sick, here I am in Paris—already I feel the difference in the atmosphere. . . . And how sad I feel to have left behind so many good and affectionate friends ! You, dear Sybil, are the kindest and sweetest person that it is possible to imagine, and never will I forget all the con- sideration which you showed us, nor your infinite patience. . . . I love your country almost more than I do my own ! I wish I had known it earlier so as to learn the language, and then I would have appreciated all the perfection, the

[1] Puccini seems to have shared Dickens' hatred, but not Mr. Bumble's contempt, of 'the Law'.
[2] " Too much blood, too much blood ! " (*Turandot*, Act 2.)

"TO DEAREST SYBIL, UNIQUE AND RARE CREATURE"

(1907)

charm and the refinement of your tongue; but it's too late now, and I have to content myself with hearing the words in my own language and reading in your eyes what you would say in your own.

I kiss your hands as those of a Queen of kindness and thoughtfulness, and I press them affectionately as those of my dearest and most devoted friend."

HOTEL BELLEVUE
PARIS
[*June* 1907]

" Last night I went to Ducas—what a blue-beard ! [1] Impossible—I think it's nearly, or very nearly, better to hear a *Tosca* at Covent Garden ! *Butterfly* is being given in Vienna in November, and *Manon*, *Tosca* and *Butterfly* in Brussels—though *Butterfly* isn't certain because they haven't got a woman to sing it yet.

I've had to stop writing because I've had a visitor— Savage [2]—he's always talking to me about operas—God ! I've had enough of it—still. . . . .

I'm so fond of you, dear Sybil, and I can never thank you enough for all your kind attentions.

I'll write to you to-morrow *at greater length* ; but this time it will be true—you'll see."

HOTEL BELLEVUE
PARIS
[*June* 1907]

" I'm leaving to-night—I've seen *Savoia* ; he wanted to see me to talk about the music of the Revolution which I have found here in large quantities—it will be useful to me for Marie Antoinette. Oh my dear, I shall certainly do it—

[1] *Ariane et Barbe-Bleue*, by Paul Ducas, first produced in Paris in 1907. Some critics describe it as " derived from the Puccini school " ; evidently its indirect begetter either did not recognize, or did not relish, the derivation.

[2] The impresario of the *Butterfly* tour.

what does it matter if it's *sad* ? It will be so impressive
that it will hold the audience enthralled—if only there had
been a chance of making room for your 🎼 ! [1] But it
isn't possible because the tenor parts are small ones. I'm
writing to Pavone [2] about the 200 [lire] to be given to the
old man, and telling him to pay it in my name—I shall do
The Girl of the West too, be sure.

I am happy because I have *work*, and I am longing to
get down to it, now that I have heard the sort of stuff that
is being given here—these two subjects have given me the
courage of a lion."

On his way through Milan, Puccini sent my mother a
present—and a poem. Here is the poem, as rendered into
English by my father.

June 26th, 1907

" Dearest Syb, I'm far from sorry
    To leave at once for rural Torre,
    There to bare my manly form
    To the sun, the rain, the storm ;
    While my Maiden from the West
    Lies uneasy on my chest,
    And I study ' con amore '
    France's Revolution's story.
    I am sending you to-day
    A parasol of colours gay.
    Tosti receives a pencil ' chic ',
    Caruso gets a walking-stick.
    And these souvenirs all three
    Poorly voice a memory
    Of the many joys I knew—

[1] Caruso.
[2] Ricordi's London representative.

Happy hours I spent with you—
When I wandered at your side.
But while I blister in the heat
Forty Celsius is no treat !
And though a bachelor's life is merrier
I'd gladly marry Madame—Perrier !
Warm as sunny Italy
Is the love that comes from me.
When will come that month remote
That demands an overcoat?
In my idiotic way
I could write the live-long day—
But what's left of my poor brain
Wisely bids me to—refrain."

From ' rural Torre ' a perfect deluge of letters descended
on my mother. " I'm anxiously awaiting *The Girl* ; I've
heard no more of Marie Antoinette—everybody is sleeping
like silk-worms in this heat." A few days later : " I am
waiting for the copy of *The Girl* ; I think I shall do it before
Marie Antoinette—but not with Illica ". This sounds
ominous enough for poor Illica ; but worse is to follow :
" I'm waiting anxiously for *The Girl* ; I've signed an agreement with the Poet, who is awaiting it no less anxiously ".
" The Poet " was Carlo Zangarini, of whom we shall hear
more in the following chapter. Two days later the first
part of the translation arrived.

TORRE DEL LAGO
July 8th, 1907

" I've read the first two acts of *The Girl*—I like it very
much. The first act is very muddled, but it contains distinct possibilities. The second act is most beautiful ; I'm
anxiously awaiting the other two acts. That poor translator
(who is a bit of a traitor too)—only 200 francs ! It's

terribly little ; I'll tell them to give him another 100— would you mind handing it over to him when he has finished the translation, and I'll pay you back after?

Au revoir at Abetone, because so far no buyer has come forward—and thanks for everything."

TORRE DEL LAGO
July 12th, 1907

" I'm waiting for the second and third acts [1]—they are sure to be here to-morrow. I've already sent on the first two acts to Ricordi senior. It's quite certain that *The Girl* is the opera I am going to do ! You can rest assured, and please say whatever you like, for it gives me the greatest pleasure that you should enter into my most intimate affairs, my *very own* affairs—have you any means of obtaining, in America or in London itself, some early American music and some modern music too ? I'm writing on my own account—but as I need as much as possible in order to *get the atmosphere*, will you look round too—I should be so grateful if you would.

We are well—at the beginning of August we (like you) will be at Abetone—is it true Caruso is coming too? Do you think it's a good idea? Enough—Au revoir."

With the receipt of the third and fourth acts, Puccini was at last able to gain a more or less comprehensive picture of Belasco's play. It must be borne in mind that he had only seen it performed once in New York ; in the circumstances there could be no finer illustration of his swift and unerring theatrical instinct than the following letter, written on the very same day on which he had set eyes on the manuscript for the first time—and that, too, in a translation which he feelingly describes as " vile ". Already he has completely visualized, as though he had

---

1 He means the third and fourth acts.

seen it himself countless times on the stage, that scene in the vast Californian forest which was of his own devising, and which was to make the ending so much more dramatic than that of the play.

TORRE DEL LAGO
July 14th, 1907

" The third act doesn't appeal to me much! But I think it would be possible to rearrange it if one takes three things into account : the scene where he is brought on, bound—I should make the scene of his sentence and of the insults of the sheriff take place then—*no school episode*—then *she* arrives, surprised, and there is a big scene in which she pleads for his freedom—everybody being against her except Dick.[1] Finally the cow-boys are stirred to pity, and she bids a moving farewell to all—there is a great love duet as they move slowly away, and a scene of grief and desolation amongst the cow-boys, who remain on the stage in different attitudes of depression, misery, etc., etc. But the scene must take place outside the *Polka* in a big wood, and in the background to the right there are paths leading to the mountains—the lovers go off and are lost from sight, then they are seen again in the distance embracing each other, and finally disappear—how does that strike you? In this way I mix the third and fourth acts together—tell me your opinion—I need the original, because the translation is *vile.*"

TORRE DEL LAGO
July 18th, 1907

" If you sent me the original it would be better—it would save time and I could send it to the librettist, whose mother comes from Colorado and who knows English. About the music, good—many thanks—You are so good

[1] In the actual score of the opera her supporter is *Nick*, the bar-tender of the ' Polka ' Saloon.

and so kind. They've promised me the car for the 27th, and we'll see if they keep their word ; if so, *ça va sans dire* that it will be there to meet you at Pracchia."

TORRE DEL LAGO
July 22nd, 1907

" It's days since I had a letter from you, and it's almost too hot to breathe ! I am waiting for the original manuscript —the matter is urgent because the other subject [1] is going forward, and I should like to have *The Girl* ready at once. I foresee that I shall have to go to Abetone in a carriage drawn by horses ! The car is still delayed ! ! ! And now my small car is damaged, and so I have become a pedestrian !

Thank you for the Indian songs you have sent me ; I've also written to America to get them—and I await those which you promised me. I'm well—and you? Always, I have no doubt, a model of beauty and the picture of health."

TORRE DEL LAGO
August 4th, 1907

" DEAREST FRIENDS,

" Welcome—I can't come and fetch you, because the use of the car hasn't yet been allowed by the authorities— it hasn't got a licence—and I might get into trouble. To-morrow everything will be in order—if it were at night I would come, because the night is made for mysteries and for crimes ! So take a carriage and drive out to us—lunch at midday and dinner at seven and then a drive in the darkness —I'll take you wherever you like—welcome—we are *over-joyed* to see you ! "

After a short visit to Torre del Lago, we all went to Abetone where once again we spent a very happy summer.

[1] Marie Antoinette.

Puccini was rather restless and could think and talk of nothing but *The Girl* ; it was nearly four years since he had finished *Butterfly*, and he could scarcely contain his excitement at the prospect of being able to get to work again. As soon as we had left, he retired to Chiatri, where he anxiously awaited the arrival of " the poet " with the preliminary draft of the libretto.

CHIATRI
September 19th, 1907

" By now you will be at Folkestone surrounded by all your dear ones ; I'm still here at Chiatri. Zangarini is coming on Saturday—I'll let you know my impressions at once. I've just had a telegram calling me to Berlin for the last rehearsals of *Butterfly* : but I can't go and I've telegraphed to *Savoia* to go instead. There's Zangarini on Saturday, and on Tuesday they're giving me a gold medal at the theatre as a gift of the municipality, so I can't be absent—besides I really have very little wish to go away at present."

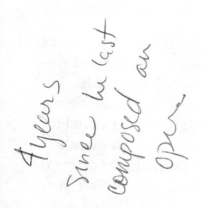

CHAPTER TWO

A LIBRETTO IN THE MAKING
(October 1907–September 1908)

AND now a new figure appears on the scenes; that of Carlo
Zangarini, one of that race of men apart known variously
as " my poets " (sometimes with a capital, and sometimes
with a small, ' p '), " my collaborators ", " my librettists "
—though all too frequently, as the work progresses, the
generic designation is preceded and amplified by a disparag-
ing epithet. We have already had cause to remark on the
overwhelmingly important part which they played in his work
and—one might truthfully add—in his life. He was utterly
dependent upon them; unless and until they had furnished
him with the material in exactly the shape in which he
wanted it, he could not write a bar of music; however
much he might rebel, he remained their slave. Which did
not prevent him rebelling—at least on paper.

A whole volume—and a very amusing one at that—
might be written about his relations with his various
librettists; it would in its way, I venture to think, be at
least as interesting as those innumerable studies of Napoleon
and his Marshals with which the world has been inundated.
As regards his later operas, Signor Adami, the gifted author
of *La Rondine*, *Il Tabarro* and part-author of *Turandot*, has
already, in his preface to the *Letters* and later in his all too
short biography, given us many delightful side-lights on
their work of collaboration as viewed from the angle of the
librettist; needless to say, it is not always the same as that

e composer. The volume that I have in mind, therefore, would doubtless reveal many differences ; but such ' sound and fury ' as it might contain would signify nothing ; for these ' differences ', if we may judge from the example of Adami, who had, perhaps, more to put up with than any of his predecessors, left not a trace of bitterness or resentment behind. On the contrary, writing eleven years after the composer's death about one of these periodical divergencies of opinion, he says : " I understood then that Puccini was always right, and that the alterations which he was constantly demanding and on which he insisted so obstinately were based upon something, which one could not hope to fathom, in his soul and in his creative mind. The trouble which all this work involved was completely forgotten in a burning desire to assist in giving concrete shape to the realization of the Maestro's ideas. And the continuous criticisms in his letters, summary yet clear as crystal, indicated in a few strokes the path to be followed."[1]

We have seen how, with every new opera that they wrote, the team-work between Sullivan and his two Gilberts, as I have called them, became not only more perfect, but progressively smoother until, with *Butterfly*, complete harmony may be said to have reigned. But now, with one Gilbert dead and the other out of favour, it was necessary to look elsewhere ; eventually the choice fell on Zangarini. " A present from *Savoia* "—as Puccini was later to call him.

I do not know with what hopes, or with what fears, the new poet approached his task ; it was scarcely to be expected that he, a newcomer, *nondum subactus ferre jugum*, would be able to succeed, where his two illustrious predecessors had so often failed, in completely satisfying his exacting task-master at the first attempt. Puccini's constant

[1] See *Puccini*, p. 89.

grumblings and complaints need not be taken too seriously, however ; it is only necessary to quote from a letter which he wrote to Signor Giulio some years later, when he was looking for a successor to the *Fanciulla*, and thought that he had found it in *Anima allegra*. " I should suggest to keep Adami and associate Zangarini with him. I should not like to leave him out of it. He defers to me and is fond of me, and since I shall be the director of all the operations, I shall make the two librettists vassals to my Doge." [1] And this of the man who had been rudely offered the unattractive alternatives of ph-otographing and fr-eezing himself, and was shortly afterwards ' discharged on account of incompetence ' ! The fact was that Puccini was burning to start work on his beloved *Girl*, and his impatience at any delays was apt to bring about explosions of wrath which were neither meant, nor taken, very seriously. I remember meeting the kindly poet at Abetone, and I feel confident that he, like Adami, preserves nothing but feelings of admiration and affection for the terrible Doge whose vassal he had become. [2]

Zangarini's task was, in many respects, more arduous than that of his predecessors. Both the atmosphere and the dialogue of this story of the wild and woolly West were extremely difficult to transpose into Italian ; the names themselves—Billy, Wowkle, Johnson, Wells Fargo and the

---

[1] See *Letters*, p. 244.

[2] Since writing the above I have received a long letter from Signor Zangarini which more than confirms my assumption that he too, like the other " vassals ", treasures nothing but unclouded memories of those days when he was privileged to collaborate with the Maestro—memories which, he says, will always remain " sacred and unforgettable ". He even goes on to confess, with striking self-effacement, that the real librettist of *The Girl of the Golden West* was not himself—but Puccini ! However, I must not further anticipate Signor Zangarini's own reminiscences, which are now in course of preparation and which should prove a valuable addition to Puccinian literature.

rest—have an air of incongruity in their Latin setting, in the same way as Pinkerton's interruption of his aria, *Dovunque al mondo*, to enquire whether his friend the Consul will have a " Milk-punch or whisky ? " always leaves an English audience with a faint feeling of embarrassment. Also, owing to the shortcomings of the 'traitor-translator', it was left to the librettist not only to adapt, but to re-translate, the play ; and although Zangarini's mother came from Colorado, his grasp of our idiom does not seem to have been quite perfect—if I may judge from the following ode indited to my mother from Torre del Lago in the intervals of libretto-making, which I found amongst her papers. True, it is signed " *Charlie* Zangarini " ; but its inspiration seems to derive at least as much from the paternal, as from the distaff, side.

Torre del Lago
October 18th, 1907

" With a smile of Minnie
and a wish of mine,
With the voice of waters
from the lake divine,
let, good Muse, my verse
everywhere you go,
bring salutes and kindness,
english So and so ! . . . [1]

Charlie Zangarini "

Confronted with a task of extraordinary difficulty, Zangarini did his best, and succeeded at first in wringing from his impatient and exacting task-master the admission

[1] The exact meaning of the Address is not altogether clear ; but lest there should be any misunderstanding about the poet's flattering intentions, I hasten to add that the expression ' You so-and-so ' as a term of disparagement was as yet unknown to Hollywood—or to Colorado.

that he had " worked well ". Later, it is true, Puccini insisted on the addition of a second librettist in the person of
Guelfo Civinini ; but I hasten to add that his statement that
Zangarini had been " discharged " is not in the least borne
out by the facts, since a few months later we find him complaining that " these two librettists are a perfect plague ;
one of them has hurt himself, and the other takes not the
slightest notice ".

TORRE DEL LAGO
October 1st, 1907

" *The Girl* is in course of construction ; so far Z. has
drawn up a rough draft of the first and third acts—but the
latter is not right yet. I'll let you know about it later.

The second performance [of *Butterfly*] in Berlin was as
great a triumph as the first ; they're giving another three
performances this week. I've not yet had any news about
the *première* in Prague which took place last night."

October 1st, 1907

" Just this moment had a telegram from Prague about
the complete and ' *absolutely thundering* ' [those are the
words used] success of *Butterfly*.

To you, dear friend of mine and of my *Butterfly*, I
send the news the very second I have received it, in the
confident knowledge that it will give you pleasure."

TORRE DEL LAGO
October 6th, 1907

" You're naughty to complain and abuse your friend
Giacomo who is as lazy as a rock and only writes to a
certain beautiful, elegant lady who never ceases talking—
but never mind, I don't bear her a grudge and I continue
to think of her and all the hours that have gone by. It
rains every day here and I'm bored—but I don't feel like

writing—my senses are dulled and I'm waiting for Zangarini, who ought to be here any day now. And I wrote to you the other day, asking what letter I should send to the pianoforte people, and I've had no reply ! "

TORRE DEL LAGO
October 13th, 1907

" Zangarini has been here since yesterday—he'll stay on until *The Girl* is finished. So the time when I can get to work is approaching, much to my delight. Nobody has sent me any Berlin papers, so I couldn't pass them on to you ; but I know that *Butterfly* is being given three times a week.

Thanks for your telegram and the note-paper which, as you know, I am eagerly awaiting—parcels are a weakness of mine. I'm longing for the arrival of the piano."

TORRE DEL LAGO
October 15th, 1907

" At midday to-day just as I was going to lunch, I had the charming surprise of the letter-case—most beautiful and exactly the right size. Thank you so much—it shall repose on my heart (but my pocket is on the right side—what a shame !) Now I shall simply have to get a green suit, and then I shall be entirely in green—unlike myself who am already tinged with the yellow of autumn ! *Hélas !*

Continue to maintain Tosti's spirits with your smile—at least *he* is there to enjoy it ! *The Girl* is making progress ; the Poet is here and at work—he has nearly completed the first act. But he won't let me read anything until he's finished it, and then we can discuss it."

In the meanwhile—since there was nothing for him to do until Zangarini's work was completed—Puccini paid a

short visit to Vienna to supervise the rehearsals of *Butterfly*.
It was characteristic of him that he had no great love for the
capital of the mighty Austro-Hungarian Empire ; but when,
as a result of the War, Vienna fell on evil times, his feelings
changed completely, and he was never tired of proclaiming
his affection for the poor abandoned city which had lost
everything but its love for music, and for its kindly inhabitants whom he declares to be " the nicest people in the
world—after Sybil ". [1]

> HOTEL BRISTOL
> .VIENNA
> [*October* 1907]

" I think of you so often and wish you were near me—
here, all by myself, I feel so sad. The rehearsals are going
only so-so ; the Drèss rehearsal is on Monday and the first
night on Thursday—but the opera isn't as well done as I
should like. The artistes are hard and unsympathetic—they
haven't got the diction or the naturalness which is necessary
in *Butterfly*. The *mise-en-scène* is going to be nice—Kurz [2] is
fairly good, not very intelligent, but I don't dislike her.
The rest are heavy, as I said.

I'm staying here till Friday and then return to Milan
and Torre del Lago, where I hope to start work on my dear
Girl—and I hope the piano will have arrived too ; I've been
notified that it has left Hamburg."

> HOTEL BRISTOL
> VIENNA
> *November 1st*, 1907

" It's been a magnificent success—ten calls after the first
act, fifteen after the second, fifteen to twenty after the third
—in spite of the fact that the woman was weak and the
tenor worth little. But it was the opera itself which affected
people—I'm simply delighted about it.

[1] See p. 321.   [2] Selma Kurz.

I had a talk with the Queen Mother of Spain, and she told me the Queen is always singing and playing *Butterfly*.

They've given me a magnificent Ehrbar piano of the Erard type all in yellow olive wood which goes well in my room at Torre—I'm very pleased with it."

MILAN
November 5th, 1907

" I have had an awful lot to do for *The Girl*, which is well on its way and which I can promise you will be a great success. Then there was Giulio Ricordi's refusal to allow *Tosca* to be given at La Scala ; in the end I succeeded in persuading him to change his mind, and it's going to be performed with a splendid cast and a magnificent *mise-en-scène*—I'm very pleased about it. It appears that in Brussels they haven't got any singer suitable for the rôle of Butterfly, and it may not be given ! I'm so annoyed because I should have seen you there, but I hope to see you in Rome or perhaps at Torre on your way through.

I have heard of the kindness which you have all shown to Fosca [1]—thank you so much. Do you know that *Butterfly* is now going to be given in twelve different opera houses in Germany ? My affairs are going splendidly ; in France and Belgium this winter there have been twenty-four performances of *Bohème*, fourteen of *Tosca*, and four of *Manon*—*Butterfly* is being given at the Reale in Madrid, but in France little or not at all, owing to the stupid concession which Tito, and I too, made to Madame Carré on the occasion of the success in Paris, reserving her the right to create the part in Brussels and five other towns : Niçe, Bordeaux, Lyons, Marseilles and Aix-les-Bains. And now Madame Carré can't leave the Opéra Comique, and so in these five principal Opera houses *Butterfly* can't be given— and this silly concession holds good for two years !

---

[1] Puccini's stepdaughter.

How pleased I am with *The Girl* ! How I adore the subject—The first act is finished now, but it will be necessary to return to it later, as it needs to be made clearer and to be smartened up. The second act is nearly finished and, as for the third act, I'm going to create that magnificent scene in the great Californian forest of which I spoke to you at Abetone."

GRAND HOTEL ISOTTA
GÈNES
[*November 8th*, 1907]

" I'm here for a performance of *Butterfly*, but I'm off to Torre to-morrow. I came here to help at a couple of rehearsals, so that the opera should suffer the least possible ill-treatment.

I feel well and I am entirely taken up by *Minnie*. The poet hasn't quite finished, but I shall soon have the libretto complete. I think the third act is going to be simply marvellous—if only the poet will understand me ; but I'm going to make every conceivable effort so as to be certain of getting what I want.

In Vienna things continue to go splendidly at the Opera, the house *completely sold out*—and in Berlin too it is being performed three times weekly. But that's enough about my affairs—I am sure I am boring you.

It's your turn now to write seldom ! Except about Opera I've nothing to tell you—everything's as usual. I'm just off for a week's shooting in Sardinia—then I've got to go back to Milan for the rehearsals of *Tosca* at La Scala, and then to Rome for *Butterfly*, where I hope to find my dearest *chatter-box* ! When are you going ? Will you promise to stop at Torre ?

Do write to me at once to Torre, and then I can get your letter before I leave for Sardinia.

All my most affectionate thoughts to you, who are the

nicest of all ladies, just as I am the best man, in the world."

TORRE DEL LAGO
November 22nd, 1907

" The work on the libretto of *The Girl* is still proceeding ; Zangarini had taken too many liberties with the original and for the greater part it hadn't come off—the characterization and language of the cowboys and Minnie were defective. But now, with the assistance of his mother, who teaches English, he writes that things look quite different and that I shall be pleased with it—we'll see.

Good for you that you have got a green dress—how I envy you ! *I* haven't succeeded in finding a suit with a touch of green in it !—I'm very unhappy about it ! I'm feeling well ; I go shooting—but I'm vegetating. However, I shall soon have some work to do."

MILAN
December 23rd, 1907

" The first night of *Tosca* is on Monday—are you sunning yourself with your usual friends—the Italian band ? Is the chief of the brigands there—the distinguished mastersinger of well-known melodies ? [1] Is he behaving like a *pig* ? Are you in good spirits there—has your fit of depression passed ? I feel like blowing my brains out—Zangarini is keeping me waiting. Still, he has already worked well—and I think that it will be a *chic* libretto."

MILAN
[January 8th, 1908]

" It was incredibly full for *Tosca*, and a splendid performance, especially the orchestra, and the *mise-en-scène* was magnificent.

[1] Tosti.

I'm still waiting for *The Girl* ! That Zangarini is beginning to annoy me—we've given him an *ultimatum* which expires on the 15th, and if by that date everything isn't ready, he can go and fr-eeze himself and we'll get another librettist. In Vienna *Butterfly* plays to full houses—twice a week."

MILAN
January 11th, 1908

" I've still had nothing from that *pig* of a Zangarini ! And on the 15th he has to send the whole book ; if he hasn't done the work he can go and ph-otograph himself. We are both well ; we've got a vague idea of going to Cairo in February—but I'm afraid that, as usual, we shan't make up our minds. I wrote to you a few days ago, but perhaps you didn't get it. There have been 250 performances of my operas this year."

MILAN
January 30th, 1908

" At last *The Girl* has arrived ! I've had so much work to do with Tito and Zangarini these last days ! The result is a really beautiful libretto—it is not fully built, but the foundations have been laid.

We're off to-morrow for Cairo ; I shall stay at the Hotel Continental. Do write to me there ; I hope to see you in Rome. Tell me if there was an interview of mine in the *Daily Telegraph* and if it was *decent*—sometimes the reporters change things, and lend you words which you've never used. There are huge audiences for *Tosca* at La Scala, and it's the real *clou* of the Season—and to think that it was given as a stop-gap ! "

The only record of the Egyptian trip consists of a couple of postcards and a long poem too full of obscure allusions to allow of translation. On his return to Milan, his differences of opinion with Zangarini came to a head. " I'm at daggers drawn with that wretch of a poet ", he writes, " because he doesn't want to have a collaborator— but to-morrow the matter will be decided with the assistance of a lawyer."

MILAN
April 8th, 1908

" Will you please send the Queen's [1] photograph to Torre, and also Lady de Grey's address, *written clearly*. I am at open war with Zangarini—to-morrow a decision will be arrived at through the intermediary of lawyers. I *will* have a collaborator."

Three days later he announces that the battle has been won : " Zangarini has had to submit to accepting a collaborator—I'm waiting to hear from Tito and hope that the *other* librettist will soon be here. In the meanwhile I am making a start."

TORRE DEL LAGO
May 2nd, 1908

" I should have liked to come for a short time to London, but I don't think it is going to be possible, as I have work to do. The second librettist is due on Tuesday ; the other has been discharged on account of incompetence —what a lot of time wasted ! The first one was a present from *Savoia* ! The second one too, for that matter—all the same I hope this one will be better. How are you ? Do give me the news of Covent Garden and of my London

[1] Puccini had expressed the desire for a photograph of Queen Alexandra, whom he greatly admired. My mother was able to gratify his wish through the good offices of her friend, Lady de Grey (afterwards the Marchioness of Ripon), who asked my mother in return for a photograph of Puccini, " to add to my necessarily small collection of rare great musicians ".

friends. Love to David—affectionate regards to my dear
darling,

from

NOTI BOI " [2]

TORRE DEL LAGO
May 11th, 1908

" What a splendid pipe ! Thanks—it's the pipe of my
dreams. I have received the royal photograph, for which
many thanks. I'll write to Lady de Grey, but it doesn't look
like the Queen's photograph ! If she were like that, God
knows she could rule the Indian Empire as well !

The poet is here and at work—I'm feeling bad-
tempered ! I'm bored, and I can't move from here—I
should so much like to come to London, but I can't ! "

MILAN
May 23rd, 1908

" *The Girl* is going well—now. The first two acts have
been done again by the new poet and now I'm at work ; in
a few days' time we shall go to Salsomaggiore for ten days
or a fortnight, then to Chiatri for a bit, and from there, as
usual, to that uncongenial Abetone ! But I shall be working,
and so I shan't feel the boredom. Please send me again,
clearly written, Lady de Grey's address, which I've lost.

I hear *Savoia* is coming to London—how are you enjoying yourself ? So this year I shan't be seeing you ! It's sad,
terribly sad ! "

CHIATRI
June 22nd, 1908

" I've taken refuge here in order to work, but I'm doing
very little ; undoubtedly *The Girl* is more difficult than I

---

[2] ' Naughty boy '.

thought—it's on account of the distinctive and characteristic features with which I want to endow the opera that
for the time being I've lost my way and don't go straight
ahead as I should like. I may also be influenced by my
physical condition and the appalling boredom of this
cursed spot. Lucky you who live in a country of great re-
sources—In Italy I can't find a single town that is possible
to live in. Wherever you go, you see envious faces and you
are treated as Cain treated Abel—It's like this in our
country especially for anyone who rises above the common
level, and to a peculiar degree in the realm of Art.

I was glad to hear the news about *Manon* ; the Italian
papers registered its success, but call it ' *Manon* ' *tout court*,
as though it were Massenet's opera ! [1] Do you ever see
Emmanuel ? [2] Oh, why won't he write an article on the
English stage and also say something about Italian Art in
London ? For so many years now our poor art has honour-
ably held its own, and the newspaper correspondents never
even mention it.

Write to me, and go on being fond of me, as I am of
you.''

CHIATRI
June 26th, 1908

" I've had your nice telegram—thank you. So the second
performance [of *Manon*] also went well ? I'm glad. I'm
feeling a little better now and I'm less bored—is it just
habit ? Or is it the nice warm weather ? Or is it *The Girl* ?
Anyhow, for the past two or three days, I've felt less unhappy—but how difficult it is to write an opera at the
present day ! I hope to do something which you will like—

---

[1] The full title of Puccini's opera was *Manon Lescaut* ; that of
Massenet's, *Manon*; in practice, however, they were generally both called
Manon.

[2] The London correspondent of the *Corriere della Sera*.

I am most anxious that it should please *you*, who are my dearest and most beloved friend, loyal and sincere."

CHIATRI
July 5th, 1908

" Thank you for the article of E[mmanuel] in the *Corriere*, and thank him so much for me—or better, *give me his address*, and I'll write to him.

I'm working, sometimes well, sometimes not so well—but progress is slow—and I feel worn out. I should like to see this work, which is *most difficult*, go forward more quickly. And you—are you enjoying yourself ? I'm like a convict here in this dull, deserted, dreary, desolate spot—Good-bye, dear friend, and give my love to Angeli, and to Tosti, who has ceased to write to me."

TORRE DEL LAGO
July 12th, 1908

" Those two librettists are a perfect plague—one of them has hurt himself and the other takes not the slightest notice, and I need them to correct the first act by shortening and re-writing it. . . . But enough of this—would you be kind enough to give me Caruso's address ? I want to write to him, especially as I didn't take any notice of the death of his father.[1] Good-bye, my dear—I'm so disappointed I shan't see you this summer, but I hope that after Venice you'll come to Torre. Elvira will be simply delighted—and I ? At the very thought of it my bad temper vanishes ! "

CHIATRI
August 2nd, 1908

" We are off to Abetone because the *Lavli Hit* [2] has driven us away. I'm taking *The Girl*, who is in course of

---

[1] Caruso's father had died in the previous May.
[2] The ' lovely heat '.

construction, with me in my luggage—up to the present she doesn't seem too bad to me."

TORRE DEL LAGO
August 30th, 1908

" And now you've been robbed ! Poor Sybil, and that it should happen in Milan ! Have you made every enquiry ? I heard from Leonardi [1] that it took place at the station— But one gets over everything, and you of all people . . . so you like the Lido ? I shall go to the Bologna circuit on Sunday with my poet—will you be coming ? It's not far from Venice.

As for the piano, I don't know to whom to write in order to protest—it seemed a good one when it arrived, and I hoped that it would improve once it had been *broken in,* but instead it has become, after a few months, a regular charabanc. I'm going to call the Opera either *La Figlia del West* or else *L'Occidente d'oro* [2]—which of the two titles do you prefer ? "

TORRE DEL LAGO
September 3rd, 1908

" I too (if I go) don't know where to stay in Bologna— because I hear it is very difficult indeed to find anywhere to spend the night. I would leave on Saturday morning, but alas ! I shouldn't be able to come on to Venice because the poet has to go to Milan and I must come back here to work. I shall be away till Monday. I'm a *Pig,* it's true, but a *good Pig*—and you who are so good and kind will forgive me for not coming to Venice—but don't forget that I am expecting a visit of yours to Torre. I have bought a piano, because it's impossible to work with the other one—It's better to await your return to London before writing about it."

[1] The husband of Fosca, and Elvira's son-in-law.
[2] *The Golden West.*

TORRE DEL LAGO
[*September 21st, 1908*]

" Thank you for your dear letters. . . . Here life is much the same as usual—Civinini has left, and now I am seriously getting to work. I had a letter from Caruso telling me amongst other things that Ada has gone off with only one dress (unlucky woman, you will say) and without a penny. He's free now and glad to be able to devote himself to his boys, to whom he hopes soon to give a good mother—he writes from London. Goodbye, my dearest friend, and thank you for your charming visit, which brought a beautiful ray of sunshine into my life."

1908 had been a sad year for Caruso ; he had scarcely had time to recover from the death of his father when the news reached him that Ada Giachetti, the mother of his two boys, had run away from him. They had come together eleven years before when Caruso, who at that time enjoyed the princely *cachet* of fourteen shillings a day,[1] had first sung ' Rodolfo ' to her ' Mimi ' at Livorno —with such success that the opera had to be repeated no less than twenty-six times during the sultry month of August. Although Ada was never as good an artiste as her sister Rina, whose popularity at Covent Garden in the rôle of Butterfly had been second only to that of Destinn, her wider knowledge of the operatic stage enabled her to be of material assistance to the inexperienced young tenor. She was also an extremely attractive woman, and Caruso was still very much in love with her at the time she left him ; in the previous year we had travelled out to Italy with him, and I remember how, directly he caught sight of her on the platform at Milan, he had leapt out of the

[1] See Key and Zirato, p. 88.

train whilst it was still moving, and thrown himself passionately into her arms.

The news of her flight had been broken to him in London, whither he had come to sing in a concert at the Albert Hall ; what made the pill even more bitter to swallow was that Ada had run away with his chauffeur. His biographers give a dramatic account (which has since served Hollywood in good stead on more than one occasion) of how, having previously assured himself that grief had not impaired his voice, he deliberately chose to open the concert with *Vesti la giubba*—the lament of another poor player who had been similarly betrayed. " He began the recitative to the *Pagliacci* aria in a voice touched by an emotion deeper than any he had known before. Yet only Paolo Tosti and one other friend, who were of the thousands that thronged the auditorium, realized what Caruso was experiencing in those moments. He sang the lament with a pathos and passion I have never heard him put into the aria before. It was not to be wondered at that the people went mad. If they could only have known ! All they saw, as they applauded frantically, was a man, with face unnaturally pale, who came again and again before them." [1] The " one other friend " who shared the secret with Tosti was my mother.

As far as he was able to do so, Caruso remained faithful to his promise to devote himself to his boys—though the hope of " giving them a good mother " was not realized until more than ten years later when he married Miss Dorothy Benjamin in New York. The younger boy, Mimmi, came to live in London with the invaluable Miss Saer, first in Maida Vale and later at Cricklewood, where they remained until the outbreak of war ; Caruso came over to see him whenever he could, and his letters to my

[1] See Key and Zirato, p. 258.

mother are full of expressions of gratitude for the kindly interest which she took in his poor motherless boy. He also announced his intention at one time of sending his elder boy, Rodolfo, " to school with Vincenzino " ; but eventually he decided to leave him in Italy under the care of his aunt Rina, and so I was deprived of the pleasure of welcoming the great tenor's son as a fellow-Carthusian.

CHAPTER THREE

TRAGIC INTERRUPTION
(October 1908–July 1909)

a Spiritual sadness *P's depression: "my complaint"*

WE have already had occasion to remark on those bouts of melancholy—" my complaint ", as he calls it—which recur intermittently in Puccini's letters. Despite his healthy enjoyment of life, a certain spiritual sadness, peculiarly his own, pervaded his whole being, just as it pervades his music ; in the main, however, these fits of despondency were due to dissatisfaction at his enforced idleness, and disappear as soon as he sees work—or even the prospect of work—before him. But the letters that immediately follow are utterly different in tone from those that went before, or those that follow after—even those written during the blackest period of the War ; that characteristic note of ' humorous despair ', as I have called it, is replaced by a horror at the ugliness of life so intense that it came near to driving him to suicide. For the first and only time in his life he who had so poignantly portrayed the tragedy of others on the stage found himself face to face with tragedy in his own home—and it very nearly killed him.

A careful reader of the *Letters of Giacomo Puccini* may, in the chapter on *La Fanciulla del West*, have noticed, and perhaps wondered at, a gap of more than a year that follows the letter of September 21st, 1908.[1] I too might similarly have drawn a veil over the pitiful little tragedy which caused such a stir in the Press at the time, and which

[1] See *Letters*, p. 183.

gap of a year +

brought his work to a complete standstill, had
for the treatment meted out to Giacomo by
biographers. For the part which he played in that
drama, from which doubtless many of these lying legends
arose, so far from reflecting the slightest shadow of dis-
credit upon him, only serves to reveal the true nobility of
his character—his patience, his long-suffering, and his
amazingly forgiving spirit. For this reason, whilst I have
as far as possible suppressed any passages which might
cause unnecessary pain to others, I have thought it right
not to pass over this unhappy episode in silence, but to
allow Giacomo to speak for himself.

What is now known as the ' love-life ' of any prominent
man must, I suppose, always be of interest to a certain
class of reader ; in the case of one who spoke the language
of love to thousands through his music, it was inevitable
that an additional curiosity should have been aroused concerning this aspect of his private life. To his friends, Guido
Marotti and Ferruccio Pagni, in their *Giacomo Puccini intimo*
(written only two years after his death) belongs the dubious
honour of having been first in the field to satisfy the
popular want ; but their slily salacious hints and rather insignificant little anecdotes are as nothing compared with
the efforts of a later biographer, Herr Richard Specht, who
is not in the least deterred by his own admission that he
only met the composer once in his life—at a banquet in
Vienna a year or two before his death, when his ' love-life '
may be presumed long since to have come to an end—from
giving his readers the most intimate details concerning
Puccini's innumerable ' amours '. Fortunately for the biographer, the composer had inadvertently signed his own
death-warrant on the title-page of one of his operas, and
the self-affixed label is gummed on with typical Teutonic
laboriousness—Puccini is the " male *Butterfly* who sips each

flower and changes every hour ". [1] I do not know from what source Herr Specht pretends to derive his information, for he is careful not to tell us ; but I am absolutely certain that the picture he draws of " a perfect troubadour ", " a male siren " who " never lost himself in adventures, but always sought them and found them ", [2] is utterly and ludicrously unlike the original. But is not, after all, the most irrefutable answer to these charges to be found in his twenty years' correspondence with my mother, which reveals a constant and unswerving attachment, only severed by his death—surely a man capable of sustaining with a beautiful woman a friendship so alien to the traditional ' Latin temperament ' deserves something better than to be charged with ' butterfly morality ' ? [3]

In clearing Giacomo's name of a wholly unjustified stigma, the last thing I could wish to do would be to blacken the memory of Elvira—a lady from whom I received nothing but kindness, and for whom I have always retained a feeling of sincere affection. Nevertheless it would be useless to deny that, although she was a loving, faithful and devoted wife, her uncertain temper and, above all, her violently jealous disposition must have made her at times an exceedingly trying companion—and it was to these defects in her character that the tragedy of Doria was directly attributable.

The domestic problem in the Puccini household had always been an acute one ; for Elvira was one of those unlucky women who seem constitutionally unable to ' keep ' servants. But for some time past there had been one infallible stand-by, the little maid, Doria, whose devotion to her mistress was only exceeded by her adoration for her master. I remember her well ; for it was she who looked after us when my mother and I stayed at Chiatri and Torre

---

[1] See Specht, p. 91.　　[2] Ibid., p. 25.　　[3] Ibid., p. 91.

del Lago ; there was literally nothing that she would not or could not do, and the whole household revolved around her. " I'm rather put out by the confusion at home ", wrote Giacomo on his return from America in the previous year. " There's nobody to wait, and no cook—Doria has to do everything."

And Doria, who was herself little more than a child, continued to do everything with that selfless devotion which is as rare as it is beautiful—until one day, when certain whisperings (we need not concern ourselves either with their source or their ignoble cause) reached Elvira's ears. At once the whole household was thrown into a state of violent turmoil, and for weeks Giacomo had to stand by helplessly and witness Doria's persecution ; for he realized that his interference would merely fan the flames of his wife's unworthy suspicions. But, once roused, Elvira's insane jealousy could not be stilled, and at length she hounded the wretched girl out of the house with every circumstance of ignominy, having been careful to inform the whole of the village that her dismissal was due to her immoral relations with her employer. Thus dishonoured, and in a sudden access of despair, Doria took poison and killed herself. Nor was this the end ; for her relatives, dissatisfied with the story and anxious to clear her name, demanded a post-mortem examination, and when it was proved before witnesses that she was a *virgo intacta*, brought suit against Elvira, who was condemned to a heavy fine and five months' imprisonment.

These tragic events explain the gap in the *Letters*. The *Girl* was laid on one side for a whole year ; for, as Puccini cries out in despair, " How can one keep one's brain clear for work and hope to find inspiration ? It's impossible—impossible ! " He who loathed any form of notoriety now found himself faced with a public scandal of which the

Press and all those who were jealous of his success were not slow to take advantage ; his good name had been traduced by his own wife without a shadow of justification, his home—that beloved ' Eden ' of Torre del Lago which had been his one refuge from the world—had been defiled. But what affected him most profoundly was not the scandal attaching to his name, but the vision of that wretched girl driven by calumny to taking her own life ; for months to come it haunted his dreams and robbed him of all peace of mind. Those who saw him at that time were deeply shocked by the change that had come over him, and there were many times when, as he says himself, he fingered his revolver lovingly. . . . There never was a man to whom all forms of unkindness and persecution were more abhorrent ; those, like Specht, who suspect that " a trace of cruelty must have lurked in some secret corner of the soul " [1] of a composer who could make such fluent music from the horrors of the torture-chamber, must surely be disabused by these heart-rending letters of his that follow.

He would have been less—or more—than human if he had not cherished some momentary feelings of vindictiveness against those who had broken up his life. And yet, but a few days after the tragedy had occurred, he goes out of his way to absolve Elvira of the main responsibility ; what other man, I wonder, in such circumstances would have shown such a nice impartiality in his judgment ? It is true that he left her for a time ; but, in the face of the advice of nearly all his friends, he soon decided that the separation should only be temporary ; and although he cried to Heaven to harden his heart against those others whose lying tongues had brought about the disaster, it was not long before he forgave them too—just as he forgave so many others who had done him an injustice.

[1] See Specht, p. 22.

His decision to take Elvira back and start afresh was only arrived at after a severe internal struggle ; in the end he did so partly for the sake of Tonio, partly for the sake of his home, and partly for her sake—for, despite everything, he was still fond of her. When her sentence of imprisonment was pronounced, he promptly decided to obtain its annulment by secretly paying an immense sum of money as compensation—though cynics remarked that a man who was actually prepared to *pay* in order to be deprived of his first chance of peace and happiness must have taken leave of his senses. But Giacomo did not heed them any more than he heeded those of his friends who seriously advised him to insist on a permanent separation ; and on the whole he was probably right, for his generosity was to receive its reward.

TORRE DEL LAGO
October 4th, 1908

" My life goes on in the midst of sadness and the greatest unhappiness ! I don't write to you about it, because I don't want to put it in a letter—I should like to talk to you and perhaps then my spirit would find solace. When you write to me, don't say I have written in these terms ; but there are days when I should like to leave my home—but the opportunity never occurs because I lack the moral strength to do it. And yet I *want* to do it—and I'm certain that you would understand if you knew the circumstances. As a result *The Girl* has completely dried up— and God knows when I shall have the courage to take up my work again ! "

HOTEL BELLEVUE
PARIS
[*October* 1908]

" I'm all by myself and I've taken refuge here ! I couldn't stand it any more ; I've suffered so much. Elvira has given Doria notice, saying that she is a . . . without a *shadow* of proof.

Life at Torre had become absolutely unbearable for me ; I'm only telling you the truth when I say that I have often lovingly fingered my revolver ! And everyone (including you) says that I am the happiest man in the world !

I'm going to stay here a short while, and then out of force of habit I shall have to return to that Hell. I'm so unhappy, though a little less so here because I'm away from them all."

G. RICORDI ET CIE.
PARIS
October 13th, 1908

" Your letters have cheered me up—I thought you might have been angry with me for something I had written. You really are an angel, and I am so fond of you—I should so much have liked to see you, but I can't—but if by any chance I can, I will, if only for a short time. Yesterday Elvira let me know through the agency of a friend, who telegraphed to me, that she would be glad to join me here. I replied ' *most certainly not* ' and I added that I should be returning at the end of the week to Italy, or rather, home.

I have experienced many kindnesses here."

HOTEL BELLEVUE
PARIS
[Undated]

" I arrived an hour late, and went to the Opéra Comique where *Tosca* was being given. A great success and a full house. The King of Greece [1] was there and I was presented to him. He was *charmant.*

Well ? Here I am—to-morrow I leave for Milan. I

[1] King George I, who came to the throne in 1863. He was assassinated in Salonica in 1913 and was succeeded by his son, Constantine.

found a telegram here from Elvira, speaking of Tonio—
nothing else. Now I go back to that hell of indecision—
we'll see what will happen and how things go. I've come
back here feeling rather sad—I had become too used to your
kindness ! Oh ! how quickly the days passed in London—
they are unforgettable. You were so good to me and I feel
so fond of you, dear Sybil—in all the world there is not a
person like you ! Thank you, thank you for everything."

HOTEL REGINA
MILAN
October 30th, 1908

"I'm still here—I'm expecting to see Tonio this
evening.

I'm rather—in fact I'm very much—concerned about my
poor beloved Minnie. I'm neglecting her too much ; but
the day will come when I will give myself over entirely to
her—even if it means sacrificing my night's rest for her sake.
At present I only manage to sleep with the help of veronal,
and my face is all mottled like a Winchester gun ! "

TORRE DEL LAGO
December 20th, 1908

"I can write a little more freely to-day because Elvira
has gone to Lucca where her mother is ill—it's a ghastly,
horrible life—enough to drive one to suicide !

My work goes on, but so slowly as to make me wonder
if it will ever be finished—perhaps I shall be finished first !
As for the ' Affaire Doria ', Elvira's persecution continues
unabated ; she has also been to see the Priest to get him to
talk to her mother, and is doing everything she can to drive
her out of the village. I've seen the poor girl secretly once
or twice—and the sight is enough to make one cry ; in
addition to everything else she's in a very poor state of

health. My spirit rebels against all this brutality—and I have to stay on in the midst of it ! ! If it hadn't been for my work which keeps me here, I should have gone away, and perhaps for ever. . . . But I lack the courage to take action, as you know. Besides, I'm not well either ; all these upsets are bound to leave their mark in the end, and it's my work especially that suffers. How can one keep one's brain clear for work and hope to find inspiration ? It's impossible —impossible ! I can only go on, hoping for the best and that things will settle down again. . . ."

TORRE DEL LAGO
[*January 4th,* 1909]

" I'm still in a state of the greatest unhappiness—if you only knew the things my wife has been doing and the way she has been spying on me ! It's an appalling torment, and I am passing through the saddest time of my life ! I should like to tell you everything, but I don't want to torture myself further ; it's enough if I tell you that I don't want to live any longer—certainly not with her. To go far away and create a new life ; to breathe the air freely and rid myself of this prison atmosphere which is killing me— Elvira keeps on talking of leaving, but she doesn't go. I wouldn't mind staying here by myself ; I could work and shoot—but if I go, where should I go to ? And how should I spend my time—I who have now grown accustomed to the comforts of my own house ? In short, my life is a martyrdom ! I'm working, yes, but not as I could have wished."

ROME
January 27th, 1909

" I'm in the depths of despair, and my position is irretrievably ruined ! Doria has poisoned herself with sublimate and from one moment to another I expect to hear news of her death—You can imagine my state of mind ! I am done for—the poor child's relations are going to bring an action against Elvira for persecuting her—it's the end of my family life, the end of Torre del Lago, the end of everything. I don't know what I shall do ; I am really weary of life, which has become an intolerable burden. It's impossible to forecast the consequences of this ghastly tragedy, if Doria dies—and she certainly will die, if she is not actually dead at the moment in which I write ; last night I heard that her condition was practically hopeless !

Tosti and Berthe are here and console me a little ; but of what use is it ? Dear Sybil, how wretched I am ! Be sorry for me, you who know me so well and who are a true friend and genuinely fond of me. Good-bye, good-bye—I don't know what I shall do ! Stay here—or go away? But where? Oh God ! what a dreadful misfortune this is !

I'm at the Hotel Quirinal. Good-bye—my head is turning round and round.

Your miserable

GIACOMO "

HOTEL DE QUIRINAL
ROME
January 28th, 1909

" That wretched girl died this morning ! You can't imagine the state I am in ! Tosti and Berthe are with me and are doing their best to console me. It's the end of everything, my dear ; I've written to Ricordi's to straighten out Elvira's affairs, but I never, never wish to have anything more to do with her.

Feel for me—I am utterly broken."

HOTEL DE QUIRINAL
ROME
January 31*st*, 1909

" I'm still here and I shall remain on until the necessary arrangements for the separation with Elvira have been completed. Tosti, of whom I see a lot, cheers me up a little for all the unhappiness I have undergone. I'm a little calmer now, and my health isn't bad.

Apart from the arrangement with Elvira, it appears that other misfortunes are to follow ; poor Doria's family intend to bring an action against my wife as being directly responsible for her suicide. This may be, in part, true ; but partly it is untrue—and it is only fair to say it. I'm not going to tell you exactly what happened ; it would be too long and too tedious to relate the whole story.

The action which may be brought against my wife can have very serious consequences for her and—morally—for me too. God grant that the friends who have taken the matter in hand succeed in dissuading the family from bringing the suit !

My state of mind, although I have entered on a period of relative calm, is deplorably sad and pitiable. I am a wounded man—and perhaps one who may never recover."

HOTEL DE QUIRINAL
ROME
February 6*th*, 1909

" It's a long story and too sad for me to relate now— I'll merely give you a summary of the facts.

Elvira continued to persecute that wretched child, preventing her even from taking a walk, and telling tales about her all over the village—to her mother, her relations, the Priest and everyone. All my friends and relations and I myself told her to stop it and calm herself ; but she wouldn't listen to anyone. I made my peace with her and told her to forget about the past and be satisfied that the girl was no longer in the house. She promised to do so ; but the same evening I found her out of doors hidden in the dark, *dressed in my clothes*, to spy on me. I said nothing and left on the following day for Rome.

Elvira was supposed to go to Milan ; instead, she remained for three more days at Torre, and during that time did everything and said everything she could to the mother, repeating again that her daughter was a . . . and that we used to meet each other in the evenings in the dark. She told one of Doria's uncles that her own grand-child used to carry letters between us ; and, meeting Doria in the street, she publicly insulted her in the presence of others. Her brother wrote to me in a rage that he would like to kill me because I was his sister's lover—and that my wife had said so herself. In a word, poor Doria, faced with Hell in her own home and dishonour outside, and with Elvira's insults still ringing in her ears, in a moment of desperation swallowed three tablets of sublimate, and died after five days of atrocious agony.

You can imagine what happened at Torre ; Elvira left for Milan the day of the poisoning ; everyone was against me, but even more against Elvira. By order of the authorities a medical examination was made in the presence of wit-nesses, and she was found to be *pure*—and then public opinion turned round entirely against Elvira. There are some other painful details which I shall omit.

The position now is that I can go back to Torre, and I *shall* go back. But Doria's family have brought an action against Elvira for public defamation. We're trying to see if we can stop the action, though I'm not directly taking part in the negotiations. In any case Elvira will never be able to go back to Torre—or she would be lynched.

Darling Sybil
from her old
Bertie To

A FRIEND IN NEED—LADY TOSTI

I have been through the most tragic days of my life. I'm better now, but my gorge rises at the thought of all the barbarities committed.

Good-bye, my dear. I'm so fond of you. I'll send you a wire if I leave."

CAPALBIO
[Maremma Toscana]
February 22nd, 1909

" I go back to Torre to-morrow ; I've sent the children of one of my sisters to open the house, and they'll remain there for a bit because I don't want to be alone.

The separation with Elvira is not yet definite ; I expect news of it any moment now. And the law-suit has not been withdrawn—I hope the trial will be put off, if for no other reason so that the Press may stop writing about this beastly business. I'm still dominated by thoughts of the tragedy, but my spirits are a little better, though there's room for improvement in my health ! If you saw me, you would find me looking older. Who knows if I won't come to Nice to see you? Perhaps—it depends on how I find it at Torre and whether I can start afresh on *The Girl*. Certainly if I can interest myself again in my work, it wouldn't be convenient to move—and yet I should like so much to see you ; I feel that to talk with such a good and sincere friend as you would do me good and would give me the greatest solace. I have so many horrible things to tell you which I don't want to entrust to paper.

Good-bye, dear Sybil ; you are sure to have seen Tosti —he was with me in the days of my wretchedness, and he and Berthe were so good to me. I am deeply grateful to our dear mutual friends for the help they gave me in Rome—do tell them that. Au revoir, dear Sybil—how beastly the world is, and what a wretched life we live ! "

" I'm in bed with a slight attack of influenza—my wife is in Milan and Tonio is here with me. I am having a very sad time—I'm quite unable to work and perhaps I shall never work again. I think my life is finished, done for—I only want to die. What horrible things have happened, what barbarities have been committed—Elvira too deserves pity because the chief fault was not hers. . . ."

" I can't work any more ! I feel so sad and discouraged ! My nights are horrible ; I cry—and am in despair. Always I have before my eyes the vision of that poor victim ; I can't get her out of my mind—it's a continual torment. The fate of that poor child was too cruel ; she killed herself because she could no longer bear the unceasing flow of calumny which was spread about to her mother and her relations, Elvira saying that she had caught me in the act —the most infamous lies ! I defy anyone to say that he ever saw me give Doria even the most innocent caress ! She was so persecuted that she preferred to die—and her strength and her courage were great. If Elvira has the slightest heart, she must feel remorse !

Forgive me if I am always harping on the same subject ! "

" I've been in bed for the last four days with influenza but I'm a little better to-day ; two of my sisters are looking after me. Tonio was here, but he's gone back to Milan because Elvira hasn't been well, and he's returning to me to-morrow—he tells me that E. is in a very bad way. I am

sorry for her, but she will get better; I stand firmly by my
proposal for a separation—it won't be a permanent separation, but for the time being she must submit to this
punishment."

TORRE DEL LAGO
March 15th, 1909

"I'm still in bed, but I'm going to get up this afternoon. There is no truth in what Berthe was told; namely,
that Doria took arsenic many years ago because I found
fault with her—I think I should have heard of it before
now! But it doesn't matter—it's one of the usual lies told
to conceal the truth.

I've got to go to Milan in two or three days' time and
I shall go to a hotel—I'll write and let you know my
address. I shall only stay the time necessary to be present
at the rehearsals of <i>Manon</i>. I'm less sad—I think that if my
health allows it I shall soon take up my neglected work,
but I don't know if I shall stay at Torre. It's certain that
Elvira can't come here, so on that side I shall have peace—
but can I endure being alone? We'll see—if it weren't for
my work, I should come somewhere near you—but I can't
work in a hotel."

HOTEL DE LA VILLE
MILAN
[<i>March</i> 1909]</div>

"What do you want me to do—to go on writing to
the papers about this business? It's better to let it die a
natural death. You do well to tell the truth openly and
frankly to anyone who talks to you about my misfortunes.

I'm staying here alone in this hotel—I see my son and
a few friends. I hear that Elvira has grown very thin and
that she is wretched and unhappy—but what am I to do?
Nothing will induce me to alter my decision, and for the

first time in my life I pray that I shall not be moved by
feelings of pity or compassion.

I shall remain here for a week or so and then go back to
Torre. After that I don't know what I shall do ; I'm
thinking of Paris and also of London—the only objection
to the latter is the question of the language. But even if I
stayed in Paris, I fancy that I should visit London pretty
frequently ! "

HOTEL DE LA VILLE
MILAN
[*March* 1909]

" *Manon* had one of the greatest triumphs ever known—
it's the biggest success of the year at La Scala. I leave the
day after to-morrow for Torre—I didn't see Elvira, but I
had a talk with the lawyer and saw a lot of Tonio. I
remain as firm as Nelson's Column ! "

TORRE DEL LAGO
April 2nd, 1909

" Every day I've been meaning to write to you, but I've
never had the inclination, or rather the peace of mind
necessary.

I'm just off to Milan to hear *Electra* and then I shall
come back here—I hope to come to London in June, but
I should want a bedroom and a sitting-room, etc., etc.,
with a *bonne à tout faire* and a piano for my work, so as to
be able to strum a little even at night—but I suppose that
would be impossible to obtain ? *The Girl languishes*—my
spirit is too broken to allow me to work. I'm here with a
sister and two nephews—I shoot a little, and I'm unhappy
and bored."

TORRE DEL LAGO
April 16th, 1909

" There is no change in the situation—we're waiting for
the law-suit to come on. It appears that Elvira is going to

Munich to join Tonio and so she will be condemned *in contumacia.*[1]

I'm working a little—Carignani is coming here in a few days' time, and then I hope to work a little harder. *Electra*?[2] A horror! *Salome* passes—but *Electra* is too much!"

In the following month Puccini announced his promised visit to London, though he writes, characteristically, about the day of his arrival : " I don't know if I can manage to be in London by Saturday—certainly the prospect of seeing *Tosca* that night is no great inducement!" But whether or not he arrived in time for that particular ' execution ', he was, as usual, very sorry when the time came for him to leave.

HOTEL WESTMINSTER
PARIS
June 3rd, 1909

" I had a very good journey—the crossing was rough, but that doesn't matter to me. I hated having to leave— after all the kindness which you showered upon me.

I shall stay here four or five days—do give me all your news. I miss your delightful company—you who are always the same, always as sweet as when we first met—a real

---

[1] The Latin preposition *in* seems to have presented unsuspected difficulties to Italian composers ; for Puccini's " *in contumacia* " is matched by Verdi's " *Requiescat in pacem* ". (Toye, p. 157.)

[2] According to Specht (p. 1), Richard Strauss once said that " there are two kinds of work that make their way whatever happens : the creations of the very greatest masters, and utter trash " ; it is hard to avoid the suspicion that he included himself in the former, and Puccini in the latter, category. Puccini was less sweeping in his assertions ; he would have been far too modest to think of including himself amongst " the very greatest masters " ; indeed he often said that, after studying the score of one of Wagner's operas afresh, he felt like adopting another profession in despair. On the other hand, as we see here, he was no great admirer of the music of Richard Strauss.

friend in whose presence one's soul can be at peace—and
mine is always so heavily charged with anguish !

Go on wishing me well."

HOTEL WESTMINSTER
PARIS
[June 6th, 1909]

" I'm still here ; I shall leave on Wednesday evening—
unless anything occurs to prevent me, because Gatti
Casazza of the Metropolitan is here, and then they're
talking of giving *Manon* here next year with Cavalieri. I'm
fairly well, and the time passes reasonably quickly. In the
evenings I go to the theatre—last night I went to see the
Russians, where there's a ballet of Cleopatra which is an
absolute marvel. To-night I'm going to hear *Ivan le Terrible.*
To-morrow the lawyers are meeting in Milan to decide
about the law-suit ; they wanted me to be present, but I
refused—I've had a telegram that the case looks very black
for Elvira. I insist that the reconciliation shall take place
after the case has been heard, but pressure is being brought
to bear on me to become reconciled first. I'm sticking to
my guns—it remains to be seen what action they'll take
against me."

HOTEL WESTMINSTER
PARIS
June 8th, 1909

" Ten o'clock Tuesday morning—had your letter and
telegram about *Tosca.* Thanks. I leave to-morrow (Wednesday). I've had enough of Paris and I have to go back on
account of Mademoiselle Minnie. I shall see Elvira, but I
shall stay at the Hotel de la Ville, not at home ; I'll let
you know what is arranged. It's certain that we shall soon
be reconciled—it's hard—yet I must do it if only for my
son's sake. But if my conditions are not accepted and
carried out, I and my *Innovation* will always be ready to take
flight."

TORRE DEL LAGO
June 16th, 1909

" Forgive me for having ceased to write to you. I came on here from Milan and I'm all alone, my sister having left to-day. It's raining, and I'm unhappy, with *The Girl* in front of me—silent. It's eleven o'clock at night—what great, what immense sadness !

Elvira's lawyers are doing their best to ruin her and me by giving conflicting advice, but I can understand that they want to pile up the costs so as to make a better meal, and in order that the case should be more sensational, thus giving them additional advertisement. The law-suit, which looks rather black for Elvira, will be heard on July 6th ; I've done everything I possibly can here by speaking to Doria's brother, but he is implacable. He's determined to bring the action, failing which he has sworn to kill Elvira —and I believe he is quite capable of carrying out his threat. I am not personally involved ; in fact he told me that he wishes me well, but that, before she died, Doria bade him avenge her on her mistress, though no harm must befall her master because he had always been so good to her, etc.— that, in a word, is the wretched story I have to tell. Outside I hear the rain beating against the plants ; it's cold, and I'm alone in this room. In the house there's only an old cook who—to make matters worse—cooked me a most horrible dinner to-night. I'm going to bed—what is there for me to do ? I can't work—it's a real crime that is being committed, to torture in this way a poor fellow who has never done anyone any harm—or at least has never intended any."

TORRE DEL LAGO
July 4th, 1909

" Long live Vini ! [1] Congratulate him from me—you

[1] I had just been elected to a scholarship at Charterhouse. It was

are all delighted about it, and that gives me pleasure too. Lucky you!

Tuesday is the great day of the law-suit—we'll see what happens. Afterwards I shall go to Bagni di Lucca—and I hope to find a little peace there. It remains to be seen whether Elvira's character has altered a little—it ought to have done after all the sad events that have occurred. To me she now writes very sweet letters; as I've said, we'll see. But if my life is made impossible, I shall come back, like a bird in the woods."

Torre del Lago
July 7th, 1909

" The sentence was a heavy one—five months' and five days' imprisonment, in addition to heavy damages and costs!!! Elvira, so as not to have to be on the spot, allowed herself to be sentenced *in contumacia*—that is, without giving evidence or defending herself.

I'm utterly disheartened by this new blow which has befallen me. There have been too many, far too many, dear Sybil—my powers of resistance are breaking down!

I'm leaving for Bagni di Lucca—Tonio and Elvira join me to-morrow."

Grand Hotel des Thermes
Bagni di Lucca
July 15th, 1909

" Still nothing settled—Elvira is remaining on in Milan because Tonio is ill. I've been taking steps to have the sentence withdrawn by paying down a large sum of money —and this without Elvira's knowledge. I thought it best to make a clean cut of the whole thing.

typical of Giacomo that, in spite of all his troubles, he not only found time to write to me but also sent me an electric clock which reflected the time on the ceiling, and thus served doubly to brighten the life of a ' new-bug '.

I'm all alone and extremely unhappy—there's not a living soul here and I can't work. I'll try again to-day, because my piano has arrived—I spend all my time motoring about the place in connection with this settlement. Yesterday I went to Montecatini, and to-morrow I'm going to Pisa where I hope to be able to conclude the arrangements with these legal sharks."

GRAND HOTEL DES THERMES
BAGNI DI LUCCA
July 26th, 1909

" I was in Milan because Tonio had been ill. Now all three of us are reunited again here, and it seems as if life is going to be less unpleasant. Elvira seems to me to have changed a great deal as the result of the hardships of the separation which she has endured—and so I hope to have a little peace and to be able to get on with my work."

" It seems as if life is going to be less unpleasant "—at this point one can fittingly bring this unhappy chapter to a close. Henceforth there are only a few distant echoes of the tragedy in his letters; from now on he was able to find, on the whole, that atmosphere of tranquillity in his home for which his soul and—above all—his work craved. I do not pretend that Giacomo was a saint, nor that, for all his sweetness of character and real goodness, he can at all times have been particularly easy to live with ; but undoubtedly most of the domestic differences that had arisen in the past had been directly attributable to Elvira's besetting sin of jealousy. Some of its manifestations had not been without their ludicrous side; there was, for instance, the enormous umbrella, not unworthy of Sarah Gamp herself, with which she was wont to threaten any comely young singer who happened to call on the Maestro—and which, on occasions, she did not hesitate to apply to the more prominent portions of their anatomy; there were, too, those chilling anaphrodisiacs which—as she confessed to him many years later, to his immense amusement—she had regularly mixed in his coffee whenever an even moderately attractive woman had been invited to dinner. But now that Farce had given way to Tragedy, Giacomo was to reap the reward of his forbearance and generosity ; for the wife whom he took back against nearly everyone's advice was a chastened woman, and henceforth there were no more of those terrible ' scenes ' which had made his home-life so wretched. As time goes on, his references to her become increasingly affectionate, and the picture which he draws of them growing old, and coughing, together (" What a duet ! ")[1] is the one on which I prefer to linger. Nothing could be more moving than the sad little letters which Elvira wrote to my mother after her ' angel ' (as she always called him) had been taken from her ; although she had the love of her children and of her grandchildren to comfort her, I fancy that she was not sorry when the time came, a few years later, for her to join her Giacomo in the grave.

Incidentally—and quite indirectly—the Doria tragedy led to a temporary estrangement between Elvira and my mother. Although Puccini could not be certain, he surmised that the same persons who had lied to his wife about his relations with Doria had not scrupled also to poison her mind against my mother. " But this fancy of hers too will, I hope, disappear one day," he writes—and it was not long before this hope was fulfilled ; for when Elvira accompanied him to London for the *première* of the *Fanciulla*, a complete reconciliation took place, and thenceforth until the end of her days she continued to correspond most affectionately with my mother. She told me herself after the War that my

[1] See p. 340.

mother's belief in ultimate victory, so confidently asserted
even during the blackest periods of the War, had done
more to sustain her courage than anything else ; for she
had an almost superstitious belief in ' Sybil's judgment '.
Amongst all the scores of his operas, with their tenderly
affectionate inscriptions, there is one which, necessarily,
lacks the accustomed signature, but which I treasure no less
than the others ; for on the fly-leaf of *Turandot* is written :

> " To Sybil
>
>   our faithful friend
>
>   from Elvira and Tonio."

And in this very opera—in almost the last notes of
music, in fact, which he ever wrote—it is possible to find a
distant echo of the tragedy which had so profoundly moved
him at the time. Unlike the novelist, the musician is
generally spared the tiresome inquisition of those who
claim to have identified the ' original ' of this or that
character ; but would it be too fanciful, I wonder, to find
in the devoted courage of the slave-girl, Liu, who fell on
the sword of her tormentors, an echo of the poor little
maid whose strength and courage, too, were great, and, in
the exquisite dirge which follows Liu's death, a reflection
of his own misery fifteen years before ? To me, at least, it
does not seem fanciful.

CHAPTER FOUR

WORK RESUMED
(August 1909–October 1910)

AND so Puccini was able to turn again to his beloved *Girl*.
I often wonder, however, to what extent " Minnie and her
friends " suffered from their temporary abandonment. It
seems reasonable to suppose that the " lack of genuine inspiration ", of which the critics were later to complain, was
due, at least in part, to the breaking of the original thread ;
unlike a human friendship, a musical composition cannot
always be resumed at the point at which it was put down.

BAGNI DI LUCCA
August 22nd, 1909

" I am a little quieter now and I am working. The suit
and the judgment against E. have been annulled, the civil
action having been withdrawn—I'm still at Bagni di Lucca,
and I have a lot of work before me. Life runs on monoton-
ously, but fairly peacefully—I've got my work, and soon
there'll be a little shooting as a distraction. It's very hot at
present, but the hotel is high up and one's all right and the
heat not oppressive.

I'm supposed to go to Brussels in October for *Butterfly*.
We'll see if I can make up my mind to leave my work—this
opera is terrible! But it seems to me that it is beginning
to take on life and strength! Forward, and courage."

As an illustration of their different methods and the

increasing complexity of the work of orchestration, it is amusing to contrast the following letter, with its estimate of more than a year for the completion of the last act and the orchestration of the whole, " which will take a lot of my time ", with a similar letter of Verdi on the subject of *Aïda*—perhaps the most ambitious and elaborate work which he ever composed—in which he complains that the writing of the fourth act and the scoring of the entire opera " will mean at least a month's work " ! [1] If we are to believe Mr. Toye, *La Forza del Destino*, which was the twenty-third opera to come from Verdi's pen, was also the first opera which he did not orchestrate during rehearsals ! [2]

TORRE DEL LAGO
September 30th, 1909

" I'm writing to you to Venice, where I hope you still are. I have to ask your forgiveness for my continued neglect of you—believe me, every day I have thought of you and I meant to write, but I've never found time—there are at least fifty letters I ought to answer ! I'm working hard : *The Girl* goes well and I've nearly finished the second act—where there's a love duet which seems to me to have come out well.

Are you all right ? And David and the boys ? I'm very well indeed ; I'm on a régime—no bread, but douches and injections. I feel strong and my brain is clear, and now that I am so fit I hope to finish my work soon. It will certainly take me all next year—or at the very least until September —because the third act will need a lot of work—and the orchestration of the whole opera will take a lot of my time.

In my home I have peace—Elvira is good—and the three of us live happily together. *I've sold the Abetone !*

[1] See Toye, p. 153.   [2] *Ibid.*, p. 128.

My love—and write to me and tell me all your news—
and whether any of the Italian band were in Venice."

GRAND HOTEL
BRUSSELS
October 2 3*rd*, 1909

" Did you receive my postcard from Bâle sent *en
route* ? I have been here for a few days for *Butterfly*, which
is coming on next Friday. The rehearsals are going fairly
well but I am longing to get back to my interrupted work
—poor Minnie, left all alone by herself ! You know, I really
am pleased with the work that I have done."

GRAND HOTEL
BRUSSELS
[*October* 1909]

" The Dress rehearsal went very well ; to-morrow,
Friday, is the *première*, and I leave immediately after. I've
been here too long—but I had to put things straight and if
I hadn't come it would only have gone fairly well ; as it is,
I hope it will be a real triumph because the ensemble and
the cast are excellent—better than in Paris, better than in
London with all its *Divi*. But I've had to talk and work
and shout like anything in order to get what I wanted—I
also made them change all the scenery, which was ugly.
I've got to leave immediately after on Saturday, and I've
got return tickets to Milan by Luxembourg and Bâle ; I
avoided Paris so as not to waste time—I had come for a
week, and I've stayed more than two weeks. How I should
like to see you again—if I had known you would be in Paris
I would have arranged differently.

I am getting on all right with Elvira . . . life is fairly
boring, but at least we don't have squabbles and rows—of
which I've had more than my fair share ! I'm working confidently, and I'm longing to be back at Torre so as to return

to my Minnie. I've nearly got to the third act—a good step forward, in fact.

And what are you doing in Paris? Is it by any chance because of your poor sister? [1] How is she? My health is good; I'm leading a very quiet life, and I'm on a régime! In this way I hope to remain fit, with my brain alert for my work. . . .

Good-bye, dear Sybil—I think of you often and of all your goodness and kindness to me, and I'm sorry that Elvira has taken our friendship amiss. But this fancy of hers too will, I hope, disappear one day—and if it doesn't, it's enough for us that we remain what we have always been—affectionate friends, full of good and sincere feelings towards each other, and whenever we meet it will be a treat for us—that's right, isn't it?

Good-bye, dear Sybil, so many affectionate thoughts from

GIACOMO, who is as fond of you as ever."

TORRE DEL LAGO
November 9th, 1909

" I've got back to my work and let's hope that it will soon be finished. I've got to the third act, which is a bit *heavy* to do. But it will come out all right—at least we must hope so.

The weather's magnificent here and in between working I do a little shooting. So life flows on easily. Send Tosti the strangest messages you can think of! "

MILAN
December 23rd, 1909

" All best wishes to you, dear friend, to David, the boys,

[1] Mrs. Walter Behrens. She died in the following May, after a long and painful illness.

and to your parents for a Happy New Year. I ? I am at my table working. Am I alive ? I don't know myself. For the time being I have Minnie—the rest is emptiness. But at least my health is good (Touch wood !)." [1]

MILAN
January 29th, 1910

" How sorry I am about your sister ! Poor dear—what misfortunes one on top of the other ! And you suffer so much ! But what can one do—suffering is the destiny of us all, and one must try to resign oneself to it.

I'm working at my Minnie, and I'm very pleased with it—yet how tiring it is and what long hours I spend at the table. But from now on it's the only amusement left to me ; I think with dread of the day when I shall have finished my work and am left to a solitary *tête-à-tête* with myself. . . . My work is only a small thing—much too small a thing ; still—it is something !

And you—how is life with you ? Well, I hope, except for your grief over your sister's condition. . . . But your character has such wonderful poise, and something essentially English about it, too. I'm utterly different—but you know me only too well."

TORRE DEL LAGO
April 9th, 1910

" I didn't know whether you were in Paris, Folkestone, Nice or London, and in my doubt (being lazy as usual) I refrained from writing—but to tell the truth, I've been working like a nigger ! I've orchestrated two hundred large pages of the score ; all the second act where there's a duet which strikes me as being rather stiff, but we'll see. So do

---

[1] Puccini's version of ' Touch wood ! ' is always the same ; the drawing of a hand with the first and little fingers raised—to ward off the ' evil eye '.

forgive me—and thanks for the news about those *pigs* at
Nice ; I know that they murder our music, but there's
nothing to be done about it. It's always like that nowadays ;
our music is destined to be badly performed everywhere
abroad with a few occasional exceptions.

I'm living like a hermit *without emotions and without anything else*—I've still got the whole of the third act to do, and
I'm beginning to be a little fed up with Minnie and her
friends. Let's hope that the third act will satisfy me as
much as the other two—if only it were finished soon !

And tell me—shall I dedicate it to Queen Alexandra ?
And if so, what formalities are customary before printing
her name on the score ? Would you mind asking somebody
—Lady de Grey, for example ? ''

MILAN
May 10th, 1910

" It's some little time since I wrote to you—I was so
distressed to hear about your poor sister—it must be a very
great grief to you all.

I'm working to finish *The Girl*, which will come on at
the end of November in New York—it's all fixed up. And
will Covent Garden be closed in mourning for the King ? [1]
What a sad thing for everyone, the death of your beloved
Sovereign—he had such a genial and lovable personality ! I
telegraphed to Lady de Grey my condolences to the Queen.

I'm going to Paris at the beginning of June for the
Saison Italienne at the Châtelet, where, as you know, *Manon*
is being given with Caruso. If you happened to be in Paris,
how glad I should be to see you ! ''

MILAN
May 24th, 1910

" My poor dear friend ! How I feel for you—Your

[1] King Edward the Seventh had died on May 6th. Covent Garden
closed for three days, and again on the day of the funeral.

sweet Evelyn is gone for ever ! Her sufferings are at an end, but she leaves behind her so many regrets and so much sorrow for you all—One must have courage, and resign oneself to the laws of nature.

I leave for Paris on the 1st of June—do go on giving me your news."

HOTEL WESTMINSTER
PARIS
[*June* 1910]

"We are in the middle of rehearsing—*Manon* comes on next Thursday, and I hope for a great success. The orchestra under Toscanini is magnificent and the rest are good. We all know what Caruso is, and the Manon is a new little artiste who will do well.

I am here with all my family, Elvira and Tonio—in a few days' time I am going back to Italy to spend a month in that horrible Chiatri to finish *The Girl*—I shall have to work the whole of July, and up there I shall be able to finish this interminable opera."

Although Puccini makes no mention of it, considerable apprehension existed, at any rate amongst the artistes, as to the reception which might be accorded to *Manon Lescaut* by a possibly excitable Parisian audience. The new Impresario of the Metropolitan, Gatti Casazza, had inaugurated his twenty-five years' reign by bringing the whole of the company over to Paris for a brief season at the Châtelet, and on the opening night—*Aïda* with Caruso and Destinn— Toscanini had had the unusual experience of being roundly hissed by a section of the audience, determined to mark their disapproval of the conductor's and Gatti Casazza's alleged discrimination against French artistes. It might therefore have been construed as adding insult to injury to follow up *Aïda* with a *Manon* of foreign extraction. Fortunately,

as the following letter of Caruso to my mother shows,
there were no ill results.

GRAND HOTEL
PARIS
" DEAR FRIEND,   *June* 13*th*, 1910
" Here's the news about *Manon*—it's rather delayed,
but better late than never.

Well, before the first performance, people were saying
all sorts of things and were doubtful about its success on
account of the Chauvinism which exists amongst the
French because, as you know, there is already a *Manon*, and
written by Massenet.

Fortunately we all got down to work, and the first performance was a real success, not only an artistic triumph but
a triumph for Italy. Puccini was repeatedly called before
the curtain and so were the rest of us, and we're all very
pleased. The second performance is to-night. They're talking of giving some more performances of *Manon*, but I can't
go on any more as I'm longing to be home."

The second performance repeated the triumph of the
opening night—much to the annoyance of the French
Press.

HOTEL WESTMINSTER
PARIS
June 14*th*, 1910
" Last night too it was an enormous success—the receipts
were 65,000 francs. Those pigs—the gentlemen of the Press
—were full of bile against me, and who cares a fig, if the
public takes my side in this way ?

I shall leave on Saturday for Milan and then I shall
retire to Chiatri to finish the third act of *The Girl*. Everything is arranged for New York—it will be presented on
December 6th.

So you're not going to the Lido any more ? I hope you haven't taken a violent dislike to the Italians as well ? How sorry I am not to see you ! I should have been so happy to see your smile again ! And to hear you talking in that sweet way of yours ! ''

VIAREGGIO
August 15th, 1910

" So *The Girl* is finished at last !

Now I'm leading a peaceful existence ; whenever I feel like it, I go and have a dip in the sea. I'm waiting for my new car to go to Spain or to the north—I haven't yet decided which.

The Girl has come out, in my opinion, the best opera I have written. It's going to be given in London, I believe, at Covent Garden, as Ricordi's apparently haven't been able to come to terms with Drury Lane.

I send you all my most affectionate thoughts, dear Sybil —and when shall I see you again ? I should so love to ! ''

MILAN
September 29th, 1910

" Is Maeterlinck's *Blue Bird* still being given in London ? [1] And if so, will it still be on at the end of October and the beginning of November ? I wish you would find out for me—the book interests me very much,

---

[1] Maurice Maeterlinck's *Blue Bird* was given for the first time at the Haymarket Theatre on December 8th, 1909, and ran until December 19th, 1910. This was not the first time that Puccini had turned his attention to the works of the great Belgian poet ; on a previous occasion he had applied to Maeterlinck for permission to put *Pelleas and Melisande* to music—only to discover, to his disappointment, that it had already been assigned to Debussy.

I do not know what he would have made of Maeterlinck's curious fairy-tale ; for he soon dismissed the idea from his mind. Later *L'Oiseau bleu* was set to music by Albert Woolf and was accorded the honour of a *première* at the Metropolitan in 1919. It only survived two seasons.

and I should very much like to see the play on the stage.
Who knows if it may not be for me ! *The Girl* is coming
to London in May, so Higgins [1] told me yesterday—and
the Opera will be dedicated to your Queen Alexandra. So
would you please send me the *exact* dedicatory inscription—
that is to say, the name and the titles it is customary to use.
Write to me to Torre del Lago, where I go to-morrow—
I've been away from Torre for a fortnight on a motoring
trip in Switzerland.''

Torre del Lago
October 8th, 1910

" I've sent you to-day (prior to publication) a copy of
The Girl—it's in lieu of a manuscript, so I beg you not to
let any journalists see it or anyone except your friends,
because the proprietary rights, etc., have not yet been
established.

I too think that a good subject at once would be *manna*
to me. Guinera and the Quintero brothers are talented
artists ; I knew of *Tierra baja*—I asked for it many years ago
but it was already bespoken by two musicians : d'Albert [2]
and Le Borne—I arrived too late. I am acquainted with *The
Flowers (Las Flores)* of the Quinteros, but I don't care for it.

If your Spanish friend sends you some scripts of plays,
nothing could be better than if we could discover something poetic and original. I would like to put an end to
blood—but that's going to be difficult in Spain.

P.S.—If I can manage it, I should like to come to
London for two or three days about the 5th or 6th of
November—where will the *Blue Bird* be given then ? ''

---

[1] Mr. Henry Vincent Higgins, manager of Covent Garden. We shall
hear a great deal more about him after the War.

[2] *Tiefland,* as the opera was called, by Eugène d'Albert, was first
given in Prague in 1903. I can find no record of a similar opera by
Le Borne.

MILAN
October 30th, 1910

" Tonio and I leave for Paris on November 5th—if there's time, send me the Spanish play—one never knows.

God knows what sort of a crossing we are going to have, with this horrible weather—but the voyage doesn't take long. I believe Higgins is coming to New York for the *Première* (Dec. 6th). Will you be coming too ? David once said he might come. Mascagni is going to give his opera almost simultaneously with mine." [1]

[1] Presumably *Isabeau*, which had its *première* at Buenos Aires in 1911. It was only once given at the Metropolitan—in 1917.

CHAPTER FIVE

THE FIRST NIGHT
(December 10th, 1910)

EARLY in November Puccini sailed for America in the suite of honour aboard the latest luxury liner, the *George Washington*. On this occasion he was accompanied, not by Elvira (for whom, to judge from her letters to my mother at the time, one visit to New York had been more than enough) but by Tonio, who had now reached an age when he could be a real companion to his father, and by his earliest ambassador, Tito Ricordi. A remarkable change in their circumstances had come about since that day more than fifteen years before, when two shy young men had found their way to London, only to be overawed, like a couple of country yokels, by the mighty Augustus Harris, and dazzled by the splendours of Covent Garden. To his eternal shame it must be admitted that Puccini himself had failed lamentably to move with the times ; his modesty and diffidence appeared to be ineradicable. On the other hand the princely *Savoia*, like the representative of an insignificant little country that has suddenly attained the standing of a Great Power, had acquired more than enough dignity and importance for two. He regarded a luxury suite as no more than his due, and on their arrival in New York he stupefied the assembled millionaire Directors of the Metropolitan, who had arranged a sumptuous tea in honour of their guests, by declaring, in his driest voice : " I am sorry to have to inform you, gentlemen, that we did not come to

America to drink tea or to waste our time on official receptions, but to work and to rehearse." Then, seizing the
horrified composer by the arm and dragging him towards
the theatre, he concluded, " Come, Giacomo, come ".
Later he added laughingly, in extenuation of his rudeness :
" I wanted, just for once in my life, to smack a billion
dollars in the face ! " [1]

It was, as we have seen, almost exactly three years since
Puccini had been given his first taste of American hospitality
on the occasion of the *premières* of *Manon Lescaut* and *Butterfly*,
but these could only be termed 'First Nights' by courtesy,
since the audience of the Metropolitan had had to wait
thirteen, and three, years respectively to enjoy their first
hearing of works with which the rest of the world and, for
that matter, other New York audiences as well, were already
familiar. On this occasion, however, the enterprising Gatti
Casazza had been determined to make amends for past
managerial dilatoriness ; the introduction to the world of a
new opera by, and in the presence of, the most popular
living composer was regarded at the time—and is apparently
still regarded [2]—as the most important event in the long
and glorious annals of the Metropolitan Opera House—
and the favoured audience, like Mrs. Todgers, was determined to do things in style.

Judging from contemporary accounts in the Press, it
certainly did so. Unfortunately, perhaps because of the
additional strain involved in attending rehearsals, or possibly on account of the yet more lavish display of hospitality
which he was now called upon to endure, Puccini on this
occasion, unlike that of his earlier visit, does not appear to
have had time for letter-writing ; at any rate the only records

---

[1] See Adami's *Puccini*, pp. 56-57.
[2] See W. J. Henderson's Introduction to Irving Kolodin's *The
Metropolitan Opera* (1883–1935).

of the trip which my mother preserved are a postcard from *Savoia* sent off from Cherbourg on the eve of departure, and a cable from Puccini dated December 11th : " Great triumph fifty-five calls. Please inform friends Tosti, Angeli, Pavone [1] affectionately Giacomo."

The composer's elation is understandable. The reception on the opening night easily dwarfed that accorded to all his earlier works put together ; everything and everybody had combined to make of it a really memorable evening. On the stage, a magnificent cast headed by Caruso, Destinn and Amato—not to mention eight horses in the last act, of which seven were for the man-hunters and the last for Destinn ; as conductor, Arturo Toscanini ; in the audience, as many of New York's 'Upper Ten Thousand ' as could inconveniently be squeezed into the theatre, wearing as much jewellery as could conveniently be attached to their persons ; in addition there was Puccini in person to be summoned, at will, before the curtain— and there was also, for those who were interested in it, Puccini's music. It is scarcely to be wondered at, therefore, that it should have been the success of the season, during the course of which it was repeated no less than eight times ; what *is* surprising, however, is that, after being given thirteen times in all during the next three years, it should then have disappeared completely from the repertoire for fifteen years. [2] In New York, at any rate, despite its brilliant début, it has not shown any lasting vitality ; the public went

[1] Ricordi's representative in London.

[2] Its fall from favour seems only to have been gradual ; for on November 24th, 1911, Caruso writes to my mother : " I have already sung in three operas, *Aïda*, *The Girl*, and *Gioconda*, with immense success. *The Girl* was sung even better than last year and everyone was delighted with it." At Covent Garden, however, its eclipse was even more rapid and complete ; it was performed five times in 1911, three times in 1912—since which it has never been given again.

once or twice out of curiosity—and then, their curiosity satisfied, stayed away. It is possible that the indifference [1] displayed by the inhabitants of a country to whom the work might have been expected to make a special appeal is due, at least in part, to that very local colour which the composer had been at such pains to impart, either because it was laid on too heavily—or not heavily enough. But whether the music was over-familiar, or unrecognizable, to American ears, its failure there goes far to strengthen the theory that the illusion of the operatic stage is best preserved when the action takes place in another country, in another age—and in another language. Ignorance, no less than distance, lends enchantment to the view.

Elsewhere the *Fanciulla* has fared better. In Italy and at Monte Carlo it is still given regularly, though it has at no time and in no place enjoyed quite the same popularity as its predecessors. The verdict of the musical critics, too, has on the whole been unfavourable. Due credit is everywhere given for the great advance in technique, as evidenced, for example, by the composer's enhanced skill in handling crowds ; for his extraordinary power to create an atmosphere and his subtlety in introducing an American musical ' background ' ; for a few passages of great lyrical beauty [2] and,

[1] Signor Adami expresses his amazement at America's failure to respond to the *Fanciulla*, and declares that anyone who can explain this " theatrical mystery " to him is deserving of his eternal gratitude. (*Puccini*, p. 54.) I make no such claim.

[2] The tenor's aria in the last act, for instance, deserves to rank amongst Puccini's happiest inspirations, and is considered by many good critics even more moving than the somewhat similar but much more famous *E lucevan le stelle* in *Tosca*. This song, in which the bandit, with the noose already round his neck, prays that the secret of his shameful end shall be for ever kept from Minnie, who must be made to believe that he has gone far away to lead a new, and a better, life, became, for the Italian Army during the War, something like the equivalent of our ' Tipperary '. I remember one icy winter's night on the Salonica Front in 1917 ; there, in the heart of Macedonia, which

in general, for his masterly orchestration of the entire score. On the other hand nearly all the critics complain of the lack of any sustained melody—regarded as Puccini's greatest gift—and detect unmistakable signs of a flagging in his inspiration ; moreover, the rapidity of the action, coupled with the absence of the lyrical element, has led certain critics to dismiss the work summarily as mere " cinema-opera ".[1] Specht, however, attributes its comparative (and undeserved) failure not to any paucity of invention on Puccini's part, but to his deliberate attempt to stray for once from his over-cultivated pleasure garden into the world of rough and ruthless Nature beyond [2]—out of the sugar-plantation, as it were, into the jungle.

At the risk of trespassing beyond my own province, I should like to suggest another, and perhaps even more important, reason why the *Fanciulla* has not won, and is never likely to win, a permanent place in the Puccini reper-tory—and that is its happy ending. I do not mean that opera must necessarily be associated with tragedy—in *Gianni Schicchi*, for instance, Puccini proved himself abundantly capable of writing brilliant comedy—but rather that what one may call the traditional ' love-story ', with the no less traditional ' happy ending ', cut the ground from under his feet by denying him the use of that unique gift which is the real secret of his universal appeal.

If one studies his other operas carefully, it becomes plain that his genius—that quality which renders his music im-perishable—lies in his extraordinary powers of suggestion

cannot have been so very unlike the wilds of California, an Italian brigade was moving up to take over a section of the line from us, and as the troops marched past, the words of Ramerrez's prayer, sung in perfect unison, echoed through the still air, muffling the tramp of the men's feet. It was a moment that I shall never forget.

[1] See Dr. Arthur Neisser's *Giacomo Puccini*, p. 43.
[2] See Specht, p. 198.

and evocation. This gift of his has two distinct aspects ;
the one, reminiscent ; the other, prophetic. As an example
of the former, one may take the last act of *Bohème* ; except
for Colline's song to his coat (inserted haphazard at the last
moment to compensate the bass for an earlier song which
had had to be ' cut ') and the duet between Rodolfo and
Marcello, there is scarcely a bar of fresh music in the whole
act—merely variations and echoes of themes and melodies
that have gone before. It was an Italian poet who wrote that
" there is no greater grief than to remember, in one's misery,
the happy days that are gone " ;[1] it was left to an Italian
composer to express the same idea through the medium of
music. For it is precisely those pathetic little glimpses,
fluttering to and fro in the music, of a former happiness
now gone beyond recall, those evocations of a passionate
love now turned to ashes, which lend to Mimi's death-
scene an almost intolerable poignancy. *Nox est perpetua una
dormienda*—but how much deeper the gloom of that perpetual night if it be shot with memories of the bright
daylight that preceded it !

In the midst of the tempest, pale reflections of the sunshine that has gone for ever ; under blue skies, the threat
of a storm. Yet more subtle and uncanny than his evocation
of the past is his ability to foreshadow the dangers that
lurk ahead ; it is a singular gift, which, to my mind, he
shares with only one other man : Sir James Barrie. In the
earlier parts of all his other operas, the music, even when
it is apparently at its most light-hearted, somehow succeeds
in conveying an intangible, but none the less potent, fore-
boding of impending disaster, felt rather than expressed ; in

---

[1] " *Nessun maggior dolore*
Che ricordarsi del tempo felice
Nella miseria."
                          (Dante.)

the care-free love-duets between Manon and Des Grieux,
between Mimi and Rodolfo, between Tosca and Cavaradossi, between Butterfly and Pinkerton—in every case one
seems to hear in the music the fearful beating of invisible
wings, as though even in the supreme moment of their
ecstasy the poor lovers were already conscious that the first
notes of their doom had sounded. In exactly the same way,
and by the same indefinable means, Barrie manages to
convey, in the scene on the island " that likes to be
visited ", an atmosphere of sadness almost akin to terror.
Until the actual disappearance of Mary Rose at the end of
the act, there is not a word in the dialogue to suggest that
we are witnessing anything but a happy picnic—and yet all
the time one has an eerie feeling as though something evil
were lurking just round the corner, waiting to pounce upon
the care-free lovers and destroy their happiness. So too in
Dear Brutus every line of that enchanting scene between
John Dearth and his dream-daughter succeeds, beneath an
outward show of gaiety and insouciance, in suggesting an
impression of fragility and impermanence. I do not know
whether these two men, endowed with the same uncanny
gift, ever met ; I do not even know whether they were
acquainted with each other's work ; but I have often
thought, especially since Puccini's death, that it was from
Barrie—and from Barrie only—that he might have obtained
the perfect libretto.

At least it is certain that he did not obtain it from
Belasco, although, after the first night, the latter, for his
part, pronounced himself " divinely happy ".[1] As I have
tried to show, the conventional ending robbed the composer of an opportunity to display his most conspicuous
gift ; it also robbed the story of much of its interest. For
to those who are aware that Minnie and her Ramerrez are

[1] See Kolodin's *Metropolitan Opera*, p. 169.

about to be happily married, the previous vicissitudes which they have been called upon for three acts to endure assume a curious air of unreality, and one is all the time conscious that, although he does not appear to have been aware of it himself, Minnie has failed to appeal to the author of her being in the same way as had her less fortunate sisters. By comparison with his earlier heroines she appears stodgy and uninteresting ; one pictures her in after life as a superannuated barmaid with dyed hair and a middle-aged 'spread', who would have been much better dead ; those whom the Gods—and operatic composers— love should unquestionably die young. Nor was her inability to inspire Puccini surprising ; for his music was but a reflection of his own nature, and although, in the musician no less than in the man, there existed a richly comic strain which reveals itself constantly in his letters, and was later to reveal itself in *Gianni Schicchi*, deep down in him a sense of melancholy permeated his whole being, just as it ran, like a strand of gold, through all his music. The affairs of " Minnie and her friends " could not touch the heart of one who was as much the messenger of sorrow as of love, and who could only interpret happiness in terms of its evanescence. " Sorrow, sorrow, sorrow ! " he cries elsewhere, " Sorrow is of the very essence of life ! " It was the essence from which he distilled his music—and which the story of Minnie lacked.

PART IV

OUT OF WORK AGAIN

(1911–1914)

CHAPTER ONE

THE SEARCH RENEWED
(January 1911–February 1912)

On their way back from America, Puccini and Tonio spent a few days in London. There follows the usual letter after the return to Italy.

Milan
January 9th, 1911

"Here I am back again at home ; I carry with me the most delightful memories of my visit to London ! It gave me *immense* pleasure to see you again and to find you exactly the same as ever—young, beautiful, good—and so kind ! Thanks—a thousand thanks from the bottom of my heart.

Tonio sends you his love and very best thanks."

Immediately on his return to Milan he set to work to find a successor to the *Fanciulla* ; happily for him he did not know then that it would be more than three years before he would be back at work—three long, weary years of interminable searching up and down the highways and byways of the literature and drama of half a dozen nations. As ever, he began hopefully enough. "They tell me", he writes two days after his return, "that there is a play called *The Prodigal Son* by a man with some such name as Caine— do you know it ?"

Evidently my mother not only knew Hall Caine's play, but thought poorly of it ; for the subject is dropped, and a fortnight later Puccini writes from Torre del Lago that he is " off to Milan, where I hope to find a literary companion with some ideas not necessarily his own (Better if they aren't !) but with at least a sufficiently broad culture to be able to suggest something for me. . . . As things are, life bores me—I need work just as I need food." And he was to go hungry for three years ! Meanwhile my mother did her best to satisfy his wants with the suggestion of a novel —*The Fires of San Giovanni*—which, however, I have been unable to identify.

TORRE DEL LAGO
February 3rd, 1911

" Don't worry about translating *The Fires of San Giovanni*, because it's been known of in Italy for years. However, I don't know the work myself, but I'll get hold of a copy and read it—I'm sure to find one at the Society of Authors.

Thank you for troubling—let's hope that this novel will appeal to me ! In haste, because the post is just off."

TORRE DEL LAGO
February 8th, 1911

" I've read your translation, and I've been able to derive an exact impression of the thing—and, *tout court*, I must tell you that I don't care about it very much. I consider that the plot is not an interesting one to put to music—there is no fluttering of the spirit behind the words, that something which evokes music, the divine art which begins, or ought to begin, where the words cease . . . in fact, at the point at which I have now arrived in art, I need to find something loftier, more musical, and more original. It's true that there are many other things in the play which one could enlarge and bring to life, and subordinate episodes which one could make use of . . . but in my opinion *The Fires* lack the sacred flame—I'm grateful to you for the great interest which you take in me, and I'm grieved at the thought of the trouble you have taken in doing the translation for me. . . . Poor dear *Sybil*, if you only knew how pleased I would be to be able to say : ' *It's all right* and it's what I am looking for ! ' A thousand thanks and forgive me for speaking so frankly."

MILAN
March 3rd, 1911

" I hear from Tosti that you have suddenly had to leave Rome on account of Esmond's illness—poor Sybil, you're never left for a moment in peace.¹ I do hope that it's nothing serious and that you are once again in good spirits —with your usual lovely smile.

I'm still here, boring myself to death—always searching, and finding nothing. I'm in despair—I think it's the most difficult thing in the world ; it would be easier to go to the Pole . . . like Kook [*sic*].²

You'll soon be getting the *Fanciulla* in London—in May. But Destinn is on holiday and will only come for the later performances ; I think they will engage Melis, who sang it in Boston.³ I'm soon going back to Torre, where at least one can pass the time more pleasantly."

TORRE DEL LAGO
March 19th, 1911

" I wrote to you to London the other day—so you are back in Rome ? Good—I'm glad to hear that Esmond is cured.

¹ Shortly after he left Eton, my brother Esmond had a nervous breakdown ; from then until his death in 1930 he was rarely well for longer than a few months at a time. During all those long years my mother consecrated herself to him to the exclusion of everything else ; her perpetual anxiety and her utterly selfless devotion gradually wore her down too, and she only survived him by five years, dying at the comparatively early age of sixty-seven.

² Captain Cook's recent ' discovery ' of the Pole had aroused certain not unjustified doubts.

³ Actually it was Destinn and not Carmen Melis who created the part at Covent Garden.

For the present I have no librettos ; I've ordered my *yachte* [sic], and so in August I shall become a sailor, and I shall be free. . . . Give my love to that *Pig, great pig* Tosti.

I'm in very good health, but how I should love to see you again ! At the beginning of April I am going with Elvira to Nice and Monte Carlo for the motor-boat races, then to Milan till May, and then to London with Elvira. Will you be passing through Milan in April some time after the 10th ? "

MILAN
May 4th, 1911

" We shall be arriving Sunday night instead ; will you please wire and let Tosti and Angeli know—I shall be so grateful if you will. I'll come and see you on Monday— telephone to me at the Savoy. I'm longing to talk to you and see something of you again.

Lady de Grey has invited me to dinner on the 21st at her country house to meet the Ex-King of Portugal, and with this I sign myself. . . ."

The *Fanciulla* made its first appearance at Covent Garden on the 29th, but despite the presence of the composer, and although it was recognized as by far the most important event of the operatic season, its reception was a shade less enthusiastic than that accorded to any of his other operas. The *mise-en-scène* could not hope to vie in magnificence with the production at the Metropolitan ; and although the tenor Bassi did his best in the part of Ramerrez, the absence of Caruso was badly felt. Destinn, however, was still—Destinn.[1]

On his return to Italy Puccini's heart was gladdened by a letter from the gracious lady to whom he had dedicated the *Fanciulla*.

[1] She remained Destinn until after the War, when, to place her Czecho-Slovakian origin beyond all doubt, she changed her name to Destinnova. Even then she remained—Destinn.

" I came back here yesterday, to find a real Pisan heat. Everything went splendidly in Rome.

I've had an autograph letter from Queen Alexandra—most flattering indeed to me. It was nice—really awfully nice ; I was genuinely touched by it. There was also an elegant diamond and ruby pin.

Where are you spending the summer ? I'm staying here for the present, but I'm thinking of leaving soon. I want to go to Salsomaggiore."

" It's true, I haven't written to you for a long time, but I'm as lazy as an Arab. Besides, the heat here is no joke—and I'm staying on at present because I dislike having to go to an hotel where I can't have the comforts of my home. Thank you for the news you give me of *The Girl*; you are too kind and always think my music so wonderful. I feel that I am still capable of doing something better, but I haven't got a subject to which to attach myself, and nobody gives me a thought.

I've heard no mention of cholera—it may be that the Italian papers keep quiet about it and only the foreign Press talks of it ; but if there is any, it's nothing to be afraid of —I believe that nowadays this illness has lost its former force and virulence and is just like any other summer complaint. I'm going to Brescia at the end of August for *The Girl*, and immediately after to Lucca, where they are very anxious to give it—I should like to get out of it if I could, because then I should be able to wander about the sea in my little yacht which will just be ready in September. And where's Tosti and when is he coming back to Italy ? Give him my love.

Is it true Erlanger is dead ?[1] So I have heard—poor fellow !

Love to David and the others. I am well, but my soul is tired . . . empty . . . I send you all sorts of affectionate messages, and shall always think of you as my one faithful friend, kind, sympathetic and beautiful.''

ADELPHI HOTEL
LIVERPOOL
October 5th, 1911

" How sad the Northern sun is ! And without Sybil England really isn't worth very much !

I was a few hours in London—and now I'm here till the day after to-morrow, when I leave at once for Italy.

The Girl, with reduced dimensions, comes on to-morrow night. The Lord Mayor is giving me a big luncheon to-morrow at the Palace.[2] Don't write, because, as I said, I'm leaving first thing Saturday morning and I think I shall go via Milan.

If I can, I'll come and pay you a visit at Villa d'Este— I do want to see you so much.''

My mother's next suggestion for the libretto-less composer was *Sumurun*, the spectacular ' wordless play ' which had been produced at the Coliseum by Max Reinhardt earlier in the year. Although on this occasion Puccini confesses that he is not greatly ' tempted ' by the East, a time was to come ten years later when he returned to it with *Turandot*.

---

[1] It was not the composer, Baron Frederic d'Erlanger, but his father, who had recently died.
[2] Presumably he means the Town Hall.

TORRE DEL LAGO
October 25th, 1911

" I wrote to you twice—*I swear*—and you didn't get either of them—Good Heavens ! don't you believe me ? It's unjust.

Thank De Lara for his kindly action—it's so rare between colleagues to act in the way he has done.

Sumurun is in my hands, but I don't know whom to get to translate it—and to think that I was only a few steps away and didn't go to it ! It was Romeo and his lady-companion who attracted me away."

TORRE DEL LAGO
November 1st, 1911

" I will get *Sumurun* translated—thanks, but I don't want to give you the bother—the more so as the *East* doesn't tempt me very much.

I don't know whether Blackmore's novels have been translated into Italian—I'll ask whether *Lorna Doone* has been done. Are you going on reading books for me ? Your goodness and sweetness touch me.

The tour of *The Girl*, which began at Waterbury (Connecticut) has had a triumph."

TORRE DEL LAGO
November 19th, 1911

" *The Girl* was a great success in Turin. Forgive me for not writing before, but my sister has been seriously ill. In a few days' time I'm going to Naples for the *Fanciulla*. I've had *Sumurun* translated ; I shall be getting it to-morrow and then I'll let you know my impressions. I am well . . . but having nothing to do bores me—I shoot every day as a distraction—so I take a cure of oxygen, and if my spirit doesn't rejoice, at least my body does.

Do you know of any grotesque novel or story or play,

full of humour and buffoonery ? I have a desire to laugh and to make other people laugh."

TORRE DEL LAGO
December 23rd, 1911

" I leave to-morrow for Milan. The Girl went very well at Naples, although Mugnone is not a suitable conductor for this Opera, which needs life, whereas he is flabby and drags out the tempi to indecent lengths. But the performances are always crowded and that is the important thing.

I've been unable to find any translation in Italy of Garrick or the other play you wrote about ; I am always searching—but without result. There's a little thing of the Quinteros called Anima Allegra which I could have—do you know it ? I don't dislike it, but it's rather light, and now that I can have something cheerful, I'm looking for a contrast—sorrow—sorrow—sorrow, which is of the very essence of life. I want to express moral sufferings without blood or strong drama."

These last two letters are of special interest in that they contain the germ of the next work, or works, which he was to undertake. There had been, of course, touches of humour in nearly all his earlier music ; quite apart from the immortal Bohemians, there had been the lamp-lighter in Manon Lescaut, and even in Tosca—an opera not otherwise conspicuous for fun and high spirits—the Sacristan, with his stuttering fussiness so admirably illustrated in the music, had at least brought one touch of colour to the sombre background. But although Puccini could not be accused of that utter absence of humour which characterizes most Teutonic compositions and composers, such comic touches as had hitherto appeared in his operas were not more than incidental effects, deliberately intended to bring ' relief ', like the scene of the grave-diggers which immediately precedes the final holocaust in *Hamlet*. This suddenly expressed desire to " laugh, and make other people laugh ", is something entirely new ; it was to be triumphantly— and, to those who did not know him, most unexpectedly— realized, not indeed in *Anima Allegra*, which was destined to join the ghosts of the many other ' Might-have-beens ', but in *Gianni Schicchi*.

Not that he ever dreamt of providing " a feast of laughter " ; he was too consummate an artist for that, and the laughter was to be strictly limited to one course. Already, like some Escoffier preparing an appetising menu, we see him looking round for a piquant contrast ; not a violent contrast of blood and thunder, but just a nice little course of moral suffering to bring out the full flavour of the humour. On further consideration, however, he decided that two courses were scarcely enough for the evening's meal ; moral suffering, humour and—well, after all, seeing that blood and thunder, judiciously mixed, were rather a *spécialité de la maison*, why not add a Grand Guignol ' thriller ' to complete the menu ? Pathos, humour, tragedy—thus was born the *Trittico* or *Triptych*—a somewhat unusual word, de- fined by the Oxford English Dictionary as " a picture or carving (or set of three such) in three compartments side by side ". Not that we need attach any special significance to the title, since we have it on the authority of Pagni that the composer and his friends went through the dictionary one night, as a sort of after-dinner game, examining, and rejecting in turn, every word beginning with *tri*—triangle, trinomiality, trinity, tripod, and the rest—until finally the choice fell on the not specially apposite *Trittico*.[1] It was, in fact, what was known before the War, when short plays by Barrie, Galsworthy and Shaw were still fashionable, and the final curtain had not yet been rung down on the ' curtain-

[1] See Marotti and Pagni, pp. 175-77.

raiser ', as a ' triple bill of fare '. Or—to adopt a simile
somewhat nearer home—a Neapolitan ice in three colours.

The pleasant little comedy of the Quintero brothers
which begat the idea, although it was to prove one of those
' false starts ', as distressing to the composer, who saw
himself deluded of the prospect of work, as to the librettist,
who saw his work thrown away, was nevertheless an important landmark in Puccini's musical career, since it was
the occasion of his first meeting with a young and brilliant
playwright on whom he was to lean increasingly in the
coming years : Giuseppe Adami. A new vassal had been
found for the ' Doge ', enlisted, rather than conscripted,
by that amiable Press-Gangster, Signor Giulio Ricordi. I
have already commented repeatedly on the debt which the
composer owed to his publisher for providing him with his
two most famous collaborators, Illica and Giacosa ; it was
only fitting that almost Signor Giulio's last act on earth
should have been to suggest Adami as the ideal librettist
for *Anima Allegra*. The suggestion bore fruit in due season
—though from a different tree.

MILAN
December 30th, 1911

" For some time I haven't been taking veronal and I
sleep well—I only take it in moments of nervousness, as
for instance when I am putting on one of my Operas. But
after what you've told me I won't take it any more.

Here too the weather is fine, and not a bit cold. What
am I doing ? Nothing. I walk about the streets, go to my
tailor, waste a lot of money and bore myself to tears, and
some nights I go to the theatre to see plays—and always
with the thought of a subject which I can't find.

Much love and best wishes to you and the Angelis, who
really are worthy of their name, always including you as the
Archangel."

AFTER THE *FANCIULLA DEL WEST*
(1912)

GRAND HOTEL HUNGARIA
BUDAPEST
February 21st, 1912

" I absolutely must stay on here another week because the first night has been put off until Thursday week—and after leaving here I want to hear *Trilby*. Angeli wired me that it is worth seeing, and Tree promised me last summer that he would be putting it on. [1]

I am so sorry that you won't be in London ! After London I am going straight on to Milan and then to Torre del Lago, and shortly afterwards to Monte Carlo and then Paris at the end of April—in every case for *The Girl*—which is now going splendidly everywhere.

Let's hope that your poor Esmond is getting better and that he will be completely cured—it's a terrible grief for a mother to see her son in such a condition, and I am so sorry for you ! Poor Sybil ! But you are in good spirits and you still hope. One of my sisters, too, is very ill and she is going to have an operation on the liver one of these days—Let us hope for the best ! "

HOTEL WESTMINSTER
PARIS
[*May* 1912]

" Got here yesterday and found your very dear letters.

The orchestral rehearsals (of the *Fanciulla*) begin to-day, and the opera will be given on the 16th—a good number, let's hope it will bring me luck ! (Forgive me, but I *can't* get used to your new address.) [2]

I hope to be in London on the 23rd—I shall be *so* glad to see you again ! I don't know if I shall be able to go and see *Naïl*—they tell me that it is poor stuff—very poor stuff

[1] One of the late Sir Herbert Beerbohm Tree's innumerable revivals of Du Maurier's famous play had taken place two days previously on February 19th, 1912.

[2] We had just moved to South Street, but for months to come Puccini continued to address his letters to Upper Grosvenor Street.

indeed.[1] But I'll do my very best to see it. Aren't you your-self ever going to get fed up with my ' Tosche ' and company ? "

HOTEL WESTMINSTER
PARIS
May 30th, 1912

" Just off to Milan—I can't stand Paris any more ! And you who say that I amuse myself here !

Write to me to Torre, where I'm going. I hope to come to London at the end of June, but I don't yet know for certain. I'm so glad about Esmond—it must be a great comfort for you, and I hope that he will be entirely cured.

The *Fanciulla* went well here as far as the public is con-cerned, but my fellow-composers and the journalists are real enemies.

Much love to you, dear, and to David.

Your affectionate,
GIACOMO
(Rather sad, rather ill,
and rather bored) "

---

[1] Isidore de Lara's opera, which had just been given its *première* in Paris. It was given for the first—and last—time at Covent Garden in 1919 ; speaking as one of the rather scanty audience present on that occasion, I think few would have found reason to quarrel with the report that had reached Puccini's ears in Paris eight years previously. De Lara had, deservedly, many friends ; his operas, no less deservedly, few.

CHAPTER TWO

DEATH OF GIULIO RICORDI
(June 1912–February 1914)

HOTEL MARIENBAD
MUNICH
[*June* 1912]
" POOR Signor Giulio Ricordi ! You simply can't imagine
how grieved I am at his death ! From now on everything is
in the hands of *Savoia*—we're in a nice fix ! But on the very
first occasion that he tries any of his tricks, I shall leave the
firm—you can be quite sure of that, I promise you ! "

The death of Giulio Ricordi was, in truth, a double
blow. Ever since the day, nearly thirty years before, when
Le Villi, rejected by Sonsogno, had been accepted by his
rival, there had been one quarter to which Puccini could
always confidently turn when he was in need of comfort,
sympathy, advice or affection, in the certain knowledge that
he would find it. It is true that Signor Giulio had been
amply repaid not only in loving affection but more materially in the large fortune which he had amassed through the
unprecedented financial success enjoyed by his protégé's
works ; it is true too that, like other men, he had made
mistakes in judgment, and that the advice that he had
tendered so freely was not always impeccable ; he had dis-
liked the entire third act of *Tosca*, and he had tried to force
Conchita down Puccini's throat with a perseverance and enthusiasm worthy of a better play. But all this mattered
nothing ; in an inconstant and changing world one point

217

had remained fixed ; one person had remained constant and unchanging.

And now that too was gone. Puccini had lost a friend ; he had also lost a publisher. Of late his relations with *Savoia*, who now succeeded his father as head of the firm, had become increasingly strained ; but as long as Signor Giulio was alive, he was willing to make allowances for Tito's eccentricities and rudeness, and he would have dismissed as ridiculous the mere suggestion that he should seek elsewhere for a publisher. Signs, however, of the storm that was bound to burst one day were not lacking, and there is therefore nothing surprising in his threat to " leave the firm "; that, despite the utmost provocation, he never did so is but one more proof of his infinitely forgiving spirit. With the solitary exception of the *Rondine*, which was also offered in the end to Tito, only to be rejected as ' bad Lehar ', there is not a single one of his operas that does not bear the stamp of the house of Ricordi—and finally, as we shall see, it was Tito and not Puccini who left the firm.

To students of psychology that " queer capricious fellow", as Puccini calls him, presents an interesting study ; for his character was strangely compounded of opposing qualities and defects ; he was at once gifted yet vain, determined yet unstable, sentimental yet brutal. I remember once as a little boy travelling with my mother and him and—I think—Puccini, and noticing that throughout the whole of the long journey he kept his face covered up with a handkerchief and never spoke a word. I thought this rather an unusual, not to say boorish, manner of indicating one's desire for a nap—until my mother explained to me gently that it was the anniversary of his wife's death, and that he did not wish any of us to see that he was crying. And yet this was the man who could—and frequently did

—show a harshness and brutality utterly alien to the kindly Italian temperament.

But, with all his faults, Tito was a man of considerable attainments ; from an early age he had displayed a spirit of enterprise which had carried him and, with him, Puccini far beyond the frontiers of Italy; he was, in fact, the proto- type of the American business-man or ' go-getter '—the ' live wire ' equipped with driving force. The trouble with live wires, however, is that they are not as a rule particularly sensitive to the electric shocks which it is their business to administer to others ; and amongst the qualities which he had inherited from his father tact was most certainly not included. It might be rather fun for once, in his own words, to " slap a billion dollars in the face " ; but when slapping degenerated into an indiscriminate habit, not even sparing composers, it is scarcely surprising that a man of Puccini's sensitive nature should find himself bitterly hurt by such brusque treatment, and, however pacific he might be, feel an occasional urge to ' slap back '. At the very worst his ' viciousness ' was that of the Buffonian animal that defends itself when it is attacked, and I do not think that anyone who follows the relations between composer and publisher over the next few years will be disposed to dispute Puccini's assertion that " at heart I'm a decent fellow, and my feelings of vindictiveness don't last long ".

VIAREGGIO
[July 1912]
" The papers here speak of the success of Conchita [1] and also give little snippets from foreign newspapers—this is what always happens to disguise a failure. To that one must

---

[1] The first performance at Covent Garden of Zandonai's opera took place on July 3rd. It was only given one more performance during the season—since which it has never been given again.

add *Savoia's* great interest in this young author, who does not lack talent but who at present hasn't got that little something which is needed for the theatre. And then the libretto is one that I turned down—which seems to me to say something.

Is Angeli in London ? I should really like to go to Carlsbad in August—would you ask him to write to me on the subject and tell me when he's going himself, etc. ? You will be doing me a favour, and sparing me another letter. . . ."

VIAREGGIO
July 19*th*, 1912

" Thanks—I've had everything, letters and telegrams as well ! So the *Fanciulla* went well—I'm glad to hear it.

I'm playing at being a sailor—but it's not very amusing. On the contrary I'm bored at not having any work to do, and I don't get much fun out of life.

The family weigh on me !
My wife is—well, never mind !
And I have to bow my head !
A pig of a life !
Long live Anarchy ! And forward to the day of the long last sleep ! "

Apart from these trifling family troubles, which, from the context, clearly need not be taken seriously, his real cause for dissatisfaction lay in the failure of *Anima Allegra* (The Cheerful Soul) to live up to its original bright promise of providing him with the work which he needed so badly. In his biography of the composer, Adami has left us a charming account [1] of that exciting day in April of this year when he first met Puccini under the benign auspices of Signor Giulio, who was anxious at the same time to get

[1] See *Puccini*, chap. 4. " *Anima Allegra, anima in pena.*"

his favourite (and most lucrative) composer to work again, and to provide a promising young playwright with a unique opportunity to attain fame. All had gone well ; Puccini seemed enchanted with the subject and sketched out his own conception of the play ; but after the composer had withdrawn, Ricordi privately impressed upon Adami the necessity for striking whilst the iron was hot—for he knew his Puccini only too well.

For thirty days and thirty nights the young playwright toiled at his work ; at the end of the month he brought the completed libretto to the Master in what he ingenuously conceived to be its final form. Puccini, however, speedily disabused him in the following words : " Yes, on the whole I think it's good. Now we can start again from the beginning. But don't look so frightened—that's the way librettos are made. By re-making them." It was a painful, but a salutary, lesson, which was to stand him in good stead during the coming years ; for although, as he confesses, the task of collaboration with Puccini was an arduous and, at times, even a heart-breaking one, it never ceased to be wholly delightful. There must have been something very exceptional about a Doge who could thus cheerfully and callously dispose of his vassals' time—and, even of their lives—and yet retain their love.

In the meantime, however, The Cheerful Soul grew every day a shade less cheerful. Adami had done his best to strike whilst the iron was still hot; but already some of Puccini's initial enthusiasm had waned, and, with the death of Signor Giulio, it disappeared altogether. The reason adduced was the shade of Bizet, which, says Adami, every day loomed larger and larger. But, except that Spain was the scene of both actions, the story of *Anima Allegra* bears not the faintest resemblance to that of *Carmen*, and in any case there seemed no very obvious reason why Bizet should enjoy a Spanish monopoly in perpetuity. However, in order to counteract these fears, Adami obligingly offered to transfer the whole play to Flanders, on whose flat, treeless plains the shadow of Bizet could no longer prove a menace. The composer approved ; the transplantation was duly effected—and, as so often occurs in the case of successful operations, the patient died.

Once again Puccini was up against a blank wall, just as he had been after the collapse of *Conchita* in 1907. In despair he turned again to reconsider those subjects which he had rejected five years previously. But however indifferent he might be to the feelings of his fellow-workers, even he would scarcely have dared to broach again with Illica the subject of the French Revolution ; there were limits to his insensitiveness, just as I feel certain that there would have been limits to Illica's endurance. There was, however, another subject which had found favour earlier, only to be dismissed, largely owing to the objections of Giulio Ricordi ; was it, I wonder, merely a coincidence that the idea of Wilde's *Florentine Tragedy* should have been resuscitated only a few weeks after Signor Giulio's death ? At any rate the chief objection advanced by his late friend, namely that the work was " too short ", was now to be met, and Illica, who had had so many painful experiences in cutting down operatic texts, was now given the unique opportunity of expanding one. It was, as Puccini admitted, rather a tall order.

Haus Osborne
Carlsbad
[*August* 1912]

" Here I am, taking the cure, but I don't care much about it because I don't feel well—is it because it's only the first days ? Everybody says I shall benefit by it later. Let's hope so—it's raining and it's cold. What a gloomy country this is—though it's true that all the world is ugly when the Heavens cry.

So Esmond has recovered—this news gives me the greatest pleasure for his sake and for the sake of his dear little mother who must have suffered so deeply over the illness of her boy!

Angeli is a dear good fellow and is the best of company —he has the greatest faith in everything connected with this place—I, but little ; it's the only subject on which we disagree.

Do you know I'm thinking again about doing Wilde's *Florentine Tragedy* ? So you would do me a great favour by writing to your friend, Wilde's literary executor, and asking him whether this play is still *free*. Illica is trying to compose a big first act, and, if he succeeds, I'll do it—as it stands, it's too small a thing, but with a preparatory act, which must also be beautiful (it must be more beautiful and more varied than the second, so Illica has a heavy task), I'll write this opera. I've found nothing at all that is penetrating, nothing that is genuinely *alive* and stirring—misery on top of misery !

Anybody who likes can do the *Anima Allegra*, not I—it was a great mistake and I've thought better of it as I did in the case of *Conchita* (and *that* time I wasn't wrong).

Good-bye, dearest and most beautiful little lady—much love to you and yours, and enjoy yourselves."

In response to an enquiry from my mother, Mr. Robert Ross assured her that the play was still free ; it was true that a French composer, a M. Antoine Mariotte, had acquired the rights, though neither exclusively nor for an unlimited period of time. Puccini, however, need have no qualms on that score ; for the Frenchman (who seems to have been a singularly unfortunate man) had previously set

Salome to music, without taking the trouble to enquire whether he was free to do so and—worse still—in ignorance of the fact that Richard Strauss had been similarly engaged. Strauss, however, with a magnanimity which was not very flattering to his French colleague, had given him free permission to perform his opera when and where he liked, and the French *Salome* had had the honour of exactly one performance—at Lyons. The inference was obvious ; Puccini, too, had nothing to fear from French competition. With a scarcely veiled hint at Illican inadequacy, Mr. Ross added that the Irish poet, Sturge Moore, had already finished the unfinished *Tragedy* in a stage version, of which he strongly advised Signor Puccini to make use. Alternatively he suggested that the composer might prefer to set to music another play of Oscar Wilde's—which proved to be none other than the elusive *Duchess of Padua*, whose disappearance five years previously had caused Puccini (and my mother) so many sleepless nights.

HAUS OSBORNE
CARLSBAD
[*August* 1912]

" Just had your telegram—I can't fix up anything definitely as yet. It depends on the poet who is trying to invent a first act to add to it, and he'll have to find something very interesting, because the second act of Wilde isn't sufficiently so—do you understand ? So it all depends on this first act whether or not I do the opera.

And it's only right—I can't and won't write an opera unless it's really *taking* and *compelling*, and all this *au complet* ! Puccini must compose something *extra*, and it is essential that he himself should first be convinced. So you can tell Mr. Ross all this—that is to say, to wait until I make up my mind, which will be shortly. And the only reason we asked whether Wilde's play was free was so that we could get to work on it and not start off without obtaining permission. That is what you can write—do be kind and do it. But indeed you are an angel—yes, you are my Guardian Angel who thinks of me and of my art tenaciously and with the greatest affection—thank you, dear beautiful lady.

P.S.—This Mariotti (or Mariotte ?—I think he's a Frenchman) has he the right to do it or not ? Is he acting without permission or has he had a concession—even a partial one ? I must know this at once—if it isn't completely free, it's useless to discuss the matter further."

Evidently, on reflection, Puccini was ready to display the same insulting magnanimity to M. Mariotte as had Doctor Richard Strauss ; for, ignoring the ' partial concession ', both he and Illica tried their hand at gilding Wilde's lily—only to find the task beyond them.

BOSCOLUNGO PISTOIESE
[*October 7th*, 1912]

" Alas ! The *Tragedy* of Wilde has gone the way of the others—because I tried to construct a first act to it, and neither I nor Illica have succeeded—I'm here, boring myself indecently . . . and so I'm awaiting the arrival of old age . . . ! It's sad, but it's true—I feel as if I were the prisoner of . . . Zenda ! "

One of the few points of resemblance between Wagner and Puccini was a tendency, when in temporary difficulties, to ' tap ' their friends. But whereas Wagner always sought a loan, Puccini sought a libretto. And now in despair he bethought him of one friendly source which had not been tapped for many years : Gabriele D'Annunzio. Despite their agreement to differ over *The Rose of Cyprus*, the two men had remained the best of friends, and in the year following their meeting at Abetone D'Annunzio announced, with a certain vague poetic licence, which Puccini had been unable to endorse, that " my old nightingale has awakened with the Spring and would gladly sing for you ".[1] Puccini's scepticism was justified, for there is no evidence of its having done anything of the sort ; but now that the poet had taken refuge at Arcachon, the composer decided to take advantage of a visit to Marseilles to call on him in the hope that the nightingale might prove more vocally accommodating on French soil.

TORRE DEL LAGO
November 29th, 1912

" I am like a bear ! I go and shoot along the Lake every day ! I pay no more attention to Euterpe ! I live, I eat, I drink, and . . . I shoot !

I went to Arcachon after having been at Marseilles for the *Fanciulla.* I found a theme for a libretto, but Gabriele is still silent. I am waiting to hear from him every day but nothing arrives—so now I have sent him a wire to wake him up. My health is fairly good, but my hair is beginning to go white ! "

The ' theme ' appears to have been that of *The Children's Crusade* ; but alas ! the same fate overtook it that had previously overtaken *The Rose of Cyprus* ; from the moment that it had been put on paper, it mysteriously changed shape—or rather, in this case, became shapeless.

MILAN
January 27th, 1913

" D'Annunzio has given birth to a small, shapeless monstrosity, unable to walk or live ! I am as usual in mid-

[1] *Letters,* p. 237.

ocean without any hope of ever reaching harbour! I am in despair! Is there nothing to be seen in London at the theatres?

Savoia is more impossible than ever—I have found out that he is actually my enemy—or at least the enemy of my music! I am assembling the evidence together, and then he can go and—look elsewhere for a composer! But *not a word* of this to anybody. Good-bye. When are you going to Nice? I shall be there on the 18th March to hear *Marie Madeleine* of Maeterlinck."

It was not until several months later in Paris that he at last alighted on a suitable subject—or rather, as he hoped at the time, three subjects. He had picked his team for the *Trittico*, and in the following letter he announces its composition.

HOTEL WESTMINSTER
PARIS
[*June* 1913]

" I'm leaving at last on Saturday; I think I've arranged for the three operas. One is Gold's *Houppelande*; another with D'Annunzio, and the third (comic) with Tristan Bernard. The libretto of the first one will be ready *bien tôt*, and I shall start to work on it straightaway. All three will be given together on the same evening.

How sorry I was not to be able to come to London—and more especially not to have been able to see *you*! "

Of the three original members of the *Trittico*, however, only one survived: Didier Gold's one-act Grand Guignol ' thriller ', *La Houppelande*, which came to be known as *Il Tabarro (The Cloak)*. Not even in this case were the composer's hopes that the libretto would be ready *bien tôt* to be realized, and his statement a month later that he is " working " on it can only refer to the making of the libretto, which he entrusted in the first place to his friend Ferdinando Martini, the brilliant writer and statesman who had successfully governed the Province of Eritrea for ten years—and had, in fact, done practically everything there was to do except write a libretto. But as the months went by, and all that had been so far accomplished was the transposition of some of the original French names into their appropriate Italian equivalents, Martini, who was already over seventy,[1] recognized that at the present rate of progress it would take him at least ten years to finish the opera to his own satisfaction, and Puccini sadly withdrew the manuscript from his over-scrupulous friend and handed it to the more workmanlike Adami, who quickly finished it. Puccini had already begun to compose the music when, as we shall see in a later chapter, work had to be suspended to make way for the ill-fated *Rondine* ; and the *Tabarro* was not finally completed until 1916.

Of the other two members of the original cast, nothing more is heard of D'Annunzio's one-act play ; presumably his nightingale had taken another nap, and when it woke up again in 1914, the great poet had sterner work in hand than the composition of operatic librettos—he had to lead his country into the War.

Tristan Bernard's sketch, too, evaporated into space ; from the little we hear of it, however, it scarcely seems to deserve the epithet of ' comic ' applied to it by Puccini, since it told of a black man who had been ' exhibited ' in Europe, and who, on his return to his native village, turns the tables by capturing some white men and charging a fee

[1] He actually survived until 1928—so that he could have completed his task with six years to spare.

for exhibiting *them*—until such time as they shall have been eaten. Certainly nothing was lost by jettisoning such a story in favour of *Gianni Schicchi*.

MILAN
August 4th, 1913

" 33 degrees !

I'm here for a few hours and then I'm going back to Viareggio. I read the article about Covent Garden in the *Corriere*—very '*flattant*' to me ; I should like to thank Emmanuel but I don't know his address—if it's not a nuisance, send it to me.

I'm working on the *Houppelande* (one act)—health good . . . and so is my peace of mind.

All nice wishes and looking forward to seeing you again —when ? "

MILAN
December 22nd, 1913

" I wish you could find out from someone, or from a Society of Authors, about a Mr. Anthony Wharton, the author of a comedy which has been performed in Italy under the name of *MOLLIE*, though it's not its real title— I *believe* the right one is *COUNTRY* or *LILLIAN*, though I don't really know the original name of the comedy [1]— what I want to find out is, supposing I were to *extract* a libretto from it (making many changes and enlarging it greatly, because the original is a poor little thing) how much he would want. It would be a question of a *sum down* —and a comparatively small one—without royalties. It's an

---

[1] The original title of the play by Mr. A. McAllister (who wrote under the pseudonym of Anthony Wharton) was *At the Barn*. It was produced successfully at the Prince of Wales Theatre in the spring of 1912, with Miss Marie Tempest in the leading part. Puccini appears to have acquired the operatic rights, but soon abandoned the idea of setting it to music, since no more is heard of it.

awful nuisance for you—but with all the acquaintances you have it would only be a question of telephoning to find out, and I ask you to forgive me. All best wishes to you and yours for Christmas, and thank you for doing me this favour whether you succeed or not."

CHAPTER THREE

'TWO LITTLE WOOD', ETC., ETC.
(March 1914–July 1914)

In a little cottage at Massarosa, on the other side of the lake of Massaciucolli—that lake whose non-existent ' tower ' had constituted the Puccini ' Eden ' for so many years now —there lived, or there had lived, an elderly English lady, a native of Bury St. Edmunds, known to her few remaining friends as Louise de la Ramée, and to the inhabitants of five continents as ' Ouida '. As early as 1868 she had made Italy her home, and it was here that she wrote those novels which had made her both famous and rich ; but after spending many years and nearly all her fortune elsewhere, she finally came to Massaciucolli, where, early in the twentieth century, she passed away in extreme penury and was buried with a corresponding absence of pomp.

Ouida's popularity as a novelist is perhaps easier to account for than her sudden eclipse. There was no great subtlety about her writing ; her heroes and heroines were as undeniably good as her villains were bad ; but she possessed the art of telling a story well, rejoiced in purple patches, and was not afraid to be called sentimental. Also —a help, rather than a hindrance, to her popularity—the writer's sex was never for one instant in doubt, since she refused to seek expert advice on matters masculine and, as often as not, her hero would get a double ' First '—one at Oxford and one at Cambridge—row for both Universities, and distinguish himself at ' Stroke ' by rowing twice as fast as any other man in the boat. So women cried and men laughed—and Ouida became the first of a long line of female ' best-sellers '. Then suddenly the fashions changed, and her popularity vanished almost overnight; indeed had it not been for Hollywood's annual rediscovery of *Under Two Flags*, which first put the Spanish Legion on the American map and which, incidentally, would have brought the luckless authoress a fortune if she had only survived, it is doubtful whether anyone would remember her name to-day.

In addition to Hollywood's hardy annual, another novel by Ouida, written in the 'seventies and entitled *Two Little Wooden Shoes*, had, in its time, enjoyed a great vogue and been translated into a dozen different languages, including Italian. Many years before, Puccini's attention had been directed to it by a friend, who averred that it contained the seeds of an opera pathetic enough to draw tears from a stone. Puccini had skimmed through it, had been bored—and had forgotten all about it. And then one night in the spring of 1914—Adami, who was dining with him, mentions that they had drunk an excellent Bordeaux, the gift of the exiled D'Annunzio, possibly designed to atone for the ' small, shapeless monstrosity '—the composer, as he gazed across the lake to the spot where poor Ouida lay buried, ' unwept, unhonoured and unsung', bethought him again of this novel which had been waiting all the time on his door-step. As the two men explored its possibilities from memory and coloured them with the glow of the red wine—which must have been of exceptional beauty and potency—their enthusiasm grew, and Adami, mindful of Signor Giulio's advice, determined not to let the grass grow under his feet. In a remarkably short space of time he was able to submit the first rough draft of the libretto, which the other, for the greater part, approved.

At first sight there does not appear to be anything particularly inspiring about this rather lush tale of the little Flemish peasant, Bébé, who walked all the way to Paris in her sabots to find her beloved artist, only to die of exhaustion in his garden. Nevertheless the appeal that it made to Puccini was not surprising; it was very much—almost too much—in his genre, and Bébé was exactly the type of heroine with whom he could fall in love. Clothed in his music, one can readily believe that she would have extracted tears, if not from stones, at any rate from a not too stony-hearted audience—though the critics who delighted to accuse him of copying himself would perhaps have been justified, for once, in greeting it with howls of 'Bohème!'

Suddenly in the midst of their work a doubt—not a musical, but a legal, doubt—occurred to the composer: Ouida was dead, and her shade could only feel flattered by the posthumous honour that was to be conferred on her work; but had she left behind any heirs who might expect something more tangible than glory in return for the use of their property? He determined to lose no time in finding out—and in the meanwhile to suspend work on the libretto.

MILAN
[March 1914]

"I've telegraphed to 'X' because he is a literary man and must have connections—what I want is the exclusive rights to Ouida's *Two little wood Schoe* [*sic*], and I've just had a wire from Cannes in which he kindly says that he is attending to the matter. I've decided to do this opera, which will be full of grace and extraordinarily poetical.

I've made an agreement with the Karltheater in Vienna for 300,000 crowns and other amazing conditions as to royalties, etc., for a *comic opera*—a short opera in three acts

on a very pleasing subject. [1] It's a work which will entertain
me and which I shall get through quickly."

And now two events occurred simultaneously which
were to fan his enthusiasm for Ouida's novel into a white
heat. No sooner had the news leaked out about the forthcoming Puccini opera than Mascagni made a similar
announcement ; he too—or rather, as he hoped, he only—
was going to set the *Two Little Wooden Shoes* to music. I have
already had occasion to comment on that curious phenomenon of 'Two musicians in search of the same libretto'
which recurs again and again in Puccini's career. On this
occasion, unless we are prepared to believe in some extraordinary system of telepathic transfer operating between the
brains of Italian composers, it seems to have been Mascagni
who was the interloper ; but that lovable, schoolboyish
trait in Puccini's character which he never quite outgrew
made the libretto infinitely more desirable in his eyes from
the moment that it was coveted by another.

Or rather, by two others. Relations with *Savoia*, as we
shall see when we come later to examine the origins of the
Rondine, had lately been going from bad to worse ; nevertheless Ricordi's could ill afford to part with their main
asset—the more so as some of Tito's recent 'finds', whatever their artistic value, had, from the more prosaic
financial angle, turned out to be distinctly unlucrative. It
did not matter greatly if Puccini chose to write a light
operetta for Vienna ; but he must at all costs be prevented
from disposing of *Two Little Wooden Shoes* in a similar
manner. The surest way of counteracting such a disloyal
and unpatriotic move would be for Ricordi's to acquire
the operatic rights for themselves.

[1] I.e. *La Rondine* (*The Swallow*), of which more will be heard in the
next chapter.

Thus began an exciting triangular contest in two rounds, the first of which was waged in London, and the second on what may be termed the ' home ground ' of Viareggio. Developments in the first can be followed closely in his letters to my mother.

MILAN
March 17th, 1914

" I telegraphed again to-night to ' X ', because I have had no answer from London. You must know that Mascagni made an announcement about the *Wooden Shoes* simultaneously with mine—and then *Savoia* has telegraphed to his agent to *unearth* the proprietor of the book at all costs—if they get there first I'm ruined. It seems then that it is a Mr. Macmillan who lives in St. Martin Street who is the publisher and proprietor of Ouida's novels—what I require is the right to make an opera from the book, together with the cinematographic rights, and I must obtain these exclusive rights *at once*. Do you think you could look after the matter for me ? I hope to get an answer from ' X ' before this letter reaches you—but you are on the spot in London and you might be able to find out whether the others have already taken any steps.

I'm sorry you had a wretched time at Nice—poor Sibillina ! I am leaving for Torre del Lago with the rest of the family—write to me, or if you have good news send me a wire."

On enquiry, my mother discovered that not " Mr. Macmillan who lives in St. Martin Street " but Chatto & Windus were Ouida's publishers. In the meantime, however, another claimant had appeared on the scene ; the famous Mr. Tauchnitz of Leipzig, in pre-war days a monopolist of English fiction abroad, but now only one of many.

TORRE DEL LAGO
March 23rd, 1914

" Thanks—I'll go and see the lawyer to-morrow, as he is away to-day.

So it's clear that Mr. Macmillan is not the owner—but it occurs to me that the copyright of Ouida's novels may have expired. But I don't know anything about English law or about German law—for the novel was also published by Tauchnitz of Leipzig who, on enquiry, has put forward a claim ! So could you please find out for me how many years ago the book was published and whether according to English law it has become public property—and likewise how things stand in German law ? Have I explained myself clearly ? All sorts of affectionate messages and a thousand thanks for what you are doing."

TORRE DEL LAGO
March 28th, 1914

" Can you please tell me who is the publisher of the *Sabots*.[1] I know it's not Macmillan because you told me so —but I've lost your letter—or rather in the confusion I can't lay my hands on it.

The lawyer of Viareggio has been to the English Consul in Livorno, who has written to London—he'll let me know what he has found out. He says, however, that he believes the *Wooden Shoes* are public property. But what is the English law ? And when did the book come out ? "

TORRE DEL LAGO
April 3rd, 1914

" I wanted to send you a telegram, but there were too many things I had to say. First of all, thank you for every-thing, and try to obtain the exclusive right to make an

[1] Puccini shows himself a true polyglot as regards Ouida's novel, calling it alternately *Due Zoccoletti*, *Les Sabots*, and a variety of more or less weird variations of the original English title.

opera from the book—if you think wise, in my name, if not, in your name and then you can cede it to me. I'm afraid they would ask too much from me, whilst you, although celebrated for your beauty and your grace, are not yet, luckily for you, celebrated as an operatic composer—I warn you (and you can ask Chatto about it) that Tauchnitz of Leipzig (the publisher) is also staking a claim—I made enquiries and they told me that he would be satisfied with very little. They said that he was the proprietor as far as the Continent was concerned, so I imagine that Chatto is only the proprietor for the English rights ? "

But the rights of Messrs. Chatto & Windus were confined to the publication of the novel ; in consequence my mother never became entitled, even *en passant*, to set it to music. Other rights, if any, remained the property of the authoress, or her heirs—if any. But if neither Messrs. Chatto & Windus, nor Mr. Macmillan who lives in St. Martin Street, nor—presumably—Mr. Tauchnitz who lives in Leipzig, had this precious right to dispose of, who had? The answer could only be found in Italy, whither the contest is now transferred.

TORRE DEL LAGO
April 16th, 1914

" The news about the *Two Sabots* was published in the *Corriere*, together with a long interview of mine in order to make certain that I had precedence over the others. To-day I have been to the lawyer at Viareggio and I have applied formally for the right to make an opera from the *Woodschoe*—and I have agreed upon the sum of money I am to pay. I know that Tito is taking steps to get hold of it and then throw a noose round my neck, but I want to be free—and I hope that he and Mascagni, too, will arrive too late.

Thank you so much for what you have done—I have written to Leipzig to find out from Tauchnitz and I ought to hear in a few days' time. Thank you for everything—I shall be going to Paris about the 25th with Elvira for *Manon* at the Champs Élysées."

The sum which Puccini had deposited with the lawyer at Viareggio was the modest one of 1000 lire (£40). But if he hoped to get off as easily as that, he had reckoned without the lawyer, who was a very smart man of affairs. Although technically described as the ' executor ' of the late Louise de la Ramée's last will and testament, he had in reality had nothing to execute, since all the poor lady had left were a few unpaid bills to the local tradesmen and arrears of rent to her landlord. Hastily summoning a meeting of the ' interested parties ', who were none other than the butcher, the baker and the candlestick-maker of Massarosa, the lawyer explained the situation to them : the great—and rich—Maestro Puccini, whom they all knew so well, was eccentric enough to be willing to pay, to the tune of thousands of lire, for the privilege of setting to music a work by the lady who had died indebted to them all. If the creditors would leave the matter in his hands, he would see that they profited by the Maestro's harmless mania. There never was a more unanimous meeting ; after a vote of confidence in the chairman, they departed each on their several errands ; the chairman to place the matter officially in the hands of the Pretor of Viareggio, the creditors to re-examine their forgotten claims in the light of this startling and unexpected development, and to round the sums off—and possibly even up.

Meanwhile Puccini's wisdom in refusing to allow himself to be tied to Ricordi's became apparent. There was no city in the world that honoured him and his music more than Vienna, and the example set by the Karltheater over the *Rondine* was proving contagious.

TORRE DEL LAGO
April 24th, 1914

" I am still not certain about the *Sabots* but I think I am going to be the winner—I am leaving on Sunday for Milan, and on Wednesday I shall be in Paris for *Manon* at the Champs Élysées. Did I tell you that I have made a contract with Vienna for a small opera for 200,000 crowns plus 50 per cent royalties ? [1] And now another publisher wants the *Sabots* and it appears that he will give me what I have asked for : 400,000 crowns plus 40 per cent ! ! If I get my terms it will be a nice little sum of money to put by for a rainy day. And good-bye to *Savoia*—but he has really brought it on his own head—however, not a word about this to anyone.

Thanks for the news about *Bohème* with the centenarian. [2] When I get back from Paris I shall have the libretto of the *Rondine* (the little opera) and I shall start work.

P.S.—The Emperor of Austria has given me the decoration of Grand Officer of the Order of Franz Joseph."

---

[1] There seems some doubt about the sum ' down ' that Puccini actually received for the *Rondine*, since earlier on he talks of 300,000 crowns (about £12,000). But even the smaller figure, quite apart from the ' royalties, etc. ' was a fantastic sum to pay for a dozen ' numbers ' in a light operetta. The rewards for operatic composition had undergone a remarkable transformation since the days of Wagner, who—as I am credibly informed—received less for the work of a lifetime (including the majestic *Ring*) than did the composer of *Yes, we have no bananas* for that one and not particularly memorable number.

[2] Covent Garden had opened on April 20th with a performance of *La Bohème*, with Melba in the rôle of Mimi. Puccini's estimate of her age was rather wide of the mark since, according to the reference books, she was at the time a mere fifty-three. She was, however, to come appreciably nearer her ' century ' before the final curtain was rung down on her Mimi.

TORRE DEL LAGO
May 1st, 1914

" Thank you for your news and for what you tell me about the Opera—so you didn't dislike the little Bellincioni [1] in *Manon* ? In Paris too this little artiste will sing the part in succession to the Diva, Kuznezoff. [2] The man of the 400,000 crowns has accepted all my conditions and in a few days' time I shall write to *Savoia* offering him the *Sabots* and giving him the preference on the Viennese terms of 400,000 crowns in addition to 50 per cent royalties, etc. These are fantastic terms to which *Savoia* certainly won't agree, and then I shall be free and feel no scruples— indeed the debt of gratitude I owe to the house of Ricordi has been more than fully paid through the large and con- tinuous revenue they derive from my old operas—don't you agree ? And now Tito is most inconsiderate in his treatment of me—he behaves to me as though I were nothing but a bit of scrap iron."

MILAN
May 14th, 1914

" Would you believe it ?—the question of the *Little Wooden Shoes* has not yet been settled by the lawyer at Viareggio—but I think I am very near the solution. Thank you for the news about Covent Garden ; you did well to say that to Emmanuel—but will he do it ? I should be so pleased if he would.

I have started on the *Rondine* for Vienna—I shall go to the country soon and get down to work. I am engaged in underground, but not open, warfare with *Savoia*, who is pleasant enough when he writes and when he sees me ; but there's a storm brewing which I fear, or rather hope, will

[1] Bianca Bellincioni, who made her first appearance in London on April 24th in *Manon Lescaut*.
[2] Presumably Maria Kouznietzoff.

soon burst. You can believe me when I say that this fellow is a real *pig*, and that his behaviour to me is most Jesuitical; I know that he has said of me that I shall never write any more—is that the way to behave after twenty years during which I have brought honour to his firm as well as many millions of profit? And I am treated without the least respect or consideration. It's a disgrace! I wish I were ten years younger—but although I am already getting old, I can still give him a nasty pill or two to swallow."

MILAN
May 25th, 1914

"I don't think that *Savoia* can have got the *Little Wooden Shoes* because it is *free*—at least, so the lawyer at Viareggio said, as well as the publisher, Chatto."

MILAN
June 1st, 1914

"Thank you for the news about *Butterfly*, but I believe the performances at Covent Garden aren't so very good, although the artistes enjoy such a great reputation. And I don't think, either, that the *Fanciulla* will be done well—but enough; we'll see. If the 'Gods'—I'm speaking of Destinn—aren't properly 'bridled', as they say of horses, they become, in course of time, impossible performers—and the *mises-en-scène*? Horrible—and the movements and the lighting?—Disastrous—but it's the same everywhere, and there's nothing to do but to resign oneself to it.

As for the *little wooden shoes* I've found out that Tauchnitz too has no rights—it's quite free in Italy. So there's nothing more to worry about, and Mascagni says that if I do the Opera he will do it too—and let him if he wants to. I've nothing to be afraid of—by now I have become accustomed to doubles; the two *Manons*—the two *Bohèmes*—the . . . four *little wooden shoes*.

Towards the 15th of June I shall at last go to Torre and then to Viareggio for three months, where I shall plunge myself into the work of the *Rondine*. William Boosey of Chappell's has written to ask for the rights of the *Two little wooden shoes*; I've written back that I should be delighted to negotiate with him later, at the proper time—but not for the whole world; only for England and North America."

MILAN
June 22nd, 1914

" It's not true that I have come to terms with *Savoia* for the *little wooden shoes*. I've still got an offer from the firm of Herzmansky (Doblinger) of Vienna for 400,000 crowns, but for the time being I don't want to tie myself—first of all I want to finish the *Rondine* for Vienna.

I shall have so many disagreeable things to tell you . . . when we meet again. But when is that going to be?" [1]

VIAREGGIO
July 19th, 1914

" . . . Perhaps after all I shan't sign an agreement with Vienna for the *Wooden Shoes* in spite of the offer of the 400,000 crowns—I'm going to sign one instead with *Savoia* for half that amount, and that because of a certain peculiar sentimentality of mine. I've been associated with that firm for too many years—and I want to go back to them. At heart I'm a decent fellow, and my feelings of vindictiveness don't last long.

How glad I should be to see you again! I'm writing some rather graceful music for the *Rondine*—light, but, I think, interesting—and clear as the water from a spring."

Thus one competitor was eliminated from the contest—but not until after a severe struggle, of which Puccini makes

[1] They were not to meet again for five years.

no mention in his letters. The struggle was between Puccini and himself ; for one fine day there descended on him at Torre del Lago two visitors ; one was Doctor Willner, the librettist of his friend Franz Lehar and the writer of the original draft of the *Rondine*, who was now acting on behalf of the Viennese publisher, Herzmansky ; the other was a cheque in Doctor Willner's pocket for—half a million crowns ! [1] For a long time Puccini gazed reflectively at the cheque ; he had never been greedy for money—but twenty thousand pounds was indeed a ' nice little sum to be put by for a rainy day '—and certainly not one to be turned down out of hand. In the end loyalty to his old firm of publishers won the day—and for once in his life he allowed himself the privilege of sneezing at twenty thousand pounds. The two emissaries returned to Vienna, unseparated.

There remained Mascagni, the creditors—and the Pretor. Mascagni made no further pronouncement ; the creditors continued to hope for the best—and the Pretor deliberated. Since, however, there must be an end to everything, even to pretorian deliberation, the decision was at last promulgated in a beautiful letter to Puccini, which set forth that, whereas the poor authoress was dead and it was therefore impossible to assess at their proper value the fruits of her genius, and whereas she had left no heirs but only creditors who by that fact had become her heirs, it had now been decided that the aforesaid fruit of her genius in which the Maestro was specially interested should be publicly auctioned for the benefit of the creditors—with a

[1] This is the figure given—and repeated several times—by Adami, who was present at the interview and was himself to receive 50,000 crowns for his collaboration. (See *Puccini*, chap. 6, *La storia di due zoccoletti* passim.) A curious air of vagueness seems to surround these offers by Austrian publishers ; but as this particular cheque was never cashed, and as, moreover, the Austrian krone was before very long to have little value except as wall-paper, the matter is of no great moment.

minimum reserve of 1000 lire, being the sum deposited by the said Maestro.

Signor Adami, to whom I am already heavily in debt for much of the foregoing, has given us a delicious account of the auction, at which he and Puccini were present together with the whole of Massarosa and half Viareggio. The excitement amongst the creditors was intense ; for they had heard that there were no less than three buyers in the market for their property, and each new arrival was scanned with mounting curiosity. Ah ! there was the great —and rich—Puccini ; and there, doubtless, someone from Ricordi's—and there, perhaps, a representative of Mascagni. Like the Sower of the seed which fell on fertile ground, they saw themselves being repaid, some thirtyfold, some sixtyfold and some a hundredfold. . . .

After an interminable speech from the Pretor, whose day it was, and a declaration from an 'expert'—one Giovacchino Forzano, of whom we shall hear more later— that the musical rights of the novel were worth far more than the paltry reserve of 1000 lire, the auction opened briskly with a bid of 1500 lire—made by the baker of Massarosa. This was followed by progressively higher bids from the butcher and the chemist ; but when the landlord of Ouida's villa had bid 3000 lire in a firm, ringing voice, there was a long pause—during the course of which that wretched man found himself in the positively frightful position of a small peasant proprietor who, in addition to having incurred a bad debt, has agreed to pay his fellow-villagers £150 for the right to set a novel to music. But at this point a young man stepped forward and explained that he represented the firm of Ricordi's ; that he had been carefully into the legal question and had established beyond all doubt that the copyright had expired (shrieks of indignation from the creditors). Nevertheless, he added, he was prepared to acquire the rights for 4000 lire. (A huge sigh of relief—led by Ouida's landlord.) Going for the first time . . . going for the second time . . . going for the third and last time . . . the auction was over, and Ricordi's, with a nice gesture, handed over the rights to Puccini—for what they were worth.

In a letter dated March 24th, 1915, Puccini refers briefly to his (indirect) victory. " After that I'm going to start on Ouida's *Little Wooden Shoes*, which at last, two days ago, I managed to acquire—though actually it was Ricordi's who obtained it."

Thereafter there is but one more brief mention of the subject in his letters. On October 15th, 1915, he announces : " I shall start on *Two little wood* ", etc., etc.—for he can no longer be bothered to bestow the full title on the novel which he fought so doggedly to acquire, much as though Napoleon were to refer to ' Aust ', or the Duke of Wellington to ' Wat '. On reflection he had decided that instead of buying a pair of wooden shoes he had been sold what is vulgarly known as 'a pup' ; and it seemed probable that Ouida's novel would return once again to the oblivion from which it had been so suddenly, and so startlingly, rescued. . . .

But not at once. On April 30th, 1917, the public of Rome were given the first chance of hearing a new opera by the composer of *Cavalleria Rusticana*, entitled *Lodoletta*. The libretto, it was announced, was by Giovacchino Forzano, and had been taken from a novel by Ouida called *Two Little Wooden Shoes*. The public of Rome were not unduly impressed—once again Puccini's second (or was it third ?) thoughts had proved best.

PART V

WAR-TIME

(1914–1918)

CHAPTER ONE

' LA RONDINE '
(September 1914–April 1917)

NOTHING is more striking than the absence hitherto in Puccini's letters of any reference to what may broadly be termed ' the outside world '. " The affairs of political and public life ", says Specht,[1] " left him quite unmoved. All he wanted was to discover good texts for operas, and, in the tranquil seclusion of Torre del Lago, to live for the work that he loved so passionately "—and, at any rate until the outbreak of the World War, this criticism (if indeed it be a criticism) was fully justified. He was entirely engrossed in his art and in his small circle of intimate friends, and beyond that little world he had no ambition to stray—unlike so many other virtuosi, who appear to think that the mastery of a musical instrument or the gift of composition carries automatically with it the right, and the capacity, to rule and advise their fellow-men.

He was, too, in the truest and best sense of the word, an Internationalist. I do not mean, of course, that he was not as unmistakably Italian as his music ; on the contrary, his delight in the fame which he enjoyed abroad was largely impersonal, for he regarded it as a vindication of Italian Art, and himself, in a modest way, as his country's Ambassador. But, like his music, he too knew no boundaries (except perhaps the boundary which divided Torre del Lago from the rest of the world) and when he talks of

[1] See Specht, p. 21.

his feelings of gratitude to anyone who has shown him a kindness, whether he happens to be French, English, German or American, he is speaking the literal truth.

With the outbreak of War, however, and more particularly after Italy entered it on the side of the Entente, a marked change is noticeable not only in the tone but also in the scope of his letters ; for the first time he is compelled to gaze beyond his little walled garden into the great outside world beyond—only to be appalled by what he sees. He discovers in himself an unsuspected love of his country, though, like most Italians, he was a poor hater, and never succumbed to that insane ' war-fever ', from which certain elements even amongst the calm British nation, whose ' poise ' he had so often admired, found themselves not entirely immune. His was not the fiercely militant patriotism of a Verdi, whose very name, by a happy acrostical coincidence,[1] sounded an unceasing clarion call in the ears of his fellow-countrymen ; one cannot fail to contrast his rather tepid allusion to Caporetto (" Yes, we've got the Boches staying with us ! But they won't stay long ! ") with the elder man's fiery resentment at the defeat of Custozza, which he regarded in the light of a personal humiliation. In fairness to Puccini, however, it should be remembered that he lived in an age when Italy, to all intents and purposes, had already achieved her unity ; though Verdi's operas, written by an Italian for Italians, might be given at the Fenice in Venice or La Scala in Milan, they were nevertheless being performed under the hated shadow of the Austrian flag, and under the scarcely less hated menace of the Austrian censor. Only in the town

---

[1] The cries of " Viva Verdi ! " with which the composer, from the 'fifties onwards, was invariably greeted in public, were due to the simple fact that the letters of his name spelt ' Vittorio Emmanuele, Re D'Italia '.

of Trieste (which I do not believe that he ever visited) was Puccini privileged to enjoy that stirring feeling of mortification which acted as a constant spur to the elder man's patriotism.

He had no thought, for instance, of joining his friend D'Annunzio and *leading* Italy into the War ; he had far too great a horror of the sufferings inseparable from modern warfare, whether such intervention proved successful or unsuccessful. His original attitude of 'benevolent neutrality' to both groups of combatants was, of course, entirely correct ; if anything, it was a shade too correct—or so at least the French seemed to think. With a little reflection he might easily have avoided that ' incident ' referred to in his letters, which caused such a stir in the French Press at the time. But it is not necessary to labour the point, since Puccini himself implicitly admits his error, when he refers to that ' little denial '—the denial that he was anti-German —" which perhaps it would have been better if I hadn't made ". Nor must we blame the French unduly ; they felt that they had been cruelly and unjustly attacked, and they were fighting with their backs to the wall—a position which is rarely conducive to calm thinking or dispassionate judgment. As to the later attacks, however, made on Puccini by Léon Daudet in the *Action Française* for his unpatriotic action in writing an ' Austrian ' opera, it is impossible to avoid the conclusion that they were inspired by jealousy rather than by public-spiritedness ; however, they were at least useful in calling forth from him his solitary public pronouncement—a quite unanswerable letter to the Press, in which he defended himself with both energy and dignity.

For him, as for most of us, the War meant the end of his little world as he had known it. Nor was he spared the one overwhelming anxiety common to all those whose dear ones were in danger ; his only son Tonio—" a fine big

fellow and a splendid son "—was at the Front throughout
most of the War, and his father was never happy nor at rest
except during those brief intervals when he was home on
leave or in hospital. In addition Puccini's own particular
world—the world of opera—had crumbled to pieces ;
Euterpe had been silenced by the din of Mars. Many of
the big opera-houses followed the example of Covent
Garden and closed down altogether ; others were situated
in what had now become ' hostile territory '—but in any
case those little trips abroad, which had become an increasing distraction to him, were now out of the question ;
except for one brief visit to Monte Carlo for the *première*
of the *Rondine*, he never left Italy throughout the War. But
the disruption in his soul went deeper ; all sense of values
had been lost, and his life's work suddenly appeared insignificant to him compared with the tremendous and
terrible events which were shaking the world. " My poor
Art ? " he sighs. " Don't let's talk of it." He had none of
that tiresome but comforting ego-mania which enables so
many musicians to fiddle, or compose, whilst Rome burns ;
although he wrote regularly to my mother throughout the
War, references to his work—the one thing that consoled
him a little—are few and far between. Nothing is more
surprising than that that little masterpiece, *Gianni Schicchi*,
should have come into the world almost unheralded, his
only reference to it being an indirect one : " I have
finished my three operas ".

The irony of it was that at the outbreak of War he who
had so long gone hungry had not only food but, for the
first and only time in his life, a choice of food before him.
There was the *Tabarro*, which he had begun in 1913 and
had temporarily laid on one side ; and there was that ill-
fated bird, his Austrian *Swallow*.

Paradoxically, the real begetter of the *Rondine* was Tito

Ricordi. Early in 1914 Puccini had been in Vienna for a special production of *Tosca*, to which he attached more than ordinary importance, and in which, incidentally, Jeritza appeared for the first time in a rôle which was later to make her famous. He had hoped to be accompanied, as on so many previous occasions, by Tito ; but the latter announced that he was " too busy ", and sent as his substitute another representative of the firm, Puccini's very good friend, Carlo Clausetti. It then transpired that Savoia's business was the production of *Francesca da Rimini* at Naples—an opera in which he claimed a twofold proprietary interest. In the first place the music had been written by his young protégé, Riccardo Zandonai (whom we last heard of in connection with Puccini's discarded *Conchita*), and in the second, it had been 'adapted' from D'Annunzio's tragedy by Tito himself, whose name, as a special mark of favour, had been allowed to appear, together with that of the poet, on the title-page—although it would seem that his main contribution to the work had been made with a blue pencil rather than with a pen.

And so preparations for the two productions went ahead simultaneously—when, only two days before the Viennese *première*, Clausetti, to his consternation, received a letter bidding him leave forthwith for Naples. Although secretly furious, Puccini made light of the matter, and cabled himself to Tito in the most friendly terms, begging that Clausetti's departure might be delayed for two days. At once came the reply : " Impossible to do as you wish. I *order* Clausetti to leave immediately." [1]

I have already remarked that, amongst the qualities which Tito inherited from his father, tact was not included.

[1] See Adami's *Puccini*, p. 127, and chap. 7 *passim* for an excellent account of the origins of *La Rondine*.

Perhaps it would be fairer to say that his 'diplomacy', such as it was, was that of a later age with which we are now becoming only too familiar : the diplomacy of the sledge-hammer—a method both simple and effective, provided the other man decides not to retaliate. But on this occasion even Puccini was goaded into counter-attacking ; and he was fortunate enough to find an appropriate weapon ready to hand. For months past, Austrian publishers had been besieging him with requests to write an ' operetta ' for them—requests which he had persistently declined, declaring laughingly that ' it was not in his line '—a statement which was to be amply borne out by subsequent events. But now he let it be known to these importunate gentlemen that he was prepared to lend a more favourable ear to their entreaties—and within twenty-four hours the contract with the Karltheater was signed. A preliminary payment of 200,000 (or was it 300,000 ?) crowns for eight or ten numbers in an operetta to be approved of by the Master ; it was almost too easy, and it must have seemed ' a shame to take the money '. But it was not the money he was thinking of ; it was the ' bitter pill ' which *Savoia* would be left to swallow. Hitherto he had written music out of love for the subject : now he wrote it out of hatred for a publisher.

There could be no more convincing refutation of the charge of ' commercialism ' so frequently levelled at him than the subsequent history of this one work which he definitely wrote ' on commission '—and out of hatred. It is true that he recognized his own limitations even more clearly than many of his critics ; until his very last work, *Turandot*, he never attempted to reach out to the stars, but kept his feet firmly planted on the earth with which he was familiar. As Mr. Francis Toye has finely put it of an even greater musician, " Like all Italian composers, Verdi regarded himself primarily as a craftsman whose duty it was to keep abreast of the times, to write the best possible music of which he was capable consonant and compatible with particular circumstances." [1] If, then, it be ' commercial ' to recognize what one can, and what one can not, do, and to cultivate one's own garden, then Puccini, like Verdi, was ' commercial '; but even within these self-appointed limits, as he now found, it was only possible for him to write how and when he felt moved to write. He discovered that he simply could not compose ' to order '—which is surely the first thing that a commercial gentleman should learn to do.

Just eight or ten numbers . . . it ought to have been child's play . . . but, somehow, it wasn't. The first libretto despatched from Vienna he returned out of hand ; the second—La Rondine—he accepted, on condition that Adami should be given a reasonably free hand in its Italian adaptation. Just eight or ten numbers . . . a less conscientious composer would have just scribbled off the first thing that came into his head, and gratefully pocketed the cash. But this was not Puccini's way ; he was a ' good craftsman ' and within the limits of his abilities he could not be satisfied with anything short of perfection. Just eight or ten numbers . . . but they simply would not come. In despair, he asked to be relieved of his contract ; but the Austrians, who had fought so hard to get him, were not going to let him out of their clutches. One can hardly blame them.

And then Adami came to his rescue with an idea. It was, on paper, an admirable idea—supposing, instead of an operetta, he were to cut out all the distasteful Viennese-made dialogue, in the interstices of which the music was supposed to be sandwiched, and wrote in its place a

[1] See Toye, p. 137.

genuine light opera ? The idea found immediate favour ; and Puccini started to work again, happy to find himself once more in a medium which he understood. True, it meant more work for him, but he did not mind that ; it meant even more work for Adami, who reckoned that in all, in order to produce the three acts required, he had written a good sixteen ; but Puccini did not mind that either. As for the Viennese, they were simply overjoyed ; instead of buying a pig in a poke, they found that they had bought a large herd for the price of eight—or ten —piglets.

The first act was finished quickly—and then the trouble started. Put very briefly, the story of the *Rondine* tells of the pampered middle-aged mistress of a rich banker, who leaves him for a poor young artist, and then leaves the poor young artist for his own good, the comic relief—such as it is—being provided by her maid, who leaves her for a rich poet, and then leaves the rich poet because she prefers domestic service. It is all worked out on the conventional lines of operetta, the mistress disguising herself as the maid, the maid dressing up as the mistress, and so on. How to transform this into opera was a task which might have daunted anyone ; it was rather like trying to balance an elephant on a flea to their mutual satisfaction. The only logical course would have been to eliminate the flea and concentrate on the elephant ; but this Puccini was unwilling to do—sufficient liberties had already been taken with the Viennese libretto, and he felt it necessary that something, however little, of Willner's and Reichert's original work should be retained. It is a remarkable tribute to the librettist no less than the composer that they not only faced this dreadful task unflinchingly, but actually suc-ceeded in the end in carrying it through ; in his letters, however, Puccini, possibly from a sense of pride (not unmixed with shame) gives no hint of the difficulties involved, but writes airily of his work, just as though it were the simple thing which he had originally imagined it to be. Nevertheless this poor hybrid swallow, during its chequered flight, was always to suffer from its dubious origin ; it could never quite make up its mind what sort of bird it was meant to be—operatic, or operettic ; and so, as we shall see later, it flapped dolorously—and fell between the two.

VIAREGGIO
August 29th, 1914

" Your mournful tidings [1] make me think of you so much—I send you my heartfelt sympathy and my most sincere condolences.

I wrote to you some time ago in answer to your letter from Folkestone. I'm very sad ; I've worked very little, and I have little will to work—the War and other unpleasantnesses have played havoc with my brains. I'm going off to take refuge at Torre—but I hate everything ! Life is really a burden, sometimes light and sometimes as heavy as a ton of bricks—but it's always a burden !

So much love, dear Sybil, and try to take courage."

MILAN
September 14th, 1914

" During the first period of this terrible War I felt absolutely stupefied and I was unable to work any more ; now I've started again, and I'm pleased about it. *La Rondine* is the title of the small opera, which will be finished in the spring ; it's a light sentimental opera with touches of comedy—but it's agreeable, limpid, easy to sing, with little waltz music and lively and fetching tunes.

[1] My mother's father, Mr. S. H. Beddington, had just died.

We'll see how it goes—it's a sort of reaction against the
repulsive music of to-day—which, as you have put it so
well, is very much like the War !

And how will this gigantic conflict end ? England is
certain to come out of it well, because she is so wise and
so strong—and we ? Enough—we'll see ; at any rate for us
poor devils it's a great blessing not to be involved in the
conflict. Let's hope that the news about your brother-in-
law is good [1]—So many sweet and kind thoughts to you—
the only war I've had has been in my home ; but things
are going better now."

TORRE DEL LAGO
December 15th, 1914

" How are you ? I am well and working a lot—in a
few days' time I shall be going to Milan. And when is this
horrible great War going to end? It's enough to drive the
whole world mad ! Are your dear ones well? Do please give
me your news, which I hope will be good. We are all well
here—how I love the calm of the countryside ! But I have
got to spend Christmas in Milan ; it's a duty laid down by
convention, but one has to do it."

MILAN
December 22nd, 1914

" I wrote to you a few days ago but perhaps you didn't
get my letter—are you at the seaside ? I am in Milan in
this horrible spot where one never sees the sky—only
something the colour of slate which I think is worse than
London—and why do I stay here ? I can't tell you myself ;
out of habit ? Or because my family are here ? But there it
is—here I am and here I remain—but only for a short time,

---

[1] Brigadier-General H. S. Seligman, C.M.G., D.S.O., etc. (then
Major Seligman), who took ' J ' Battery, R.H.A., to France in the
original Expeditionary Force. He came through four years in France
without a scratch.

I think, until my health begins to suffer from it. But at least we're not at war ; this is a selfish remark to make, I know, but I cannot do otherwise than make it—War is too horrible a thing whatever the results, for whether it be victory or defeat human lives are sacrificed. We live in a terrible world, and I see no sign of this cruel state of things coming to an end ! I am working—but God knows when I shall be able to give this opera, which has to have its *première* in Vienna !

Love to David and to the boys and all best wishes for Christmas—this year a red Christmas ! ''

MILAN
February 11th, 1915

'' It is some time since I had your dear news. You will have heard of the uproar in the French papers against me—they are unjust and have always been against my music because it is so successful in their theatres—I made no sort of demonstration in favour of Germany and have kept myself strictly neutral as was my duty. I have feelings of friendship and gratefulness for the reception given to my music everywhere—in France, in England, in Austria and in Germany—only I happened to read in a German paper that I was against Germany and they said that I actually signed this declaration—whereas I had in fact signed nothing, for the simple reason that I was never asked to. And so I wrote a couple of lines denying this, saying that I had never taken up a hostile attitude to Germany. That is all—and from this a whole host of the basest calumnies have poured down on my head. But patience—everything will pass—as I hope this terrible War which has shaken the whole world will also pass !

Best wishes to you and affectionate regards to David and the children—has Vincent enlisted ? May God protect him ! ''

MILAN
February 23rd, 1915

" No, dear Sybil !—my little denial (which perhaps it would have been better if I hadn't made) has been travestied by my enemies in France into an assertion which is untrue. I repeat to you that it isn't the French—that is, the people of France—but those incapable colleagues, people like X, Y, Z and Co., who for a long time past have been working and writing against me—it is they who have let loose the storm. You know how grateful I always am to anyone who has shown me a kindness—that is why I am indebted to the people of France, of England, of Germany, of America, and I might go on until I had mentioned all the nations of the civilized world, because my music has found its way into every quarter of the globe—and so I must publicly show myself impartial and neutral. As an Italian, it is my duty to be bound by neutrality, and so I am—because, having a horror of war and loving my country as I do, I must pray God that it be preserved from this scourge. I have an additional reason for saying this, that I do not think my country is as yet in a position to take part in a big conflict. You will see that when it is all over—and God will that that may be soon !—all these unjust little outbursts of rage will vanish."

TORRE DEL LAGO
March 15th, 1915

" You cannot imagine what pleasure the news of *Butterfly* being done in London has given me ; I thought I had been put on the *Index* by you too—as the French have done for something which was offensive to nobody—and which was simply a correction.

I am here alone to enjoy a little of the beginning of spring—besides, life in Milan had become intolerable. I follow the phases of the terrible War and wonder when it will finish ! It's a ghastly nightmare for everybody—so much grief, so much suffering, so much inhumanity."

Torre del Lago
March 24th, 1915

" Thank you for your dear letter—I'm here by myself, and almost happy to be alone—because I couldn't stand any more of Milan and the rest . . . ! Here at least I can talk to the wall which doesn't answer me back—I'm expecting my poet to-morrow to finish my—Austrian Opera ! I wanted to break my contract, but I haven't succeeded—after that I am going to start on Ouida's *Little Wooden Shoes,* which at last I have managed to acquire, two days ago, for 5300 (Italian) lire—though actually it was Ricordi who obtained it.

I'm pleased with what you tell me about the English papers saying nice things about me ; but you people are more serious-minded and have better sense than the French—with them it is envy which has made them do and say what they have against me—and for what ? For a simple denial—for what was, in fact, a sort of declaration of neutrality, since that was how my King and my fellow-countrymen regarded it. Besides, an artist should keep entirely out of politics—at least, that is what I think. Personally I don't know what has happened to Matilda Serao [1]—that is, I should like to explain her action, but I don't want to discuss politics. I understand you, and I understand the others—may God, who has been so

[1] The famous Italian novelist and journalist, who was an old friend of my mother's, and always wrote of her on account of her singing at St. Moritz as " The nightingale of the Engadine ". During the War—or at any rate at the beginning of it—she evinced strong pro-German sympathies, and it is no doubt to this attitude of hers that Puccini, in answer to a question from my mother, is covertly referring. She died not long after the War.

frequently invoked, prevent such a tragedy from ever recurring ! ''

TORRE DEL LAGO
April 9th, 1915

" I have very nearly finished the *Rondine*. . . . And how did *Bohème* go ? [1] Oh, how grateful I am to the English for being so utterly different from those *Pigs*, your neighbours !

My family are now here for Easter—Tonio is a fine big fellow and a splendid son.''

MILAN
June 13th, 1915

" Yes, we are at war and things are going well—which is very comforting. The enthusiasm in Italy is great, it's serious and it's solid—may God protect us and may the star of Italy shine on the final victory !

It's terribly hot here—I'm in Milan because Tonio is going off as a volunteer motor-cyclist, and I want to say good-bye to him—I think he will go as aide-de-camp to a General, or in the Sanitary Corps. In August I shall pay a visit to Paris and to London—will you be there ? If not, I'll come and see you wherever you are.

I knew indirectly that the Japanese Butterfly was a disappointment—those ' gramophone ' voices are not, I think, very pleasant. I've got my Austrian opera here, and it—and I—can go to the devil.''

TORRE DEL LAGO
October 15th, 1915

" I'm really to blame for not having written to you any more—do forgive me. It's the fault of this war which has upset everyone and me specially—I've spent all the summer here and I've finished the *Rondine* for those gentlemen, our

---

[1] Although, as I have already mentioned, Covent Garden was closed throughout the War, opera—of a sort—continued intermittently to be heard, generally in English, at Drury Lane and elsewhere.

enemies, and now I've got to wait. I shall start on *Two Little Wood*, etc., etc.—my health is fairly good, but I'm beginning to grow old, that's the sickening part about it. I saw Angeli the other day in Milan and we talked about you—in fact he said that he was going to write to you.

They're doing *Tosca* again in Paris on Thursday—let's hope there won't be any unpleasantnesses. Tonio is still an officer in the Sanitary Corps—I too should be happy to see you again, you who have the secret of eternal youth—for I always picture you just the same with your sweet smile. Give my best love to David and the boys—is Vincent out in France? Good-bye, my dearest friend."

ORBETELLO
December 4th, 1915

"Your letter arrived here in the Maremma, where I have been shooting—I shall be back in Torre on Thursday. Nothing can be done about the *Rondine* because *they* are the proprietors of the libretto—so I am absolutely bound hand and foot. Tonio is well and is still in Milan with the Sanitary Corps—I am working at the *Tabarro*—a one-act play—I am well—But this War ! ! ! What sad and horrible times we are living in ! "

MILAN
December 26th, 1915

"I have left your address at Torre and I am writing to you in London to send you my dearest love and most sincere wishes for the New Year, which I pray may be less devilish than 1915 ! Let us hope for the best !

A thousand affectionate messages to you and your dear ones."

TORRE DEL LAGO
February 22nd, 1916

"I've been in Rome and I consoled myself a little by seeing the lovely sun and my friends. I was nearly all the

time with Tosti [1] and Berthe, who were as sweet and kind
as ever. Now I'm here alone and mournful as an Elegy ;
the wind is blowing and the cold has returned. Elvira
is always in such black spirits that I feel a longing to
get away—but living alone like a dog makes me so
unhappy !

With *Savoia*, more odious than ever, I entertain only the
most distant relations ; he's a most ungrateful man, and an
even more ungrateful publisher—from now on he regards
me as a piece of useless scrap-iron and never shows me the
least kindness—quite the contrary ! And this makes me
miserable—I work little or not at all at present ; as you
know, I've finished the *Rondine*—but our enemies have post-
poned everything until the end of the War. In spite of the
fact that I have the Italian rights, I can't use the Opera
because under the contract the *première* must take place in
Vienna ! You might say that in war-time contracts go to
the wall—but this isn't possible in the case of my contract
—because the lawsuit would be heard there and if I lost I
should be compelled to pay through the royalties I get
from their theatres, and besides they enjoy proprietary rights
over the libretto.

I haven't had my photo taken lately, but if I do I'll send
you one. Why don't you come to Rome ? There are lots
of English people there and I should like to go back there
again—how gladly would I tell you all my griefs and
troubles. It certainly wouldn't be very amusing for you—
but you are so good, so like an angel, that I am sure you
would condole with me, and that you would give me
solace and inspire me with courage."

[1] Tosti's death a few months later—on December 2nd, 1916—came
as a great blow to Puccini as well as to my mother. I feel certain that
Puccini must have written to her about it ; but, like a number of other
letters of his, it must have gone astray.

TORRE DEL LAGO
April 27th, 1916

" It really is an age since I have given any sign of life—
I am here by myself—Milan, with the rest of them (except
my son) bored me to tears. I am quite well, though I am
getting older—I am working at the *Tabarro* and I am well
forward. The other opera, the *Rondine*, is quite finished and
is waiting for the end of the War to undertake its first
flight, either into the heavens or down to earth.

How I long to travel ! When will this cursed War be
over ? It seems to me like a suspension of life ! And are all
of you all right over there ? Life must be pretty boring for
you—remember me to David and to your boys. When
shall we be able to travel about again without hindrance as
we used to do ? How one longs again for a little life ! Here
one languishes ; between the green earth and the sea the
seeds of hatred against this enforced calm are beginning to
develop within me. Send me your news, which always
gives me the greatest pleasure.'"

TORRE DEL LAGO
July 17th, 1916

" How are you ? Here the heat is worthy of Pisa ; I am
fed up with it but I can't make up my mind to leave—
there are a thousand reasons why. I am leading a wretched
life and my only consolation is a few hours of good
work. . . .

And the War ?—Well done the English ! [1] Let us hope
that the end will come soon and that a little peace will
return to the world—but it doesn't seem likely to me—
quite the contrary !

I saw Angeli and his wife at Viareggio and we talked a

---

[1] He is referring to our successes in the battle of the Somme, which
had begun on July 1st.

lot about you—Love to David and the boys.

Yours affectionately,

PAUVRE JACK ! ''

A brief note from Torre del Lago, dated September 19th, 1916, shows that the absurd impasse which had hitherto prevented the Swallow from making its first flight, and which had baffled the wits of half a dozen international lawyers, had at last been overcome.

" I've nearly finished the *Tabarro*, which I think will be given at Monte Carlo. Sonsogno is going to take the *Rondine*—*Savoia* has made a serious *gaffe*."

What had happened was extremely simple. The firm of Sonsogno (thus making tardy amends for their rejection of *Le Villi* some thirty years before) had agreed to relieve Puccini of all liabilities *vis-à-vis* his Austrian publishers, with whom they in turn had come to terms through a neutral channel. Puccini, however, would not consent to this arrangement until he had made one more fruitless attempt to persuade *Savoia* to take over the opera instead.

TORRE DEL LAGO
November 17th, 1916

" It's a long time since I have written to you ! I am a *great pig*—I know it, I confess it and I write it—but this War which goes dragging on and silences every thought which is not connected with it, generates in me that state of inertia which I already possess in great measure. I am at war with my publishers ; I have two operas ready and nothing has been decided—one of them has no money and the other (that's Tito) occupies himself with other matters than music—all the same he telegraphed to me yesterday and it seems that he will agree to my terms for the *Tabarro*.

I am looking for a subject in one act—something specially poetical and lofty—have you nothing in view ? I am going to give one opera at Monte Carlo—I don't know whether it's going to be the *Rondine* or *Tabarro*. It will be in March."

In the end Puccini decided that the *Tabarro* would have to wait until the original scheme of the *Triptych* had been completed, and consequently it was the *Rondine* with which Monte Carlo was honoured on March 28th in the following year.

No more appropriate setting for its first flight could be imagined. There, by the blue waters of the Mediterranean, there stood out one small oasis untouched by, and almost unconscious of, the surrounding conflagration. The Monegasque Opera House was as diminutive as its frog-like presiding genius, M. Raoul Guinsbourg, and was ill-adapted for grandiose spectacles ; but for a light opera like the *Rondine* it was perfect. Moreover, since good music was but one more bait for attracting gamblers to the neighbouring ' tables ', M. Guinsbourg could afford to do things regardless of expense, and the operatic season invariably showed a heavy loss—at least on paper. One suspects, however, that the loss to the Principality was no more than a departmental one, since, indirectly and unconsciously, the audience paid fabulous prices for their musical entertainment, not at the box-office but in the adjoining Casino.

M. Guinsbourg had enjoyed many triumphs in the past ; indeed it was his proud boast (though it is possible that some of his statements needed checking) that he had discovered and given to the world every singer of note from Caruso to Chaliapine. But a Puccini *première* represented, even for him, a remarkable scoop, and he was determined

to do things ' in style '. It was perhaps as well that the
composer was present in person to superintend the arrangements ; for M. Guinsbourg's ' style ' was not always
impeccable, and he was given to ' improving ' the original
by sundry embellishments of his own. " You had better
warn Puccini ", his more sedate colleague, Harry Higgins,
advised my mother in connection with the Monte Carlo
production of the *Trittico*, " to keep an eye on Guinsbourg.
He is quite capable of introducing a fox-trot *d'une verve
étincelante* into *Suor Angelica* suggestively performed by the
novices."

On this occasion M. Guinsbourg appears to have kept
his natural ebullience under proper control. The first
performance was in every way a genuine success ; the
public were enthusiastic ; the assembled critics of Europe—
or as many of them as could be spared from their military
duties—gave it their blessing ; and Puccini rejoiced addi-
tionally at the thought of *Savoia's* discomfiture.

HOTEL DE PARIS
MONTE CARLO
April 1st, 1917

" Thank you for your telegram and for the letters—I
enclose a newspaper cutting so that you should have an
idea how successful the opera was. I am leaving to-morrow
for Milan and on the 9th I shall go to my beloved Torre
del Lago, and there I shall console myself with work, as I
have another opera which I have begun : *Suor Angelica*, an
opera in one act to add to the *Tabarro*, which is already
finished. I have had lots of telegrams but I am surprised
not to have had one from Angeli nor from Ricordi—He
[Ricordi] said that I had written an opera that hadn't come
off, and that it was bad Lehar ! I insisted so much that he
should take the opera that I positively degraded myself
before him ! But he would not have anything to do with it

—And now he will be sorry, because the *Rondine* is an opera full of life and of melody—it will appeal to you very much. The score is not yet ready—but the moment it's out I will send you a copy. My health is not good; I have had pains in the arm for the last six months and the usual diabetes which plagues me. My brain is clear but my body is really not worth very much—but enough; we must hope for the best.

I enclose the last photograph I have had taken—And this ghastly War? My God! It is as horrible as it is endless! I cannot stand it much longer! Dear Sybil, I have always thought of you with the greatest affection, and both Elvira and Fosca and the others keep remembering you. They are all here and we are leaving to-morrow—Tonio has had leave, but I am afraid he will soon have to go back to the Front ! ! "

Despite its auspicious first flight, the Swallow never lived up to its original promise. During the following year it essayed a few further practice flights in different cities in Italy, but only with moderate success; and shortly after the War it was given its long delayed *première* in Vienna. But the performance was an indifferent one, and all interest seemed to have evaporated from it; even the friendly Viennese, who flocked to hear the *Trittico* or *Tosca*—or indeed any of Puccini's earlier works—could not be persuaded to listen to the one opera which had been specially written for them. The English attitude towards it, as we shall see later, was even more discouraging; though Puccini alternately threatened and cajoled, and though my mother made the most frantic efforts to find someone to take an interest in it, neither Covent Garden, nor Mr. Cochran, nor anyone else could be induced to give it a trial, and to this day it remains the only important Puccini opera which the English public have never had an opportunity of judging. [1]

However much he might protest to the contrary, the composer himself was never quite satisfied with it ; he made no less than two attempts to rewrite parts of it—a sure sign that he was not certain of his hitherto impeccable touch—and it is probable that, had he lived longer, he would have made yet one more final attempt to remedy its original deficiencies. I doubt, however, whether any amount of tinkering could have supplied it with the one thing really lacking ; not only was the Swallow a bastard bird, but, being born of hatred instead of love, it had no soul.

[1] Neither *Le Villi* nor *Edgar*—the works of his immaturity—have ever been given in this country.

CHAPTER TWO

' IL TRITTICO '
(June 1917–January 1919)

AT the end of 1916 Puccini had at last finished the *Tabarro*, begun as early as 1913 ; but, unlike the *Fanciulla*, it bears no traces of having been laid on one side half-way through. The scene takes place on a barge on the Seine ; the middle-aged owner of the barge, already grown suspicious of his wife, unconsciously gives the signal for her assignation with the young stevedore ; after having wrung a confession of guilt from him he strangles him and hides the body under his cloak. When his wife comes on deck, he summons her to come and sit by his side and wrap herself round with his old cloak, as she was wont to do when they were first married—and the body of her dead lover rolls slowly forward at her feet.

The music is as grim and powerful as anything that he has written. At no time has he caught and delineated the atmosphere of sullen, brooding jealousy so faithfully ; all the different ' types ' of the riff-raff that infest the riverside life of Paris are sharply and brilliantly contrasted in the music ; and as the story moves slowly and inevitably forward to its gruesome climax, the suspense is such that one scarcely dares breathe. A ' thriller ', no doubt, but one that genuinely thrills.

This Riverside Night of his, however, completed only one side of the original triangle ; the other two still remained to be found. It is clear that although he had never abandoned his original plan of a Triple Bill, there were times at which he despaired of ever completing it ; for we find him toying with the idea of presenting the *Tabarro* by itself at Monte Carlo.[1] Who was to find him those two contrasting works of pathos and humour which had originally been allotted to D'Annunzio and Tristan Bernard ? Adami searched everywhere, but in vain ; my mother searched, his other friends searched—until one day when another brilliant young playwright, Giovacchino Forzano, came to his rescue.

We have already come across Forzano as the ' expert valuer ' appointed by the Pretor of Viareggio, and subsequent librettist (for Mascagni) of Ouida's *Two Little Wooden Shoes*. It must have been in the spring of 1917,[2] shortly before the first flight of the *Rondine*, that he put forward to Puccini the suggestion for a one-act play, the scene of which was to take place in a convent. The young nun, Sister Angelica, learns that her son, whose sinful birth she has been expiating for the past seven years, is dead ; in despair she poisons herself with herbs from the convent garden—when a vision descends to her from Heaven of the Madonna bearing a son, which she gently places in the little nun's arms.

Puccini was delighted with the idea. His ancestry and the early years of his life spent at the organ at Lucca had imbued him with a sentimental love for ecclesiastical music ; and the setting was an additional attraction, for his eldest and favourite sister, Romelde, had gone early into a convent, where he loved to visit her as frequently as he could. In those quiet, cloistered surroundings, his weary soul always found peace. . . .

[1] See p. 267.
[2] See Puccini's letter dated April 1st, 1917, in which he mentions that he has ' started work on *Suor Angelica* ' (p. 268).

Yes, he would certainly do *Suor Angelica*; but despite—
or perhaps because of—the War, he still wanted to " laugh
and make other people laugh ". Had Forzano something
irresistibly comic to suggest ? Forzano had ; a few lines
from Dante's *Divine Comedy* had suggested to him a tale—
or, more properly speaking, an anecdote—with a fourteenth-
century Florentine setting. The rich Buosi Donati is dead,
and his aristocratic relatives discover to their disgust that
he has left everything to the Church. The hitherto despised
bourgeois, Gianni Schicchi, is called in to their rescue ; he
agrees to impersonate the dead man in bed, and make a
fresh will in their favour—but he warns them that if the
truth is discovered, they will all be condemned to have
their arms chopped off. When the lawyers arrive, he
leaves the bulk of the property to himself, and finally
drives the furious but impotent relatives from the house—
which is now *his* house.

The idea was irresistible ; Puccini decided to start on
it in preference to *Suor Angelica*, and within two months he
had completed what many critics regard as his masterpiece.
Meanwhile Forzano was putting the finishing touches to
the libretto of *Suor Angelica* ; and at the beginning of 1918
the three plays of the *Trittico* were ready. Never before had
the work of collaboration proceeded so smoothly or so
quickly ; on this occasion there were no hesitations, no
fumblings, none of that weary rehashing and refurbishing
of the text that had occupied so many years of his life. For
once he was face to face with a librettist who was also the
original source ; the idea, no less than the treatment, was
Forzano's, and the composer proved that it was not his own
excessive fastidiousness but the shortcomings of his material
that had been responsible for past delays ; given the right
libretto, he could work as quickly as anyone.

Nevertheless it is impossible not to feel the deepest

sympathy for Adami. For four years he had toiled and struggled unceasingly in the service of his Doge ; and at the end of it what was there to show? *Anima Allegra* had petered out ; the *Two Little Wooden Shoes* had been worn by another ; the *Rondine*, which he had written and rewritten until the very sound of the word must have made him feel sick, already showed ominous signs of collapsing after its first few flights. There remained only the·*Tabarro*, as finely constructed a libretto as anyone could possibly want, and the one plank of the original platform which had remained firmly in its place—and then Forzano comes along, and in a trice, with something of the impudence of Gianni Schicchi himself, he has secured for himself two-thirds of the triple crown of laurels.

But if we cannot help feeling sorry for Adami, Adami shows no signs of being sorry for himself. With characteristic sportsmanship (as rare as it is remarkable between playwrights) he cheerfully acknowledges that the better man has won ; Forzano had the ideas, and deserved his success ; for at whatever hour of the day he begins to work, the labourer is worthy of his hire. His account of the *Trittico* closes with an ungrudging tribute of admiration to the brilliance of *Schicchi* and the pathos of *Angelica*. Puccini himself seems to have felt uncomfortable about it, but Adami assured him that he owed him no sort of apology, and expressed himself as more than content at the hope held out that they might work together again later.[1] In due course he was to have his reward.

TORRE DEL LAGO

June 11*th*, 1917

" Forgive my laziness—I was waiting to get the score of the *Rondine* to send it to you with a letter, and then I went to Bologna for the *mise-en-scène* of the opera and that made

[1] See Adami's *Puccini*, p. 159.

me put off writing to you. So now I've sent you off the score—I was glad to hear of *The Girl*, etc., in London. I will write a line to Pitt.[1]

But when is the War going to end? I can't stand it any more, tied down here and unable to go to London or Vienna or Paris—it's not a life at all, to be like that. If only this massacre would cease once and for all ! With victory for our arms, *ça va sans dire.* Tonio is here on convalescent leave—I'm well and working on *Suor Angelica*— The *Rondine* is a great success ; it will go well in London because it's a melodious opera and the subject is a moral one—Angeli was at the *première* in Bologna and was simply enthusiastic about it. Read it yourself and don't be terrified by the Waltz music. . . . I'm going to Pisa to-morrow and as I pass the Tower I'll think of you.

My warmest and fondest thoughts go out to you, my dear, ever-youthful friend."

VIAREGGIO
January 24th, 1918

" I wrote to you before Christmas and wired to you on Christmas Eve, addressing it only to Redlands, Bournemouth—I don't understand why you didn't receive either. We too are by the seaside at Viareggio for the sake of convenience, because we can't run about in the car any more— however, I have got hold of a syde-car [*sic*] and I often go to Torre to shoot—(Heavens ! what a long address you've got !) Tonio is on Lake Garda, but in a quiet sector—he's in command as a motorist. Yes, we've got the Boches staying with us ! But they won't stay long ! Life is not too bad here—some days there's a shortage of bread, but one gets on all right without it. I've been to Rome for the *Rondine*, which went well. I've no desire at all to work—my health

[1] The late Mr. Percy Pitt, one of the organizers of the British National Opera Company, and an excellent conductor.

hasn't been very good, but I'm better now ; I'm certainly growing old, which is a most disagreeable thing—don't you think so ? But you, I am sure, have not changed in the slightest—I understand how you must hate having Vincent so far away ; I send him all my fondest wishes and hope that he may return to you soon safe and sound. Tonio is returning on leave shortly—it's five months since we saw him."

TORRE DEL LAGO
April 12th, 1918

" I've had your news—we are well—Tonio is at the Front—And Vincent ? Is he still in Salonica ? I've finished my three works which were to have been given in Rome now and then in South America, but it's not been possible to arrange anything here owing to lack of artistes—I'm not sorry because it wasn't a good time with this horrible War dinning in our ears ! I had arranged to give the operas before our disaster occurred ![1] . . . You say it will be over soon ? I don't believe it—there are too many complications ! How to find a way to bring about peace ? And in our favour ? Or in theirs ? But that must never be ! And every day life becomes more difficult—how is it with you ? Henceforth I am almost without hope for the future—my poor art ? Oh, the happy days of my trips to London and Paris ! But enough—let us go on hoping, and give me good news of yourself and of the world !

Your affectionate, devoted, and henceforth old, friend."

VIAREGGIO
June 8th, 1918

" I have had your dear letters—but what a terrible thing this War is ! God will that it may be as you say, that it will soon be over ! Everything is paralysed, but don't let's talk

[1] Caporetto.

about my art—I've finished the three operas, and they're going to be given for the first time in New York in November. The manager and the conductor are coming over to see me ; at present they're in New York, but they are going to make the journey on purpose to arrange things with me. I should dearly have loved to have heard this new music of mine and I hoped that the War would be over in November—but it seems as though we should never live to see the world set straight again ! My health isn't bad—but food is scarce—very little meat and that only occasionally—bad bread—I've still got my diabetes, but it doesn't trouble me much now. One spends a fortune—everything is three or four times as dear, but we must be patient and go on as long as we can. Tonio is shortly going back to the Front—it has been something to know that he was a long way off considering what is happening.

Adieu—when shall we see each other again ? "

VIAREGGIO
June 18th, 1918

" I wrote to you a few days ago—I can't understand how you didn't get my letter. I had your card of the 12th to-day—I see you have been ill, poor Sybillina! And poor Esmond ! Let's hope he will get better and return home to you restored in health. Tonio is home on leave, but he'll soon have to return to duty at the Front—and at this time that is a great anxiety for us, because, as you know, we are in the midst of a big battle. We must place our hopes in Italy's lucky star—but things are very serious.

Tito is here to make arrangements for putting on the three operas in New York and then in Rome, but not till November or December. How I long to travel ! I do so much want to see London again ! And my friends there—which means you—because, seriously, I have but few friends. I should be so happy if only this horrible War would come to an end—and I believe everybody else feels the same. Let us hope that it will be over soon, and that a little peace and freedom of movement may return to the world !

I send you my best love—and so do Tito and Elvira."

VIAREGGIO
June 29th, 1918

" I've had your dear letter with the newspaper cuttings —I'm so glad that my operas are still alive in London. There's something I want to say to you : I find myself at loggerheads with my Italian publishers, and I should not be indisposed to enter into negotiations with some English publisher. Another reason for this is that I have in mind a subject, full of emotion, in which the leading parts are those of two boys (they would be women in the Opera)— a subject which I regard as being suited to the taste of every country, but particularly to that of the British public. I am not bound in any way to *Savoia* except for the right of pre-emption, which means a sort of preference which would automatically disappear in face of a *strong* English bid with which he certainly couldn't compete. But I don't want to write direct to Boosey or to any other publisher.

For the *Rondine* I received 250,000 lire—do you think it would be possible on this basis to come to an arrangement ? It would be a question of the rights all over the world.

I warn you that in addition to this premium there are the percentages for royalties, etc., and a percentage on the publication of the music, which would be a matter for discussion and on which we could come to an agreement. If you know of anyone you could trust and who could enter into negotiations, write to me—thank you for everything you are able to do, and if you can do nothing thank you just the same.

How happy I should be to come to an arrangement with an English publisher and to be able to get out of the clutches of these publishers of ours !

Best wishes for a pleasant time in Holland, and hoping that the convulsions of the world will soon come to an end, I send you a million affectionate thoughts together with the hope that Vincent will return safe and sound.

Fosca is here and is well—and Franca,[1] who is a dear, pretty girl full of good judgment.

I'm fairly well, but I shall have to undergo a cure for my illness, which, however, doesn't trouble me much.

How I long to go to London ! If you could arrange things, in principle, with some publisher, I would come."

TORRE DEL LAGO
July 2nd, 1918

" I read ' Holland ' in your letter instead of ' Ireland '. *Errata corrige*.

I hope you received my letter all right. Be sure if you speak or write to a publisher not to put the figure in Italian lire but in sterling, at the equivalent of exchange of course, that is, ten thousand pounds.

Yesterday at the West End Hospital at San Remo a soldier who had lost his power of speech was strumming the third act of *Bohème*—when his speech suddenly came back to him ! "

VIAREGGIO
August 31st, 1918

" Not a word from the publisher so far, but I can't offer myself—which is why I don't write ; it wouldn't come well

[1] Fosca's elder daughter, and Puccini's step-grandchild.

from me. In a moment of disgust with Tito I wrote to you in order once again to put a spoke in the wheel of that queer, capricious fellow; but now we've made peace and I no longer worry about the foreign publisher—all the same if he were to make a good offer I could enter into *pourparlers* with him.

I pray Heaven that the war ends soon ! But I don't believe it—there are too many intrigues, too many questions to be solved, and then the hatred. . . . God knows how long it will be before we can settle down again—and the debts ? And the losses ? For my part I have given up hope of seeing a good settlement—I'm glad that Vincent is coming home, and glad for your sake especially—Caruso ? But is it true ?[1] Heaven knows how badly it will affect 'X'; she has been behaving in Italy as though she were the wife of the great tenor and the guardian of his son. . . . Prices here are terribly high, but if you have enough money, you can buy anything you want—we're having that awful heat which you like so much ! It's just been raining and one can breathe again—Viareggio has been crowded with people, but the sight of all this flesh in the sea disgusted me. I stay indoors a great deal—except for an occasional trip to Torre in my side-car. My operas are coming on in New York on December 14th : the conductor has been over here to get acquainted with the operas—he came in a convoy of 35 ships ! I'm rather down in the mouth ! "

VIAREGGIO
September 20th, 1918

" I've had no news of you—we're both well, but getting old, though! How time flies—confound it! Not a word from the publisher—it's obvious that he didn't want to negotiate. I'm ready with my three operas, which, as I told

---

[1] Caruso's marriage to Miss Dorothy Benjamin, rumours of which were beginning to reach Europe, had taken place on August 20th.

you, are coming on in December in New York and in January in Rome. It seems as though the War had taken a turn in our favour—at last ! Let's hope that it will soon be over—how I long to see London and my friends again ! It's a mad feeling of yearning ! Is Vincent home on leave? Give him my love, and David and any friends who still remember me—I've been staying in this boring Viareggio and I don't know if I shall move at present. But I shall certainly go to Rome in December."

VIAREGGIO
September 24th, 1918

" I'm sending you my latest photograph—it's ugly, but I haven't got anything better !

I've had Caruso's wedding invitation. The news of the marriage here came like a thunderbolt ; by order of the authorities everything was sealed up—and so, from a Princess, 'X' was thrown into the streets, to which, if the truth must be told, she always belonged. It's the way of the world.

You say the War will soon be over ? I say the contrary —with the American programme, it's bound to be a long drawn out affair. It's sad, but it is so—we've been told too often that the War was coming to an end . . . !

I'm boring myself *most terribly*; I've got so many small and big worries, and one overwhelming unhappiness—this transformation of our old world is for me, who am already advanced in years, a hardship to which I adapt myself badly —and when shall we see things restored to normal ? I despair of ever doing so.

I'm so glad about Vincent's literary success.[1] And so you have a cow and some chickens ! That will help you to pass the time and give you something fresh to eat."

[1] My first war-book, *Macedonian Musings*, had just been published.

VIAREGGIO
October 10th, 1918

" I have had your dear letter. . . . It seems as though we would have Peace soon—God will that it may be so—I shall take the train straight to London !

What horrible weather ! It's raining—and so many people are ill, but there are few deaths here.[1] Let's hope for the best—and how is the health of the people in England ? Take care of yourself—Good-bye, my dearest."

VIAREGGIO
November 5th, 1918

" A thundering victory ! It's like a dream ! To think of this time last year under the nightmare of Caporetto ! Long live Italy ! And long live the Allies !

Poor Angeli ![2] I only know that he died at the Hotel Baglioni in Florence—I too telegraphed to his wife, but I only put ' Florence ' without any other address ! And so this dear good friend too has gone for ever—how sad life is ! Here the Spanish influenza has killed off more people than the War. In Torre del Lago there were fifteen killed in the war and eighty dead from the Spanish 'flu !

I lead a quiet life, and I'm waiting for my operas to come on—but it's still some time off. Every day with my motor-cycle and syde-car [*sic*] I go to Torre to shoot—I've also got a permit to use my motor-boat, so the days don't pass too badly. I'm longing to fly away for a bit. Let's hope that Guglielmone[3] will soon abdicate and that a good Peace will come for us all to enjoy before we croak !

I'm nearly sixty, dear friend ! How unjust it is that one should grow old—it makes me simply furious, con-

[1] The epidemic of Spanish influenza had just broken out.
[2] His old friend, Alfredo Angeli, had been a victim of the prevailing epidemic.
[3] The Kaiser.

"A THUNDERING VICTORY"

(Facsimile of Puccini's Letter dated November 5th, 1918)

found it ! And to think that I won't surrender and that there are times when I believe I'm the man I used to be ! Illusions, and also a sign of—strength ! "

And now Puccini was to have his victory too, less ' thundering ' perhaps than that which had recently been gained by his fellow-countrymen on the field of battle, but still a very satisfying one. For he was at last to be granted an opportunity of listening to " that new music of mine which I should have dearly loved to have heard ".

Once again, on December 14th, the world *première* was given at the Metropolitan Opera House in New York. But on this occasion, possibly because the Armistice was too recent an event, or possibly because the composer was not present in person, the reception, although apparently most cordial, lacked some of that warmth which had been accorded eight years before to the *Fanciulla*. Although first-night audiences, as we have had occasion to note before, are not as a rule a particularly valuable criterion whereby the future success or failure of a work can be gauged, it is interesting to note that New York set the fashion by showing a very marked preference for *Gianni Schicchi*. [1]

The European *première*, at which of course Puccini was present, took place at the Costanzi in Rome on January 11th, 1919—the first time that Rome had been thus honoured since *Tosca* had made its début at the same theatre in 1900. Unfortunately either Puccini did not have time to describe it to my mother or—as seems more probable—this is one of the many letters which have gone astray. The performance, under Toscanini's bâton, took place in the presence of the King and Queen of Italy and all the Royal Family, and was one of the greatest triumphs that Puccini ever enjoyed in his native land. Within

[1] See Kolodin, p. 251.

the next fortnight the *Trittico* had been repeated six times.

" I enclose a small cutting from the newspaper about the seventh performance—as you will see, the opera is going splendidly with an immense public. I shall stay on a few days longer here, because on Saturday they are giving me a Banquet at the Grand Hotel.

Rome is more lively than ever, and the cold doesn't reach here—I am in fairly good health. In a few days' time I shall return to my usual nest, but I think I shall be bored not having any work to do. I should like to make more than one trip to London—I have such a longing to see my friends again, who now consist of you—with Angeli and Tosti gone ! I have missed them so much here—I have seen Berthe, who lives in poor *Ciccio's*[1] studio, but I have heard nothing of Mrs. Angeli—have you?

Good-bye, dear Sybil. Give me your news, which is always most welcome."

Even at this early stage in its history the *Triptych* already clearly bore within itself the seeds of its ultimate disintegration. For in planning this nicely varied evening's entertainment, Puccini had overlooked one thing : he had given the voice of the people a chance of making itself heard. If an opera is composed of two good acts and one bad one, the public cannot dictate their preference ; they must either endure the bad act with what patience they can muster, or stay away from the theatre. But with a triple bill their choice is no longer fettered ; and in the case of the *Trittico* they were not slow to give their verdict—nor managements to accept it. About *Gianni Schicchi* there could be no two

[1] Tosti.

opinions ; by public and critics alike it was acclaimed a
masterpiece. The other two operas, however, after the
initial enthusiasm, did not fare so well ; the *Tabarro* (rather
unfairly, I think) was dismissed as ' Puccini *réchauffé* ', and
never won the favour which its brilliant characterization
and powerful treatment deserved. It may have lacked some
of that youthful freshness of invention which marked his
earlier work, and it was certainly unpopular with singers
because it gave them little opportunity to distinguish
themselves individually ; nevertheless I feel that if only it
had been given a fair chance, its merits would have been
better appreciated. What really killed it was *Suor Angelica*,
which was manifestly inferior to the other two works, and
so paved the way to the complete disruption of the idea
of a ' triple bill '. It pleased no one ; in Anglo-Saxon
countries it was considered ' religious ' (in the worst sense
of that much abused word), and in Latin countries, just
dull. The monotony of contralto and soprano unrelieved
by a single male voice sent the audience off into an unre-
freshing sleep, and the patently theatrical ' atmosphere ' of
the convent offended religious and irreligious alike.

As we shall see, Puccini strove manfully to maintain his
trinity one and indivisible. For sentimental reasons, and
from a natural desire to succour the weak, he never ceased
to proclaim that *Suor Angelica* was the best of the three
operas, and he seems positively to have resented the success
of the Florentine rogue who had put his favourite nun in
the shade. He could not persuade himself to go to Paris to
hear a performance of *Gianni Schicchi* by itself, and complaints at Covent Garden's ' ostracism ' of his best work
are the burden of only too many letters to my mother—
indeed it occasioned the one slight note of acidity to be
found in the whole of this twenty-year correspondence.[1]

[1] See p. 324.

In the end, of course, *Vox populi* was bound to prevail. *Suor Angelica* was the first to disappear from the boards, but was closely followed into cloistral retirement by the *Tabarro*, thus leaving *Gianni Schicchi*, as was only fitting, ' in sole possession '. His lease would seem to be a long one ; for he appears, and invariably with immense success, whenever a suitable companion for the evening can be found.[1] The pity of it was that *Suor Angelica* was ever written ; for if the *Triptych* had only been a ' Diptych ', the merits of the *Tabarro* might have been more generally recognized, and the public would doubtless have come to associate the two works together in the same way as they did those ' Heavenly Twins ' known to an earlier generation as ' Cav and Pag '.

[1] Only recently at Covent Garden the surprising experiment was tried of giving *Gianni Schicchi* as a curtain-raiser to—*Salome* ! It was not a particularly happy one ; and doubtless Doctor Richard Strauss must have resented his work being preceded by ' trash '—but he must have been still further incensed if he chanced to read the comment called forth by this arrangement in *The Times* : " To make *Gianni Schicchi* into a prelude to something else is likely to be bad for the something else. It was particularly bad for Strauss's *Salome* last night " (*The Times*, January 12th, 1937).

PART VI

LAST YEARS

(1919–1924)

CHAPTER ONE

AFTERMATH OF THE WAR
(March 1919–July 1920)

UNHAPPILY neither to Puccini nor to Italy did their
" thundering Victory " bring that period of peace and
plenty to which they felt that the sacrifices of the War
years entitled them. A suspension of horrors does not
necessarily imply a return to contentment, and it was not
long before all the Allied and Associated Powers, in their
different ways, discovered that the fruits of victory soon
turned sour, or at best tasteless, in their mouths. Even in
this country sarcastic references were to be heard on all
sides to Mr. Lloyd George's patently unfulfilled promise
to make England " a land fit for heroes to dwell in " ;
the process of settling down again to peaceful conditions
proved far more difficult than had been supposed, and
everywhere an epidemic of strikes marked the universal
disillusionment.

But to no country did the aftermath of war bring
greater disappointment than to Italy. Despite her sacrifices,
which were at least commensurate with those of other
nations, she found herself pushed into the background at
Versailles and treated contemptuously as a poor, and not particularly deserving, relation. This attitude was none the less
resented because, compared with Great Britain and France,
she was in fact a poor country ; nevertheless she had to sit
by and watch Mandated territory being doled out with a
liberal hand amongst those who already possessed colonies

in plenty ; in addition, her own claims under the Treaty of
London were calmly ignored. It is not my business to
discuss the rights and wrongs of that famous, or—as some
think—infamous, Treaty ; but it was the price paid by
the Entente for Italy's adherence to their cause, and any
moral scruples which they may have felt about it would
have been more fittingly expressed at the time. It is true
that the United States of America were not a party to it,
and President Wilson's action in ignoring the Italian Dele-
gation and appealing direct to the Italian people is a
reflection on his head rather than on his heart. But the
attitude of certain English and French statesmen, who
openly encouraged the President to *saboter* a Treaty to
which their own Governments had adhered, is quite in-
excusable, and has moreover recently been denounced by a
distinguished English diplomat, Lord Howard of Penrith,
who was himself present at the Peace Conference, and
whose impartiality cannot be doubted. [1]

From an international point of view the ultimate consequences of our wretched diplomacy, as Lord Howard
clearly hints, were only to be felt sixteen years later, when
they led to the only breach that has ever occurred in our
friendly relations with Italy. The immediate consequences
for Italy, however, were severe, and nearly disastrous ; ill-
success abroad added to the Government's difficulties at
home, and social unrest began to assume the most alarming
proportions. Factories were seized by the workmen, and
the spirit of lawlessness gradually spread, until in the end
the country was only saved from Bolshevism by Mussolini's
march on Rome.

At heart, as I have already said, Puccini was not in the
least interested in politics. But from the date of Italy's
entry into the War until the advent of Fascism (which, in

[1] See *Theatre of Life*, by Lord Howard of Penrith, pp. 276-80.

common with the vast majority of his fellow-countrymen, he heartily welcomed) the outside course of events could not leave him unmoved, and his letters abound with references to the troublous times in which he lived. At one time he even talks of emigrating for good from his country, but I doubt whether anything short of a real Revolution would have moved him ; he was too good an Italian to have been able to endure existence outside Italy for long. Nevertheless the depth of resentment felt by his fellow-countrymen at their ungenerous treatment at the hands of their former Allies can be gauged from the fact that even Puccini (than whom this country had no more fervid nor more constant admirer) cannot resist the conclusion that ' Albion '—a designation which, on foreign lips, always presages trouble—" has once again known how to look after herself" ; and his visits to London, where he was able to feel " the heart-beats of a great country ", only served to emphasize by contrast the miserable conditions prevailing in Italy. But although he welcomed the end of anarchy, it is characteristic of him that he did not, like so many other rich men, blame ' the poor ' for what had occurred ; he recognized that their discontent was not due to any inherent wickedness or viciousness on their part, but arose naturally from their privations and sufferings.

In addition to these anxieties of a more general nature, there now intruded a personal one, which seemed at one time destined to prevent altogether that excursion to London which he had so long promised himself and to which he had been looking forward so ardently : his quarrel with Toscanini. In view of Specht's already quoted dictum that he was " a peculiarly inexorable and not always a very amiable judge of his conductors and singers ",[1] it is

[1] See Specht, p. 13.

necessary to emphasize that this quarrel was a personal one. For Toscanini as a conductor he had nothing but admiration, and he never ceased to acknowledge him as infinitely the finest interpreter of his music, going so far even as to exclaim, on the occasion of the *première* of the *Fanciulla* in New York, that " Toscanini has composed this opera a second time ! " [1]

From first to last, indeed, Toscanini had been constantly associated with his operas ; as early as 1890 he had conducted a performance of *Le Villi* at Brescia ; *Bohème*, the *Fanciulla*, and now the *Trittico* as far as Europe was concerned, were given their first hearing under his bâton ; it was therefore all the more regrettable that the trouble should have arisen in connection with the Roman triumph which they had so recently shared.

The first mutterings of the storm are to be found in a pencilled note dated March 7th ; although ill in bed with influenza, Puccini bestirs himself sufficiently to beseech my mother to intervene, if possible, with Sir Thomas Beecham or with Mr. Higgins to prevent the engagement of Toscanini as conductor for the *Trittico*, which it was hoped to present at Covent Garden, on the grounds that " he has expressed an unfavourable opinion of these very operas at Rome ". A few days later he is sufficiently recovered to go into greater detail.

TORRE DEL LAGO
March 16th, 1919

" I wrote to you a few days ago to Bournemouth—I've been ill for some days with influenza, but I'm all right now, though still a little weak. I've heard about Covent Garden—I protested to Ricordi's because I don't want that *pig* of a Toscanini ; he has said all sorts of nasty things about my operas and has tried to inspire certain journalists

[1] See Paul Stefan's *Toscanini*, p. 46.

to run them down too. He didn't succeed in every case, but one of his friends (of the *Secolo*) wrote a beastly article under his inspiration—and I won't have this *God*. He's no use to me—and I say, as I have already said, that when an orchestral conductor thinks poorly of the operas he has to conduct, he can't interpret them properly. This is the reason from the point of view of Art which I have expounded ; there remains the personal question, and I shall do all I can not to have him ; I have no need of *Gods* because my operas go all over the world—they have sufficiently strong legs to walk by themselves. If you see Higgins or any of the others tell them too that I don't want this *pig* ; if he comes to London, *I shan't come*, which would be a great disappointment to me—I can't object to this *God* because my contract with Ricordi's doesn't give me the right, but I'll do and say everything I can so that it should be known and so that he should know it himself.

Tito has been compelled to resign, and now the firm of Ricordi is in the hands of Clausetti and Valcarenghi—although Tito hasn't been very nice to me, I'm sorry about it, even if of late I've had little cause to speak in his favour ! "

The real truth, in such matters, is seldom easy to arrive at ; it is quite possible, for instance, that the offending article in the *Secolo* was, in the double sense of the word, ' uninspired '. In this connection I cannot resist quoting the comments of the most brilliant of all English musical critics on his Dresden colleagues, who were thought to have been ' nobbled ' by Wagner's rivals. " It may have been so, but there is really no need for any assumption of that kind : anyone who has had much experience of musical critics knows that they are honestly capable of making their blunders of judgment without the smallest

stimulus from others. Every artist who suffers under criticism believes the critic to be either personally prejudiced
against him or the hireling of a rival artist. The critics,
however, are generally quite honest according to their
lights ; the trouble, as a rule, is merely with the quality
and the degree of the illumination."[1]

Nevertheless I see no reason to doubt that on this
occasion Puccini stated the facts of the case as he genuinely
believed them to be. Unfortunately there are mischief-
makers in every walk of life and in every profession, and
doubtless these two great musicians were surrounded by
hangers-on and toadies, who saw a heaven-sent opportunity
to attain ephemeral importance by carrying the seeds of
discord between those with whom they were unworthy to
associate—and never should have been allowed to associate.
Such quarrels, fomented by spiteful and self-important
underlings, are only too common in artistic and musical
circles ; that this should have been the only important
example of its kind in the whole of Puccini's career proves
how utterly he was lacking in that spirit of pettiness and
irascibility which is so often the bane of the artistic
temperament. One can only regret that for once his
extreme sensitiveness should have got the better of his
natural sweetness of temper, and, by making him attach an
altogether disproportionate importance to a casual remark
which may—or may not—have been uttered, should have
caused the enrolment of yet one more distinguished name
on the already sufficiently long and diversified scroll of
Puccinian ' pigs '.

Had it not been for his preoccupation over the ' affaire
Toscanini ' I feel certain that he would have made more
than a casual reference to the important change that had
just taken place in the house of Ricordi. A certain mystery

[1] See *The Life of Richard Wagner*, by Ernest Newman, vol. i, p. 418.

surrounds the ' resignation ' of *Savoia* ; there can be no
doubt that heavy losses had been incurred by the firm
through some of Tito's more spectacular but less remunera-
tive musical discoveries, and in an earlier letter (which I
have not included) Puccini hints that a certain degree of
restraint had been put upon his impetuosity—a form of
control which he does not believe that the haughty Prince
of Savoy will long tolerate.

But whatever the circumstances surrounding his departure, it was, for Puccini, an unmixed blessing. He was
on the best possible terms with the two new *gérants* of the
firm, and henceforth complete harmony reigns between
composer and publishers ; Clausetti, in particular, was
absolutely devoted to him, and was with him in Brussels
at the end. Nevertheless—for such was his way—now that
Savoia was powerless to do him any more harm, Puccini
promptly forgot all his past sins and began to feel sorry for
him. The dispossessed Prince was to fall on evil times, but
as long as Puccini lived, there was always one old friend
ready to hold out a helping hand.

TORRE DEL LAGO
March 21st, 1919

" For one reason or another *Mr. Pig Toscanini* is not
coming to London. The papers say he couldn't come to an
agreement with the management of the theatre—and this
may be—but I think that *he* knew that I didn't want him
and that I would have created a scandal, etc., and so for
reasons of his own but especially on my account he thought
it wise not to come to an arrangement, and I'm very glad
indeed. Who *is* going to come? I don't know—I haven't
written to Ricordi's or asked them, because Clausetti is
now in charge and he is on intimate terms with Toscanini.
And I shall come to London—and now that I'm certain to
come, I am happy at the thought of returning there and

seeing you again. Elvira will be coming too—and then I may go on to Brazil ; it's not certain yet because I haven't made up my mind.

I received the Drury Lane programme ; I see that I am still at the height of my glory—good. I answered your telegram at once, addressing it to Bournemouth (which was perhaps too little) and you didn't get it—you might make enquiries, though.

Are you now in London for good ? "

And so matters rested for the present ; I am glad to be able to add, however, that it was not long before the disagreement was composed, and Toscanini's name expunged from the list of *pigs*. There is no direct reference to the end of the feud, but when my mother was in Milan in 1922 they were on the best of terms again. It was Toscanini who conducted that memorable performance at La Scala on February 1st, 1923, in celebration of *Manon Lescaut's* thirtieth birthday ; as was only fitting, it was Toscanini who was entrusted three years later with the mournful privilege of introducing posthumously to the world the unfinished *Turandot*.

Meanwhile preparations forged ahead—or perhaps it would be more accurate to say, went ahead—for the reopening of Covent Garden after an interval of five years, during which it had indirectly served its country in the rather lowly capacity of repository for the furniture taken out of the various London hotels commandeered for military purposes. One feels somehow that Covent Garden might have done better for itself and been put to more appropriate use, say as a training-ground for regimental trumpeters or military concert parties.

It is possible that, with all this furniture, a certain amount of moth had also invaded the venerable building ;

"I BELIEVE NOW THAT HE IS MY FRIEND"

MR. H. V. HIGGINS

but in any case the English are notoriously slow starters, and it was inevitable that the first season of Grand Opera since 1914 should have been of a somewhat sketchy and tentative nature. Many novelties, the most important of which was the *Trittico*, had been promised ; but in the end London, which had hitherto prided itself on leading the way as far as the works of its favourite composer were concerned, found that it would have to wait another year for the new operas ; in the meantime its impatience was staved off with liberal doses of ' the mixture as before '— *Bohème*, *Tosca* and *Butterfly*.

Many changes had taken place at Covent Garden since 1914. The old Grand Opera Syndicate had been dissolved, and Mr. Neil Forsyth, who had been Manager since 1907, was drowned in 1915. A new Syndicate was now formed under the management of Sir Thomas Beecham ; but a certain continuity of the old traditions was assured by the retention as Managing Director of Mr. Henry Higgins, who had for many years been associated not only with Covent Garden but with the Metropolitan in New York.

It is difficult to say exactly what constitutes an ' Impresario '. His powers, for instance, may vary from those of a complete autocrat to thinly veiled servitude to the whims and wishes of his ' backers '. The definition given by the Oxford English Dictionary is meagre and unenlightening : " one who organizes public entertainments ". In the popular imagination he figures as an excitable and polyglot foreigner with a silk hat, a fat cigar and a superabundance of jewellery about his person. It would be impossible to conceive anything less like the Impresario of convention than that tall military figure who was for more than thirty years, both literally and metaphorically, the outstanding personality in the operatic world of London. A former officer in the 1st Life Guards and a solicitor of repute, Mr. Henry Higgins controlled the manifold activities and cosmopolitan personnel of Covent Garden in a manner which was none the less effective for being restrained ; he possessed an infinity of tact and, when necessary, a rapier-like wit to which added point was given from the circumstance that, owing to an early operation on his vocal chords, his remarks were never delivered above a whisper. Anecdotes about him are of course innumerable ; but perhaps the best known of all is his whispered comment to the interpreter, when a certain foreign prima donna had stated her (extremely exorbitant) terms : " Perhaps you would make it clear to the good lady that I am only engaging her to *sing*." Yet although at times it could be devastating, his wit was never unkindly nor malicious, and this patient, quiet-mannered English gentleman knew how to gain not only the respect but the love of that strange assortment of foreigners with whom he was called upon to deal.

For many years my mother and Mr. Higgins had been on friendly terms ; but it was not until the reopening of Covent Garden after the War that the practice seems to have arisen for Puccini to make his wishes—and complaints —known to the Management through her as intermediary. Both from his point of view and that of Mr. Higgins this system had obvious advantages ; in her capacity of Ambassadress, my mother was able to smooth over difficulties and tone down asperities which had crept into the negotiations—although, if I may judge from the two sides of the ensuing triangular correspondence that I have seen, there must have been occasions when she would have been only too thankful to be relieved of her duties. The real trouble was that Higgins was not always master in his own house, as he admits in his letters ; and there were others behind

him who were not prepared to extend the same consideration to Puccini's wishes as he himself would gladly have
done.

Actually the correspondence seems to have been opened
by a letter from Mr. Higgins, in which he thanks my
mother for " coming to have a straight talk, which I am
sure will do good " and asks her to find out from Puccini
whether Sammarco—the obvious choice for *Gianni Schicchi*
—" is still in good form, or whether he is an extinct
volcano ".

> TORRE DEL LAGO
> *April 6th,* 1919

" I've been away for a couple of days and returned
to-day to find your telegrams, and this morning I had your
express letter. As for Sammarco, he's retired from the
field and has given up singing—he's *finished*. Ricordi's write
to me that as far as my Operas are concerned everything
is upside down—*Higgins won't have Beecham as Conductor!*
Meanwhile you write and telegraph differently—what is
underlying this contradiction ? Anyhow I tell you that *I
agree to Beecham conducting my three new Operas at Covent
Garden* ; let Mr. Higgins know. And I accept Miss
Sheridan [1] for *Suor Angelica* and *Schicchi*—in case they can't
find someone better for *Suor Angelica*. I don't know if
Madame Edvina [2] has enough dramatic force but I don't
exclude her for the *Tabarro*—we can discuss that—will you
please tell all this to Mr. Higgins.

Thank you for your kind intervention—and forgive me
if I have taken advantage of your dear friendship."

---

[1] Miss Marguerite Sheridan.
[2] Marie Louise Edvina, chiefly famous for her singing of French
rôles, although she had also made a name for herself in *Tosca*.

" Just had your telegram from Bournemouth. I wired
to Higgins and told him I accepted Edvina for the *Tabarro*
and he answered me as he did you : *Crains soit trop tard*—
So I'm still waiting, but I have little hope—besides, what
artistic ensemble have they got ? I'm very much afraid, and
I certainly wouldn't give the Operas with Mugnone—it
would ruin everything. I have two proofs of that—of the
Rondine in Milan, and the *Fanciulla* at Naples, and I swore
I would never have him again for important performances.
They made a mistake to engage him—they should have
engaged Panizza,[1] who has done very well and developed
into a first-class conductor—but they wouldn't do it."

Although there was now no *Trittico* to supervise,
Puccini paid us his long-expected visit early in June. He
seemed to have changed but little during the long interval
since we had seen him last ; his hair had begun to turn
white, but it was as abundant as ever ; his movements were
perhaps a little slower and more measured, but the oncoming of old age over which he continually laments in his
letters was with him a very gradual and almost impercept-
ible process, and no one would have guessed that he had
turned sixty ; and he looked, as he always did until a few
months before his death, the very picture of health.

Above all, he had retained that simple boyish outlook
on life, that keen appreciation and enjoyment of its ' little
things ' which never deserted him. Back in his beloved
London, he was exactly like a schoolboy on the first few
days after term ; he must go everywhere and see everything

---

[1] Ettore Panizza. Recently Puccini's favourable verdict has been en-
dorsed by the audiences at the Metropolitan in New York, where he
succeeded Tullio Serafin in 1935.

—and everything that he saw delighted him. Apart from Covent Garden, to which he only went reluctantly and to please my mother, there were all the theatres, including of course *Chu Chin Chow*, which was nearly as old as the War. But although he was eagerly on the look-out for a new subject, it would be idle to pretend that the idea of *Turandot* came to him from this other gorgeous spectacle of the East ; indeed the only thing that impressed him about the performance was an elderly gentleman in the front row of the stalls who had brought the score with him, and who was quietly and solemnly conducting away by himself as though he were at a Bayreuth Festival. This was too much for Puccini's sense of humour, and for the rest of the act, rather to my mother's embarrassment (for they were in the stage-box), the real conductor had two assistants to help him ; one in the front row of the stalls, and one in the stage-box. . . .

And again of course there were the shops. His wardrobe had become sadly depleted during the past five years, and had to be restocked from top to bottom. My mother calculated that to walk from one end of Bond Street to the other took nearly two hours, for there was scarcely a shop-window that did not retain an excellent print of his nose. I remember on one occasion accompanying them to my hosier in search of ties which, as he admitted, were a special weakness of his. By a bit of sheer bad luck his eye chanced to rest immediately on a large pile of them taste-fully assembled in a corner of the shop. I say bad luck, because these were not just ordinary ties ; before I had had time to intervene, Puccini had enrolled himself an honorary member of the Brigade of Guards, the Old Etonian and Old Harrovian Clubs, and the Rifle Brigade. He was on the point of joining the Royal Artillery when I emitted a shocked protest ; those ties, I said, were not for him. He gave me a puzzled look, like that of a child unable to understand the cussedness of its elders. I tried to explain the situation without offending him—" But that only shows their good taste ! " he exclaimed triumphantly ; and as my mother clearly felt that the three regiments and two schools in question could only feel honoured at this involuntary addition to their membership, and as the hosier (probably because he didn't understand a word of Italian) maintained a strict neutrality, I found myself outraged but outvoted ; " Only for mercy's sake," I begged, " don't wear them until you get home." I had done what I could for the conventions, and at Viareggio or Torre del Lago it wouldn't matter so much. . . . A few days later he invited me to lunch with him at the Savoy, where, as usual, he was staying. He was wearing a nice dark blue suit, and a blue tie to match, streaked with those jagged red lightning effects which he had so much admired. . . . I offered up a silent prayer that no one would notice it . . . and I fancied that the famous twinkle in his eye was rather more pronounced than usual. . . .

TORRE DEL LAGO
July 7th, 1919

" I got back to Pisa yesterday at four o'clock ; it was raining and there was a strike on, which was half a revolution, on account of the high cost of living—Poor Italy ! An excellent journey, and no bother at the frontiers—I saw Tito in Paris at the Westminster ; the business with the publisher is off—now he's thinking of going into the cinema business ! It made me rather unhappy to see him— all the same he was fairly calm.

There's a real ' Pisan ' heat here—I preferred the cold of London. I've got back into my house, but I was better off at the Savoy—how good and kind you were to me ! I am really touched by it ! Go on giving me your news and

I will give you mine—I'm just off to Viareggio in the car ;
I hope they won't take it away from me, because there are
riots there owing to the high cost of living, and it appears
that it's half Bolshevik—we'll hope for the best.

Love to *dear Vini* ! and to David."

TORRE DEL LAGO
July 29th, 1919

" Thanks for your letters—I see that you are better—
but to have to lie up must be a hard thing for you. I'm
going to perspire for a week or ten days at Monsummano
—go on writing here. Poor De Lara ! Still—I knew the
opera[1] already, and it couldn't have much of a success—
although it contains good things here and there. . . .

My health is good—except for the pains which wriggle
about from one place to the other. . . . We shall have to
take a little trouble with Madame X for next year—I'm
afraid that Beecham won't do what he promised to do. I
hope to have *Sly* to work on soon ; it has changed very
much for the better in the many discussions I have had
with the poet.[2]

I'm now engaged in making a few small alterations in
the *Rondine* because it is going to be given this winter in
Florence, Naples and Palermo."

TORRE DEL LAGO
August 31st, 1919

" I enclose a list of my operas performed during the six
months from January to July—how are you ? I hope you
are cured ; it's an annoying illness, but it passes quickly
and leaves no trace. I am working at present on rewriting
the *Rondine*—it's going to be made much simpler and much
more easy to sing. It would be just the thing for a London

---

[1] *Naïl.*

[2] Giovacchino Forzano. We shall hear more about his *Christopher Sly*
later.

theatre. But will Mr. Cochran take it ? You might send the theatrical notes to Kalisch,[1] whose address I don't know."

" I think of you so often, poor dear, with that insistent sciatica ! Good heavens, how long it lasts ! As a rule those kinds of illnesses disappear pretty quickly—do please let me have your news—and I hope that it will be good news and that you will have got out of bed.

I am still here leading a very retired life ; I have re-done the *Rondine* and made it simpler, too, for the voice—but I haven't heard a word from Mr. Cochran. And Beecham, with his English music ! He was going to send me some Elizabethan publications, but nothing has come."

According to Mr. Higgins, the failure to produce the *Trittico* in 1919 had been due to the dilatoriness of Ricordi's, who had turned down every tentative suggestion of his, and had then gone to sleep ; according to Ricordi's, it was due to the dilatoriness of the management of Covent Garden, who had never even woken up. But now that the preparations were already on foot for the second post-war season, both parties agreed to forget their grievances and unite in an effort to make a real success of the production in 1920. It is needless to add that the composer himself lent his co-operation freely, though not uncritically, and even before the turn of the year his unofficial Ambassadress at the Court of Covent Garden found herself extremely busy. There were three whole casts to be decided upon—not to mention the thorny question of the conductor. Toscanini was ruled out—or had ruled himself out ; Mugnone was vetoed by Puccini and

[1] The late Mr. Alfred Kalisch, the musical critic.

Ricordi's ; Panizza was apparently not to be had ; in the end, however, the matter was settled to everybody's satisfaction by the selection of Maestro Bavagnoli. Similar difficulties were experienced over the cast ; and when one after another of the composer's suggestions had proved inacceptable, he was driven to enquiring mournfully : " Then who *is* going to sing my operas ? " Mr. Higgins did his best, but was compelled to write repeatedly to my mother : " I am not the boss of this show, and merely act in an advisory capacity ".

Eventually, however, the main rôles were filled ; Dihn Gilly, Tom Burke and Quaiatti for the *Tabarro* ; Gilda Dalla Rizza—Puccini's own choice—as Suor Angelica ; Ernesto Badini as Gianni Schicchi, supported by Burke and Dalla Rizza as the young lovers. It cannot be said that the casting, at any rate of the female parts, was an ideal one ; Quaiatti proved at once shrill and ineffective, and Dalla Rizza, as Puccini afterwards admitted, failed to repeat in London the success which she had won elsewhere.

The season opened early in May, and shortly afterwards Puccini, together with Forzano, arrived in London to superintend the rehearsals. But the duties of his Ambassadress did not cease at this point ; on the contrary, they were redoubled ; for at his special request (and with Mr. Higgins' whole-hearted approval) she generally accompanied him to rehearsals, where she was often able to smooth his ruffled feelings. Covent Garden had not yet recovered from the after-effects of the War ; indeed in the following year it closed down altogether. As a consequence, the standard of performance fell far short of what Puccini felt that he had a right to expect ; on at least one occasion he stamped out of the theatre, vowing that he would never allow the operas to be given, and was only induced to return through my mother's intervention. The tribute which he paid later to her tact and her courtesy was fully deserved.

Despite certain obvious shortcomings in the production, the first night, which took place on June 18th, was a wonderful personal triumph for Puccini. He was, as the critic of *The Times* remarked, the darling of the opera-going public ; " what mattered most to them was that he was present and could be called on to the stage at the end of each opera as often as the audience wished. They took full advantage of this opportunity, as well they might, for what would Covent Garden be without Puccini ? It was a unique chance to offer him the personal tribute of thanks." [1]

I have the liveliest recollections of that evening ; for it was the only time that I ever saw him at one of his own *premières*. He spent most of the evening popping in and out of our box in the greatest state of suppressed excitement ; I realized then what a terrible strain these occasions imposed upon his nerves. As the evening wore on, however, and his success seemed to be confirmed, he grew a little calmer, and he was obviously delighted with the warmth of his reception. During one of the intervals the King and Queen, who were present in the Royal box, sent for him to offer him their sincere congratulations. This, too, touched him very much—though I regret to have to add that his irreverent eye seemed to detect, not indeed in Royalty itself, but in those attendant on Royalty, a curious resemblance to a group of wax-work figures at Madame Tussaud's.

A few days later he was able to leave for Italy, confident that the *Trittico* was now firmly established in London. Unfortunately, as the following letters show, the work of disintegration had quickly set in ; for the British public

[1] *The Times*, June 19th, 1920.

had not been slow to make up their minds on the respective merits of the triple bill, and even in the ecstasies of the first night a carefully trained ear could have distinguished between the tumultuous applause that greeted *Gianni Schicchi*, the sincere but rather more restrained applause for the *Tabarro*, and the applause for *Suor Angelica* which was little more than perfunctory. Puccini composed : the public disposed.

TORRE DEL LAGO
June 27th, 1920

" I had an excellent journey back—yesterday I rested and had a really good sleep ! I needed it—in Paris I found Schnabel, Guinsbourg and Dalla Rizza—I went to the Opéra Comique to hear two acts of an impossible opera— *Lorenzaccio*,[1] and to the Opéra to hear the last act of *Romeo* sung by Muratore [2] very well.

I am still deeply moved by all the kindness which a certain dear lady showed me during my stay in London— the lady Sybillina. You were a real angel of goodness, of kindness, of tact and of courtesy—thank you—a million thanks. I enclose a small cutting from a French newspaper which I found in the wagon-lits [3]—it will please you. Alfa Bedolo has written a fine article on the *Trittico* in London— I haven't got his address, so would you be kind enough to pass on to him this card which I enclose. A thousand thanks.

I found Elvira well, and Franca thanks you so much for the scarf which you gave her—she has already put it on for the first time this evening in the garden.

I've telegraphed to Ricordi's so that they too should

---

[1] By Ernest Moret.   [2] Lucien Muratore.
[3] I still have the cutting ; it was a review of a book of mine on M. Venizelos which had just come out. On the back of it Puccini wrote : ' *Dans le train. Gazette Illustrée. Bravo Vini !* '

take steps to get a woman for Suor Angelica in London—
I don't like the idea of this opera becoming a *Cinderella*.
I'm waiting to hear from you about it. Much love to
Vincent, who is so sympathetic and so full of good sense
for one so young—and to you, my very dear friend, a host
of affectionate thoughts and the most grateful thanks."

TORRE DEL LAGO
July 1st, 1920

"I am so sad here, so very sad—how different the life
is from London ! Italy is really in a bad way . . . and I
can't stand Torre much more. I wouldn't mind leaving
Italy either—certainly if things don't improve I shall have
to come to a decision of one sort or another—but it's going
to be difficult for me, who am already an old man, to see
good order restored in my country. What a contrast I find
here with the orderliness and prosperity of London ! There
one really feels the heart-beats of a great country, whereas
with us it's a disaster—oh, the War ! and oh, the Allies !
In this way one advances like a crab !

And *Suor Angelica* ? How annoyed I am that Higgins
won't put it on again and so gives satisfaction to that *pig* of
an X ! Give me the operatic news and commend my Suor
Angelica to Higgins ; by excluding her in this way they
are casting a shadow over my big success—I've telegraphed
to Ricordi's about it, and I like to hope that the management of Covent Garden will do everything in their power
to restore the opera to its place."

TORRE DELLA TAGLIATA
ORBETELLO
July 5th, 1920

"Forzano is working on the second act of *Cristoforo* [1]—
but I have little hope for it ; he says it's going to be mar-

[1] *Christopher Sly.*

vellously good—we'll see. I believe Fosca is going to Viareggio to-morrow and Elvira has some idea of joining her. I shan't ; I can't stand all those people—it's the sort of crowd that doesn't suit me. I understand the crowd in a big city but not that of a bathing-place—And when are you going to Aix ?

And *Suor Angelica* ? Have they found a woman, or have they let me down ? I believe the latter—tell Mr. Higgins that I am very grieved to see my beloved little nun treated in this way.

How I miss those happy days in London ! And how divinely kind you were to me ! Dear, sweet Sybil—I feel so fond of you ! "

> TORRE DEL LAGO
> *July 15th*, 1920

" I very much dislike the *Trittico* being given in bits—I gave permission for two operas, and not *one*,[1] in conjunction with the Russian Ballet ; this is a real betrayal and Higgins ought to have stopped it—the mistake was not to have inserted in the contract what we wanted done. Next year we'll see that different arrangements are made—I should be inclined not to allow any of my operas to be given, and then we'll see how they will be able to carry on without them—I'll tell Valcarenghi my idea when he comes here shortly.

I'm sorry Bavagnoli is not staying on—but on the whole what he has written to me about the massacre of our art is right. . . .

Life is the very reverse of pleasant in Italy just now ; after my visit to London I am more conscious than ever of our misery here ! We must hope for the best, but I don't

---

[1] The worst had now occurred ; first of all, *Suor Angelica* and now the *Tabarro*, had been dropped, leaving *Gianni Schicchi* to be companioned by the Russian Ballet.

think I shall ever see the old prosperity return—Curse the
War and other things as well, which I won't mention to
you. I don't mean by this anything against your country—
let that be clearly understood—though now, as always,
Albion has known how to look after her own interests."

The act of bad faith of which Puccini complains was
due in the first place to a genuine misunderstanding.
Documents were produced for my mother's benefit from
both sides, from which it appears that when Gilda Dalla
Rizza, the original Suor Angelica, had to leave, the
management of Covent Garden instructed Ricordi's agent
to find someone to take her place. For some obscure reason
these instructions were either never passed on or not
carried out ; and in view of the public's lack of interest in
the opera, which had become more noticeable at the second
(and last) performance, the management were probably not
sorry to have a good excuse for dropping it altogether.
Some rather acrimonious correspondence follows, in the
course of which numerous additions are made to the
' piggery ', and Puccini expresses the cryptic desire to " tie
up all three in a sack together : the Purge, the Ship and
Higgins ! " One could hazard a guess at the identity of
the former ; but the ' ship ' must ever remain, as far as I
am concerned, as mysterious as a ' Q-boat '.

In the end, of course, Puccini unreservedly accepted Mr.
Higgins' explanation, and the incident was closed ; but for
months to come, the ' ostracism ' of his beloved little nun,
not only in England but elsewhere, remained a very sore
point with him.

CHAPTER TWO

THE BIRTH OF 'TURANDOT'
(July 1920–August 1921)

MORE than two years had elapsed since the completion of the *Trittico*, and still no successor had been found. Doubtless that rather insistent note of irritability that characterizes his letters at this time was due, at least in part, to what Specht calls his "almost morbid suffering during the pauses of his creative work".[1] What irked him most was that these pauses were not of his own volition, but were due solely to his dependence on others to find him a suitable subject. "If only", he sighs to Adami, "I could be a purely symphonic writer ! I should then at least cheat time . . . and my public. But that was not for *me*. I was born so many years ago—oh, so many, too many, almost a century . . . and Almighty God touched me with His little finger and said : ' Write for the theatre—mind, only for the theatre '."[2]

There were two doors through which he hoped to escape from this prison of hateful ease, and the keys were held respectively by Forzano and Adami. At first it had seemed certain that Forzano would be the chosen one ; it was he who had accompanied the composer to London and, in the intervals of rehearsing the *Trittico*, the possibilities of the new subject which had occurred to him some months before were eagerly discussed. Once again this brilliant young writer had displayed his singular ability to elaborate

[1] See Specht, p. 223. [2] See *Letters*, p. 265.

an idea suggested to him by a few lines in a masterpiece of
literature ; just as *Gianni Schicchi* had been inspired by a
fragment of Dante, so now from a few lines of Shakespeare
was born *Christopher Sly*, originally in the form of a poem,
and afterwards as a play.

At first it had appealed immensely to Puccini, as well it
might ; for the subject was original and dramatic, and had
been handled with masterly skill and vividness. The play
enjoyed an enormous success throughout Italy, and when
later my mother had succeeded in interesting Mr. Matheson
Lang in it, the English version, despite a comparatively
short run, won the unanimous approval of the critics.[1]
Unfortunately—for I think the subject would have suited
him admirably—Puccini's enthusiasm for *Sly* was not
maintained, and in a brief note from Bagni di Lucca dated
July 28th, he writes its obituary notice—and at the same
time records the birth of its rival.

" Thank you, but no Spanish dramas for me—perhaps I
shall do an old Chinese play, *Turandot*. The poets Simoni
and Adami are coming here.

Sly is no good. Forzano is unhappy about it, and so am
I—for his sake. But what can I do ? "

Perhaps after all Puccini was right. Although he could
have had no inkling that he had but four more years to
live, he was only too well aware that the days of his pro-
ductive activity were numbered ; unconsciously he was
seeking for something entirely fresh and original to crown
his life's work, something quite outside the beaten
theatrical track with which he was so familiar. It is true
that *Sly* was, in many respects, an original subject, but it
lacked that element of fantasy and mysticism for which,

---

[1] It was given at the New Theatre on August 31st, 1921. Matheson
Lang gave a really memorable performance in the title part.

almost without knowing it, he was looking. As a young man, he had thought of writing an opera on the subject of Buddha ; now that he was nearing the end of his days, his soul yearned once more to be translated from the earth into the clouds. . . .

With the collapse of *Sly*, it was only natural that he should have turned again to the other librettist of the *Trittico*, who had worked so hard for him and, on the whole, so unprofitably. Adami had long ago despaired of finding anything single-handed ; he had therefore taken unto himself another young writer, Renato Simoni, who was, amongst other things, something of an authority on China ; between them they happened to chance one day, in course of conversation with the composer, on the name of Carlo Gozzi, whose fantastic comedies had once been the delight of Venice. Each play in turn was recalled, only to be dismissed with a shake of the head, when suddenly Puccini himself exclaimed : " What about *Turandot*? " The quest was ended.

A Persian legend from the *Thousand and One Nights* ; a Chinese fairy tale of a cruel Princess, whose hatred at last turned to love ; a Venetian Masque ; a play of Gozzi, a poem of Schiller, an overture of Weber—from such discordant elements was Puccini's masterpiece born. The story of the next four years is the story of its gradual growth ; a story of hope alternating with despair, of a grim fight against time—and finally of a triumph which the composer himself was never destined to witness.

TORRE DEL LAGO
August 4th, 1920

" I enclose a letter from Ricordi's as a proof that no letter or telegram ever reached the house in London ; you might let Higgins see it. How sorry I was that you didn't come to Viareggio—I was most comfortable at Bagni di

Lucca. I am going, at the beginning of September, to Munich and to Vienna for ten or twelve days to hear Strauss's *Donna Senza Ombra*,[1] and some other new operas. I need to hear good performances and new music of whatever nature it may be. I am waiting for the libretto of *Turandot* to decide whether or not I shall do it—*Cristoforo* has collapsed.

This winter, I want to make a long journey ; I shall go to Constantinople, then perhaps to India, Japan, and China—Torre del Lago doesn't suit me any more. Curse these modern industrial developments ![2] It has lost its peacefulness. In November I shall go to the Maremma—Good-bye, dear Sybil, or I should say, *Lady of the Opera Hotel*—a good title for a film."

I have already quoted Mr. Toye's remark that Verdi regarded himself primarily as a craftsman " whose duty it was to keep abreast of the times " ; and in a footnote he adds : " The first act of Puccini's *Turandot*, with its choruses *à la* Moussorgsky, is a good parallel instance ".[3] It is interesting to note that, at any rate in this respect, Puccini was a true ' successor ' of Verdi ; he always liked to keep himself up to date, as this letter shows, and the influence of contemporary music is apparent, in a greater or lesser degree, in every opera that he wrote. It was natural, therefore, that when the critics had grown tired of accusing him of copying himself they should be driven to accusing him of copying others—whether it happened to be Wagner, Strauss, Debussy or Moussorgsky. Such charges, however, were as baseless as the similar ones of ' Meyerbeerism ' or ' Wagnerism ' brought against Verdi ; both Italian composers absorbed whatever they found admirable

[1] *Die Frau ohne Schatten*, first produced in Vienna in 1919.
[2] See p. 329.   [3] See Toye, p. 137.

in their contemporaries, just as Puccini, even more than Verdi, drank in the ' local ' music of the country in which his opera was set ; [1] but every bar of their music bears the unmistakable imprint of their own signature and their own idiom.

On this occasion his anxiety to refresh his mind with new music " of whatever nature it be " seems to have called forth a shocked protest from my mother, who was not as internationally-minded as he, and could not understand his willingness to fraternize so soon with our late enemies.

TORRE DEL LAGO
September 3rd, 1920

" Calm yourself, I'm not going to Germany at present. What you tell me about Higgins is really strange—what interest could Ricordi's have in hiding his letter ? *That letter certainly never arrived* ; of that I'm sure. And next year if they don't give the *entire Trittico* you can say that I shall consider it an affront and that I shall never set foot again in Covent Garden—but I don't believe they would treat me like that. I should also like to give *Rondine*—I think it would be a great success in London.

Forzano wired me to go to Cento (a small town near Bologna) where they are giving the *Trittico* with Bavagnoli, Badini, etc. ; but I have little wish to go, because that district is known for the violence of its demonstrations— and I've no desire to be made a target. I'm waiting for the first act of the Chinese *Turandot*. Forzano writes that he has

---

[1] Most of Verdi's operas could be, and several of them in fact were, transposed from one country and one age to another without any apparent incongruity. Even in the case of *Aïda* he definitely rejected the idea of writing ' Egyptian ' music, though he went so far as to examine an Egyptian flute in the Museum at Florence—only to compare it unfavourably with the primitive pipe in use among the urchins of his own village (Toye, p. 158).

changed *Sly* a lot and that it will soon be given in prose—
so I shall have a chance of seeing it. You did wrong not to
come to Viareggio—it would have given us such pleasure.
I haven't set foot in it this year because there were too many
War profiteers and too big a crowd of silly people—I preferred that little spot, Bagni di Lucca, a place much favoured
by elderly English people ; this year too there were lots of
them, very kind and very nice—they had the surnames of
well-known shoe-makers—*Lobb*—and of gun-makers—
Greener. There was also a Mrs. *Tailor* and another called
Krips—what an imbecile I am—you can see that I have
become senile ! But be patient—I'll go to Chicago to the
doctor who rejuvenates you with glands. Constantinople ?
When ? I don't remember having written about it—Oh,
yes, I do—it was an idea which lasted exactly one day."

TORRE DEL LAGO
September 5th, 1920

" Would you please ask the photographers, Swaine's of
Bond Street, to send me six copies of the pose with the
cigarette held in my hand ? I haven't got the number of
the negative, but they're sure to understand. Thank you—
and forgive me if I keep on worrying you as if you were
my Agent, but the *Lady of the Opera Hotel* never refuses anything to the author of those *cochonneries* which are performed
at Covent Garden. How are you ? I hope your health is
quite restored and that your leg isn't giving you any
trouble ; I am well but I am still waiting for the libretto !
I don't know what to do with myself—I really am a useless
being ! I wish I were in London ! "

TORRE DEL LAGO
September 12th, 1920

" The earthquake was felt severely here, but it didn't
do any damage either here or at Viareggio—it appears that

a cornice in a church collapsed, and a bit of the plaster fell from my ceiling—that's all. On the other hand, sixty or more kilometres from here towards the mountains it did huge damage, destroying small villages entirely. The tremors still continue ; last night too towards four I felt the house dancing—but it's nothing. We are on sand here, like Viareggio, and they say that an earthquake can't do much damage—so we'll hope for the best.

Tell Higgins not to allow Signorina *Carena*, who is at present singing Angelica at Cento most beautifully and who had a great success at Lisbon, to slip through his fingers. It's a marvellous voice—*firm* ; she hasn't too much temperament—but that's an advantage for English audiences.

Unpleasant things are happening here—factories being seized by the workmen ! We'll see how it all ends—certainly things look very nasty at present, and the exchange gets worse and worse for us ! I think I shall go to Vienna in October for the *Rondine* and the *Trittico*."

TORRE DEL LAGO
September 20th, 1920

" What's all this about Giordano and *Turandot* ? [1] There's not a word of truth in it—it's a mere invention.

Has —— gone to prison ? I should be neither surprised nor displeased to hear it—a little black bread wouldn't do him any harm at all !

I'm waiting for the First act of *Turandot*. I may go to Vienna in a few days' time for the *Rondine* ; as soon as I'm certain, I'll let you know.

---

[1] Presumably my mother had heard rumours that the composer of *Andrea Chenier* had also embarked upon a *Turandot*. It would not have been very surprising, as he was practically the only Italian composer who did *not*, at one time or another, clash with Puccini over a libretto !

I believe now that Higgins is my friend. I didn't before, but I do now—and it's entirely thanks to you."

From Puccini's innumerable messages to Mr. Higgins not to let So-and-so " slip through his fingers ", one might suppose that it was the custom for the management of Covent Garden to hibernate during the off-season. That this was very far from being the case is apparent from the following letter of Mr. Higgins to my mother, written directly he had heard of the projected visit to Vienna.

7 Bloomsbury Square
October 7th, 1920

" Chere Amie,
    " . . . I have also made acquaintance with Mme. Jeritza (Czech) from the Vienna Opera House, whom I know to be good though I have never heard her. She is going to sing Tosca for Puccini at Vienna. Do ask him about her. Everyone (including Beecham and Ziegler of New York) assures me she is quite remarkable—she's tall, slight, fair and good-looking. She wouldn't sing for me yesterday but is coming to Paris for three months at Xmas to study and I am to hear her then. She is married to Baron Poppe, and I suppose she is called Baroness Momme. . . ."

From Vienna Puccini gave the desired information—though he concludes (rather unfairly in the circumstances) with the usual entreaty to Mr. Higgins not to allow Mme. Jeritza to " slip through his fingers ". Covent Garden closed down in 1921 from lack of sufficient support ; but in the following years the British public were given plenty of opportunities to admire her acting, her singing, and her beauty.

HOTEL BRISTOL
VIENNA
October 17th, 1920

" It's true that I am a *pig*—a real *pig*, because it's such a time since I have written to you. So I beg you to forgive me, and tell you that I am being fêted here in a dreadful, atrocious, indescribable manner. The *Rondine* went well but I wasn't satisfied with the performance or the *mise-en-scène.* It was given at the Volksoper, and the *Trittico* is coming on next Wednesday at the former Imperial Opera House. I think it will be a magnificent success. Jeritza is really an original artiste—perhaps the most original artiste that I have ever known. She has all the gifts necessary to make a real impression—I heard her in *Tosca,* and in the second act she does certain things simply marvellously. She would like to come to London, but she wants to do the *Tabarro* and *Angelica.* Tell this to Mr. Higgins—certainly the management of the Opera House will do all it can to keep her. The other night for *Tosca,* in a house of 300,000 crowns, the public was simply overflowing. She is a magnificent Giorgetta in the *Tabarro*—That is the news I have for you.

I am well but tired out by the rehearsals and the agitated life I am living. Elvira and Tonio are here. The *mise-en-scène* is magnificent, especially in the *Tabarro.* There is also another artiste, Lehmann,[1] who sings Angelica—She's a first-class singer and she too (she's a German though) would be very much liked in London. Jeritza is a Czecho-slovakian."

BRISTOL HOTEL
VIENNA
October 25th, 1920

" It's getting near the time when I leave, and I assure you that I am longing to go—there are too many fêtes, too

[1] Lotte Lehmann, whose subsequent triumphs all over the world have fully confirmed Puccini's judgment.

many invitations. The newspapers were excellent, but I haven't kept them ; that is, I never took the trouble to get them, but just had them translated out loud.

I have got to stay a few days longer because I have an Italian luncheon and another Concert in my honour ; so I shall leave on Tuesday so as to be in Torre on the evening of the 4th. I can't stand any more of this life—to be truthful, I have had fête upon fête, and these Viennese have no equals in courtesy. Jeritza is really the artiste for Covent Garden—tell Higgins not to let her slip through his fingers —as well as Lehmann, who sang Angelica amazingly well.

I am going to rewrite the *Rondine* for the third time ! I don't care for this second edition ; I prefer the first—the edition of Monte Carlo. But the third will be the first with changes on account of the libretto ; Adami has been here and has come to an agreement with the publishers and the Viennese librettists. It appears that next year they will give the *Rondine* at the ex-Imperial Opera House—because this time there was a rather mediocre performance of it at the Volksoper, a theatre of only the second rank. And *Turandot* ? I haven't got the libretto yet, but the plan of the opera is beautiful, and I think that I shall do it.

So many affectionate thoughts,

from your

really old

GIACOMO

P.S.—Tell Mr. Higgins that I should very much like Jeritza to be *engagée* through my intermediary—but certainly not because I want to make any money out of it ! "

[TORRE DEL LAGO]
November 22nd, 1920

" That tenor X wouldn't do for London in my opinion —he has, or rather he had once upon a time, a most

AFTER THE *TRITTICO* AT COVENT GARDEN
(1920)

beautiful voice, but he's lost it, and besides he never keeps in time—all the same in certain operas he's still good.

I'm not working because they haven't given me the libretto yet—if they wait much longer, I shall have to get them to put pen, paper and ink-pot in my tomb ! What a cheerful idea ! That's how I am—just like that ; in a few days' time I go to the Maremma to get far away from everyone—there I hope to find solace. I spend my time unprofitably—sometimes, stupidly, shooting.

Why do you tease me about Vienna ? You don't know the Viennese, because if you did you would change your opinion of them. They're the nicest people in the world—after Sybil. That's all.

Tell me *frankly* whether Higgins intends to do the *Trittico* again. If he does, he mustn't forget to engage Carena for *S. Angelica* and the *Tabarro*. Are you going to Monte Carlo ? Guinsbourg wants to give me De Sabata to conduct the *Trittico* but I don't want him—because although he's an excellent musician of the other school—that is, the modern school—he can't, and does not know how to, conduct my music. To-night I'm not feeling at all well; I've caught cold and I've got a pain on my chest. . . . Supposing it's pneumonia ? It would be welcome because it would bring my wretched, stupid life to an end."

The usual letter of Christmas greetings, sent from the famous Torre della Tagliata, whither he had repaired with his two librettists to examine their handiwork, contained sad news : " *Turandot* ? Adami has brought me a first act which won't do—I'm very much afraid I shan't have the libretto as I want it ! "

Adami has himself left us an account of that terrible ' Christmas reading '. As already mentioned, Simoni was an expert on China, and knew its customs and its literature from top to bottom ; profiting by this knowledge, the two young enthusiasts determined to crowd into the first act outside the walls of Pekin every inch of local colour possible. They did so—and the result, in their humble opinion, was most beautiful and original. Unfortunately when the time came to lay their offering at the composer's feet, it was discovered that their enthusiasm had destroyed their sense of time ; the reading of the act took over one hour. Puccini had listened with growing stupefaction, and when at last Adami had rung down the curtain, he gasped for breath. " But this isn't an act ", he groaned ; " it's a conference. Do you think I can possibly put a conference to music ? "[1]

The two young men sat down to work again—with a shade less enthusiasm, but with a sterner eye on the clock. Three weeks later Puccini was able to give a much more satisfactory report.

MILAN
January 15th, 1921

" At last I've got a fine first act for *Turandot* ; I'm here and I feel well, after my horrible stay in the Maremma. Tito is here in Milan, still the Prince of Savoy without a crown.

What Higgins and company say about *Suor Angelica* grieves me—and I don't believe that the English public is against the opera owing to its religious setting. It is due to two unfortunate events that occurred ; the first was that Dalla Rizza's voice didn't appeal to the public very much, and the second was that she had to leave, and it wasn't possible to *consolidate* the success of the opera. I beg of you to insist with Higgins that if he is really my friend, as I believe, he should give me this satisfaction and not make me unhappy by seeing this, my favourite opera, put on one

[1] See *Puccini*, p. 177.

side—it would break my heart. In Stockholm, too, a few days ago *Angelica* had the biggest success of the three—it's only a question of finding the right artiste—and I would suggest to Higgins either *Lehmann* who sang it in Vienna or Carena who sang it recently in Italy.

Will you succeed? It grieves me very much to see my *Trittico* thus brutally torn to pieces. I hope you enjoy your stay in the country—but I can't remember your address and I'm writing to London."

MILAN
January 20th, 1921

" *Turandot* is coming out well ; it will be an original libretto and one full of emotion. We're working in order to complete it, and we are really on the right road.

I have protested to Ricordi's for giving permission for *Tabarro* and *Schicchi* without *Angelica*—it makes me really unhappy to see the *best* of the three operas laid on one side. In Vienna it was the most effective of the three with the good Lehmann (she's German, it's true) but a fine, delicate artiste—simple and without any of the airs of a prima donna, with a voice as sweet as honey. *Caracciolo* is fairly good ; above all, she's a real artist, but she hasn't much of a voice.

Thank you for what you are doing with Higgins about S. *Angelica*. But one must always bear in mind the question of the singer ; personally I am in favour of Carena. And is Bavagnoli going back to Covent Garden ?

I saw Tito the other day ; he is well and still gives himself the airs of a Prince, but I believe he's rather on the down grade. This year the ' Frog ' [1] isn't going to do *Rondine*—I wrote to him to protest, but good-naturedly and without any bitterness.

As to what you say about the ' religiosity ' of the

[1] M. Raoul Guinsbourg.

subject of *Angelica* which cannot appeal to the English, I permit myself to say that I am not of your opinion. The thing is, and I've said it already, that the opera didn't have time to find its way into the public's ears—because the story is really one of passion and it's only the environment which is religious. And besides, why was Max Reinhardt's *Miracle* at Olympia such a success ? There you have Madonnas and churches, etc., to your heart's content.

When are you going to Monte Carlo ? I don't know yet, but I shall certainly be there in March."

MILAN
January 25th, 1921

" I have had your letter addressed to Torre—I have taken information on Caracciolo. She's a good artiste, very intelligent, with a beautiful voice but not a big one— I still hope that *Suor Angelica* will not be banished by Higgins, or put on one side. Tell him that I suffer from this *ostracism.*

All goes well here—the mournful accounts in the foreign press of the riots in Italy are not true. There's a little trouble here and there, but generally speaking the Italian people are quite calm—the only thing is that the exchange is ruinous, and the question of the bread shortage is serious and will have to be dealt with. The cost of everything is simply enormous, and this is a great misfortune ! We have here a sun which is worthy of rich people ! You, too, are not so happy with that Ireland of yours—every country has its own misfortunes.

Turandot is taking on a most beautiful appearance and I shall get a unique libretto ! I haven't seen *Sly* because the run of the play was over here, but for me the subject is not suitable in spite of the great success that it's had in the theatre. Every day I have conferences with Simoni and Adami over *Turandot,* and I hope to start work soon."

Puccini's satisfaction at having at last found a libretto to his liking was heartily shared by at least one other person —if not by two. " Your news of Puccini is very good ", wrote Mr. Higgins with brutal frankness to my mother. " It is much better that he should concentrate on a new work rather than waste time trying to revivify dead horses like the *Rondine* and *Suor Angelica*."

Although I have no knowledge of diplomatic usage, I assume that, however much an Ambassador may secretly sympathize with the views expressed to him by the Government to which he is accredited, he does not always feel himself bound to pass them on textually if he thinks that they may prove unpalatable at home. In this case I am grateful that my mother refrained from doing so—or poor Mr. Higgins would infallibly have found himself relegated *en permanence* to the piggery from which he had so recently been rescued. Not that his troubles, or my mother's, were yet over ; despite the fact that *Turandot* had now taken on " a most beautiful appearance ", Puccini was not going to abandon his nun or his swallow without a further struggle.

> MILAN
> *February 3rd,* 1921

" I've had a wire from Hamburg that there were forty calls and that the *Trittico* had an enormous success. The same story, too, in Stockholm—*Suor Angelica* led the way in order of popularity, then *Schicchi* and the *Tabarro* last. Tell Higgins that he is making a mistake to put *Angelica* on one side ; it was never properly heard in London last year, and the *mise-en-scène* was ridiculous. But I don't want to insist—I am just as happy if they don't give the *Tabarro* or *Schicchi* either, and if they don't open the theatre at all—I shall be happier still ! So that's the end of the business—I can't get over this exclusion of *Angelica*, which, for me, is the best of the *Trittico*. Erlanger too is quoted in Italy as having said that the opera was unpopular and that the subject didn't appeal to the English.[1] And yet in New York, with Farrar, who has no voice left, it had a great success, and then the part was taken up by Raisa and sent the public of Chicago and New York into a delirium of enthusiasm. No, no, no, those gentlemen of Covent Garden are more invincibly obstinate than the Germans—they had better change the name of the theatre, because the word ' Covent ' must disgust them. Good-bye, dear Sybil—shall we see each other at Monte Carlo ? The *Trittico* is going to be done on March 19th—will you be there ? I should hate it if I didn't see you ! "

MILAN
February 22nd, 1921

" Welcome—I think I have already written to you to Monte Carlo. There's nothing new here ; Spring is beginning and I don't care about the town—I should prefer to be in the fresh verdure.

I hear that they have already started engaging the artistes for Covent Garden—so there will be a Season after all.

I'm not sure yet when we shall be coming to Monte Carlo. I'm not very keen on it and if it weren't for you I should definitely say : ' I'm not coming '—still, we'll see.

I'm not anxious to be there for the rehearsals ; *entre nous*, I don't care for that conductor ;[2] I tried not to have him, but I couldn't succeed in getting rid of him. He's a good musician but he's one of those *d'autre rive*—and he

---

[1] When I taxed him with it, Baron Freddy d'Erlanger admitted the truth of the report which had reached Puccini's ears ; but at least he had shown on a previous occasion the courage—or should one say the cowardice ?—of his own convictions, in resolutely refusing to entertain Tito Ricordi's suggestion that one of his own operas which had a religious background should be given in London.

[2] De Sabata.

can't love or have any feeling for my music. But Guins-bourg has got him on the brain and there was no way of side-tracking him. It must be lovely there, with this sun ! But I prefer wilder country and one where there are fewer *nouveaux riches*.

Tell me what you think of the performances at the Casino—I'm sorry that Melba is ill, but I think that Mimi will be pleased to be *unsung* by her ! "

TORRE DEL LAGO
[End of March, 1921]

" How sorry I was to have to leave you like that ! [1] Poor, sweet friend ! Believe me, I thought so much about you during the long journey ! I like to think that you are better—I *do* hope you are. And do you really intend to leave on Wednesday ? At any rate the ' Frog ' thought of reserving you the *Salon-lit* : but before I left I told Gilda to remind him ! Please let me have your news.

I got home at one o'clock at night. Gilda will have told you how she accompanied me in the car as far as Ventimiglia —how courteous they were to me ! If you see Willy [2] give him my best regards—I like that man so much, even though he does write against me behind my back.

Poor Sibillina ! How it hurts me to know that you are suffering so much ! But I hope with all my heart that the illness will soon disappear.

Good-bye, sweet friend. I care for you so much—and you really deserve that I should ! "

MILAN
April 21st, 1921

" I'm still here—waiting for the third act of *Turandot*, which is delayed because the poets refuse to produce it. I

---

[1] My mother had had a severe attack of sciatica on the Riviera, and had to be brought home to England by a doctor.

[2] The French novelist, and creator of the immortal Maugis.

too am not well ; for several days I've had a pain in my mouth (my teeth), aggravated by bad temper, by lack of faith, by being tired of life—in a word, nothing is right for me—and you, poor dear ? Still those awful pains—but why the devil isn't there any cure for that cursed illness ? If you knew how often I think of you ! My poor Sybil ! Cheer up and let's hope that when the warm weather comes —for it's still cold—you will recover, and for good. Elvira too has been very ill, but she's better now ; as for me, I'm very, very down. I don't seem to have any more faith in myself ; my work terrifies me, and I find nothing good anywhere. I feel as though, from now on, I were finished— and it may well be that this is so ; I am old—this is literally the truth—and it's a very sad thing, especially for an artist. And then Milan stifles me with its affairs, its commerce, etc. ; there's not a breath of art here—the most profound indifference for everything which isn't *money*, and greed to accumulate a fortune—*Cambronne !*" [1]

At the beginning of May he started to work on the first act of *Turandot* ; from then until the end of July, when he had finished it, he had little leisure for letter-writing beyond an occasional line to report progress—" I have begun work on *Turandot*" . . . " I feel old and I haven't got the will to work any more—how I long for London ! " . . . " *Turandot* is progressing, but it's very difficult and troublesome work."

On August 2nd there occurred an event which profoundly stirred the whole Italian nation : the death of Caruso from pleurisy at Naples. In laying the blame on

---

[1] It is rather ironical that this distinguished French General should only be remembered as the utterer of an impolite little word. I suspect that Puccini learnt the *mot de Cambronne* from his new friend, Willy, in whose novels it appears with unblushing frequency.

the American doctors, whose faulty diagnosis was supposed to have been responsible for the catastrophe, Puccini was merely endorsing the view held by the vast majority of his fellow-countrymen—who were almost inclined to treat it as a *casus belli*. " Poor Caruso ! " he writes. " What a sad destiny ! It has made me dreadfully unhappy—so an Italian doctor [1] has cured you, and the American doctors have killed Caruso ! " The world was certainly the poorer for the stilling of that incomparable voice.

Early in August my mother and I went for a few weeks to Viareggio. We stayed at an hotel, but we saw a great deal not only of Fosca and her children, who were spending the summer there, but also of Giacomo and Elvira, who came over constantly from Torre del Lago to superintend the work in progress on the new villa which they were shortly to occupy.

For Puccini had at last been evicted from his earthly paradise. Those " industrial developments," of which he complains earlier, took the form of a peat factory erected near his villa at Torre del Lago, which offended no less than three of his senses ; with such an unsightly, noisy and smelly neighbour it was no longer possible for him to work. And so, with a heavy heart, he had determined to uproot himself from the surroundings that had been so dear to him ; but even so he could not bring himself to migrate very far—only as far as Viareggio itself, where the waters of his beloved Massaciucolli found their way to the sea, near the spot where Shelley's body had been found washed up nearly a century before.

Here, at the far end of this popular seaside resort, and sheltered by the pine-trees, he had built himself a comfortable modern villa rather in the shape of a bungalow,

[1] My mother's sciatica had been cured by Professor—now Sir Aldo —Castellani.

gaily coloured and with a touch of the East about it. It was to have been ready for him to move in early in the summer, but there had been unexpected delays—involving, needless to say, the addition of numbers of house-builders, contractors, and workmen to the already over-crowded sty of Puccinian *pigs*. However, his piano had been installed in his large airy study, which was connected—as he showed us with great pride—by an inside staircase with his bedroom, and one memorable afternoon he played for us there the first act of *Turandot*, which I thought then—and still think —was the finest single act that he ever composed. Towards the end of the year his new home was at last ready to receive him, and during the three years of life that remained to him, he became increasingly attached to it, and increasingly disinclined to leave it, even for the shortest interval of time. And then, if ever he felt home-sick, he could step into his car, and in a few minutes he was back at Torre del Lago. . . .

Those were three very happy weeks that we spent at Viareggio. Except for Tonio, who was away, the whole of Puccini's dear ones were with him, and they seemed a singularly happy family. That vague feeling of tension of which, in the old days, I was always conscious when Giacomo and Elvira were together, had completely disappeared; Elvira was still a confirmed pessimist and complained—for hers was a complaining nature—at the high price of food, at the weather, at the strikes—at everything, in fact, except her husband and her family; yet age, which had destroyed her looks, had given her a new sweetness and a new serenity. As for Giacomo, he was the same as ever; tender, gentle, affectionate, gay—and yet always with that touch of sadness which lurked at the corners of his mouth even when he was smiling. Indeed the curious thing is that the imprint which he has left on my mind has never varied ; the Giacomo that I can remember strolling up and down the Promenade des Anglais is exactly the same as the Giacomo who now, more than fifteen years later, came to see us off at the station and kissed me on both cheeks, just as he had always done ever since I was a little boy. Little did I realize then—for he seemed so youthful and so healthy— that this was the last time that I should ever set eyes on him. . . .

CHAPTER THREE

'TURANDOT' LANGUISHES—AND RECOVERS
(September 1921–May 1923)

SOMETHING was wrong with *Turandot*—or was it that something was wrong with Puccini ? After the completion of that magnificent first act there follows an ominous pause during which he seriously contemplates the possibility of abandoning his task altogether—a thing which he would never have dreamt of doing before. Outwardly he had never seemed in better health than when we were with him at Viareggio ; yet it is possible that already that terrible disease which was so soon to carry him off had begun its insidious work of eating into his mental and physical powers ; for in the very first letters following our return one can detect traces of that fatal lethargy which was to defeat him in the end in his race against time.

On the surface these letters do not differ materially from hundreds of others written during the composition of his earlier operas ; there are the same alternations of hope and despair, the same striving after unattainable perfection, the same dissatisfaction with those *terrible* poets of his on whom he was so tragically dependent. But a new and disquieting note has crept into them : mistrust, not only of his collaborators, but of his own powers, and a sort of nightmarish feeling of urgency, as though he were unconsciously aware that he had little time to lose, and yet could not summon up the necessary force to complete his task. . . .

TORRE DEL LAGO
September 2nd, 1921

"I had your very dear letter from Paris ; the heat continues here, and so does the boredom—without any work to do, I feel nervous. I shall leave for Milan shortly to get together with my librettists ; my life isn't in the least happy ; I've got something—I don't know what it is—which makes me feel ill and especially depresses my spirits. Tonio got back yesterday from his trip—and how is Vincent ? He left behind him amongst us all the greatest feeling of affection—he really is a dear boy.

Elvira sends you her love. . . . In a word, I am very nearly fed up with life—and old age is knocking at the door ; for the time being I must try to keep going, but I don't think it will be for long. I agree that this letter isn't a gay one ! Forgive me—and I ask your pardon, dear Sybil, if I wasn't very attentive to you when you were here—I've had so many small and big worries these last days.

Good-bye, my dear.

With all fondest wishes to you, Vincent, and David."

TORRE DEL LAGO
September 20th, 1921

"I wrote to you some time back to London. As regards the *Rondine* I have found out that the new edition won't be ready for another month, but as soon as I get it I will send it to you. It's necessary to find a *woman* ; for the rest, one can easily make shift ; but one must have a woman, and one with a good voice. I remember two years ago at Covent Garden I heard a good Mimi—I don't remember her name, but she might make a good *Rondine*. I think, if one searches hard enough, one ought to be able to find one —it would be a good thing for me and for the opera if one could succeed in putting it on in London. Thank you for all you are doing and all you are going to do. I leave to-morrow for Milan, where I shall get going with my librettists on *Turandot* ; let us hope that we shall succeed in building up a good sequel to the first act—if not, I shall put it on one side and look for another subject."

TORRE DEL LAGO
October 20th, 1921

" I'm off to Bologna for the *Trittico* ; it's going to be done at La Scala too in January. I'm fed up with Torre del Lago, and shooting too doesn't interest me any more. Now, as to the carpet. . . .

Turandot languishes. I haven't got the second act as I want it yet, and I don't feel myself capable any more of composing music ; if I had a charming, light, sentimental subject, a little sad and with a touch of burlesque in it, I think I could still do some good ; but with a serious subject—a *really* serious subject—no. My health is good (touch wood !)—but I am *âgé*. It's only too true—and I am bored with the world ; I should like to take flight to other countries—but all by myself. Good-bye, dear Sybil, and regards to all your dear ones.

Your affectionate and eternally discontented,

GIACOMO "

Meanwhile trouble had arisen again over the ill-fated *Rondine*. My mother had at last succeeded in unearthing a Theatrical Agent, who hoped in turn to find some Management to put it on ' for a run '. The difficulties to be faced, however, are clearly set forth in the following letter of Mr. Higgins, to whom she had appealed for advice.

" CHÈRE AMIE,
        " I have your note. The objections to the scheme for producing the *Rondine* ' on a run ' are as follows :

The heavy cost of production.

The necessity for introducing a good deal of comic *spoken* dialogue, involving considerable modifications in the musical score.

The writing of a part for a low comedian.

When *Véronique* was produced in English all these difficulties were faced by George Edwardes and the modifications agreed to by Messager who co-operated. But would Puccini fall in with British views on these points ? There would be absolutely no chance of Sonsogno bearing any part of the cost of production. If the book is really a good one—I mean as good as say the *Cloches de Corneville* or *Véronique*—it would require little alteration, but if it had to be re-written to suit British taste, it would involve all sorts of modifications in the musical score.

If you will send me a summary of the story, describing the details of each act, and a copy of the vocal score, I will see what can be done conditionally on being given some mosaic waistcoat buttons ! "

Some of these objections, though not all (for I refuse to believe that she had the courage to mention the ' low comedian '), my mother must have passed on. Needless to say, Puccini rejected them ; there were limits to the concessions which he was prepared to make to " British taste ". The fact was that the poor Swallow's hybrid origin was bound to prove fatal to its production anywhere except at Covent Garden—and not even the bribe of a full set of " mosaic waistcoat buttons " would have induced Mr. Higgins to consent to that !

TORRE DEL LAGO
November 5th, 1921

" I'm getting up to-day after a week of influenza—the *Trittico* went well at Bologna, but it was *S. Angelica* which triumphed, with twelve curtain calls.

I've sent you two copies of *Rondine*, one for you and the other for the man ; but as to what you say about changing the ending and adding some prose, it's impossible—because the present ending is different from the one in the Monte Carlo edition ; it's not a *happy* ending, for that wouldn't be possible in the case of the *Rondine*. Besides, this is a lyric opera—small, it's true, but not an operetta with numbers between which you can insert fragments of dialogue. I conclude by saying that perhaps the *man*, being a man interested in Operettas, is not the kind we want ; in this case somebody different is wanted—and possibly the sort of man I'm thinking of doesn't exist—if that is so, Good-bye to *Rondine* in London, unless they have lyric opera in the Covent Garden repertory—that is, if Higgins wants the theatre to be as it used to be.

I'm still at Torre del Lago ; I've got to go to Rome for three days for the musical Commission at the Ministry of Fine Arts, but I shall come straight back here. The carpet hasn't arrived—nor has the cold either.

Turandot will end by going to the wall because the libretto of the second act is no good—and I have done the first act ! I'm looking for something else with Forzano with an eye to London."

November 19th, 1921

" What you tell me about the Jazz-band Fox-trot music stolen from my operas disgusts me, but does not surprise me.[1] . . .

---

[1] " Are you aware ", wrote Mr. Higgins to my mother, " that there is a rag-time dance published by Ricordi of New York and sold by Ricordi of London based on the most popular airs in Puccini's operas ? If you doubt it, order the composition here and you will get it. Is Puccini aware of this outrage ? Anyway you might get a copy and send it him—a similar infamy has been perpetrated by others here in the case of the Meistersinger ! "

Puccini took the matter up with his lawyers ; the ' outrage ' was at

Heaven only knows what the Carl Rosa executions will be like ! But I thank God that they are executing me at all —what gives me pleasure is the thought that the English public still cares for me. . . .

I'm well—but I'm not working. *Turandot* has sunk into oblivion. I'm still waiting for my poets, but they don't stir—I'm looking for another libretto with Forzano.

P.S. of Forzano's :

My dear kind Friend,

We're hoping to find something worthy of the *Great Man* ! We're going to use all the brains we've got !

Did you get my letter ?

Affectionately,

Forzano ''

Hotel Quirinal
Rome
[*End of December*, 1921]

'' I've had your letter—I'm glad that Forzano's *Chinese Play* won your approval. I liked it too in many places—but I've got *Turandot* and I can't change now. You say I should use the music I've already written, but it's not possible— you know how I fit the words exactly to the music.

I heard *Romeo* [1] last night—a disaster ! Ugly ornamentations in the orchestra and shrieks from the stage—no heart, no emotion. And the libretto too was bad ! Very far from Shakespeare !

To-morrow we start our sittings at the Ministry ; afterwards I return to Viareggio, and hope to start working again.

once suppressed, and although in the end he decided not to take the case into Court, he received heavy compensation. This did not prevent other composers of ' original ' rag-time melodies from ' lifting ' large sections of *Madama Butterfly* en bloc.

[1] Riccardo Zandonai's latest opera, which had just had its *première* in Rome.

So all is well with you in England—and Esmond is much better—Good—*all rigth* [*sic*]."

My mother's suggestion was not quite as outrageous as it might at first sight appear. There had been occasions in the past when he had not scrupled to make use of sundry passages which had originally been intended for another context ; to give but two examples, there was the opening music sketched out for Ouida's *Two Little Wooden Shoes* which later served him for a very different setting in *Suor Angelica* ; and there had also been the occasion when he crept silently into the Museum in Milan to ' steal ' the only surviving copy of that *Capriccio sinfonico* which had first brought his name before the musical public ten years earlier, and which he now proceeded to incorporate, note for note, in the first act of *Bohème*. He made what use he could of unconsidered trifles (of his own, of course), and although it would have been a thousand pities if the masterly first act of *Turandot* had had to be broken up, I have not the slightest doubt that large quantities of salvage would have found their way into Forzano's *Chinese Play*.

Via Buonarotti
Viareggio
December 23rd, 1921

" The carpet has arrived ! Excellent taste—most agreeable, and it looks well in the dining-room. A thousand thanks, dear friend.

That's all right about the *Rondine*—as soon as I get to Milan, which will be in a few days' time, I'll put the idea forward to Sonsogno's, and they can then get into touch with the English agent, who has written to me and whom I'll answer to-morrow.[1]

[1] My mother had heard from the theatrical agent that he had ' succeeded in interesting one management in *La Rondine*'. But the interest

I arrived to-night straight from Rome, and passing through Torre del Lago I found your letter. I'm writing to you immediately after dinner—and then I'm going to bed.

I've been in Rome at the Ministry after spending ten days at my Tower in the Maremma, where the weather was lovely, though there was no shooting. I'm going to sell it, because although it's a lovely spot the arrangements for food and for letters are too difficult and the roads are impossible.

As you see from the address, I'm writing from my new home—the house is most agreeable and I hate to have to go to Milan, but I've got to go for the *Trittico* at La Scala and for the libretto of *Turandot* which is still unfinished ! I wasn't satisfied with this libretto and I said so ; the papers published the news of my disagreement with the Poets, who were simply furious. And now they've recognized how wrong they were and are going to work enthusiastically along the lines of my suggestions—And we'll see—certainly, as I see the opera, it's a very beautiful thing—but shall I be able to do it, and shall I be able to do it well ? I'm a little doubtful because it is the type of opera that terrifies me ; I should have preferred something of a different kind— and I've got an idea : *Cagliostro* : this idea occurred to me in the train to-day when I was reading a review about him. He seems to me a great character, this Count Cagliostro— do you know Dumas' novel ? But it would need a lot of historical research in order to construct a play for the stage, half heroic and half comic with a touch of the fantastic too —But enough, we'll look into this subject too—Best wishes to you and Vincent and Esmond and David for a happy Christmas and a prosperous New Year."

apparently soon evaporated, as nothing more is heard of it—only sad little queries from Puccini : And *Rondine* ?

" I'm here for the rehearsals of the *Trittico*—I left Viareggio with genuine regret because the house is most agreeable to live in and your Dutch carpet keeps one's feet nice and warm at meal times !

I had all your express letters—as soon as I've finished with the *Trittico*, I'll take steps through my lawyer.

In Brussels *Gianni Schicchi*, performed by itself, had a great success. I am fairly well, but both Elvira and I have got a cough—what a duet ! We are ancient—that is the cruel truth !

And *Rondine* ? "

Farewell, Milan, I turn once more
Sated, to Viareggio's shore.
For there a happier life I'll lead
From Ricordi's presence freed,
While the Scala fades from view,
—Its singers and relations too.
Ah ! there beneath a shelt'ring pine
Blackbird and thrush and finch combine,
Hailing the Spring till starlight falls
To pipe Puccinian madrigals,
And every sylvan joy enthrals.
There on the mead, in shady bowers,
Health and contentment shall be ours.
But should satiety assail my soul
Torre del Lago is the goal.
For on Milan I turn my back,
Nor tread again the beaten track." [1]

G. PUCCINI

[1] Once again I am indebted to my father for his rendering of Puccini's verse.

" I would have written to you, but I thought you were still in Paris—I'm working, and I'm most comfortable in this house. How is Esmond ? And Vincenzo ? Give him my best love—how hard this work of *Turandot* is ! But I like doing this opera. The third act is still missing but the poets write to me that they are making good progress with it.

I've had the document from New York which the Italian Ambassador in Washington sent me, and it's a serious business. . . ."

" I ask pardon of my dear friend for her lazy correspondent ! I am going through an ugly period. I work little or not at all—and my nerves have completely got the upper hand of me ! Will this state of affairs pass and shall I be able to work again ? I hope so. . . .

I told Forzano what you had written ; he's very sorry but he hasn't been able to finish *Lorenzino*—it really is a pity.[1] On the other hand he has written another play in Florentine dialect which had a great success recently —I hope to start work again. . . . But I still haven't got the complete libretto . . . those lazy fellows keep me waiting."

" *Turandot* goes slowly forward—I shall start again on my interrupted work at Viareggio. I'm fairly well—and I'm most comfortable in the new house at Viareggio. I shan't go to Paris although they're doing *Schicchi* in October ; but

---

[1] Forzano had been commissioned by Mr. Matheson Lang to write a second play for him : *Lorenzino de' Medici*. It was not completed in time, and has never been given in English.

I'm very little interested in the performance, as I should have liked them to give all three operas together. They made over a million at La Scala, and next year it appears that they're going to do a special performance of *Manon*, conducted by Toscanini.

All the world over my operas still hold their own—I've had quite a good six months—about 400,000 lire."

VIAREGGIO
June 16th, 1922

" Thank you for your letter and the newspaper cutting about Covent Garden. I see, I see that for many years I have reigned over Covent Garden and I am glad of it ; but now that I am an old man I think I might have received some form of recognition from your great Country. The father no less than the son, the present King, loved and love my music ; I know that, whether at the Opera or at Court, they wanted and they want songs from *Bohème*—And never once have they thought of that author who, too, has reigned for so many years in their home on the throne of the music of the theatre. That's the end of my outburst, which is moreover a passing thought that has just come to me, and has died as quickly as it was born ; for if there is one man in the world who does not care for knick-knacks to be put on his evening dress, I am that man—and the real meaning of my outburst is that I love your Country and want to go on reigning there. And since 1894 !—*Manon*.

Yours affectionately,
GIACOMO THE FIRST "

I do not know whether this sudden whim of his to receive an English decoration was ever gratified, but in any case I am certain that he never gave the matter another thought. It was the literal truth that there was no one

alla cara Sybil
il cacciatore
Vecchio Amico

Giacomo Puccini

Milano
29.12.22

Boon!
1958

HIS FAVOURITE SPORT—AND AN ALLUSION TO THE
COVENT GARDEN PROGRAMME (see p. 9)
(1922)

who cared less for honours and rewards than he ; although
he was genuinely gratified when, a few months later, he
was created a Senator by Mussolini, he preferred to alter
his title and sign himself *Sonatore del Regno* (*Musician* of the
Kingdom). Nor, although he was a convinced Monarchist,
was there the faintest trace of snobbishness in his character ;
he was on the most intimate terms with the Italian Royal
Family, but there is not a single mention of the fact in
all these letters ; indeed such few references to Royalties
as appear are generally to be found tucked away in a
postscript.

MILAN
January 6th, 1923

" I've had your dear letter. We are well—I'm fed up
with Milan and want the sun ; in a few days' time I'm
going to the Maremma for a week and then come back to
Milan—to see if I can succeed in extracting the third act of
Turandot from these *terrible* poets of mine. *Manon* is still
going splendidly—to-night is the fifth performance.

I hear that the Carl Rosa are still giving my operas in
London. I hope you won't have the courage to go and
attend the *executions*. Nothing new here—the usual life ;
I'm going to have a day's shooting near Milan on Monday.
Dear Sybil, you are a real angel of goodness and of loyalty
—such a rare thing in these out of joint and indifferent
times. I set the greatest store by your friendship, and I am
only remorseful because I have not been as nice to you as
you deserve—forgive this nervous, thoroughly discontented
man if he was not sufficiently attentive in keeping you
company—I always have a thousand things in Milan to
take up my time."

MILAN
January 11th, 1923

" Oh, that Melba ! Duse, Sarah—it's enough, it's too
much. The house is still sold out for *Manon* here ; there

have been six performances and the takings are half a million lire—tell that stupid old Higgins.

They're giving me a banquet on Monday and on Tuesday I'm going to Viareggio, then to the Maremma for a week—after that I'm going back here to have the libretto completed. I've been at home (in bed) for three days—a sort of mild influenza, but I'm better now. It does nothing but rain—rain—rain—I'm going to the rehearsals of Franchetti's *Colombo*—I told Forzano about Lang."

VIAREGGIO
January 26*th*, 1923

" I've got a marvellous new car, an eight-cylinder limousine Lancia—90,000 lire ! I came to the conclusion that one only has one's life once.

What a curious and interesting man that must be who waits outside Covent Garden the whole of a winter's night to hear *Bohème* ! I haven't had the newspaper—it would have given me pleasure to have it—perhaps it's at Milan ?

The *thirtieth* anniversary of *Manon* at La Scala on February 1st—there's going to be a so-called night of honour. I think in March I shall go to Vienna to see that doctor ! I've met a South American gentleman here, sixty-seven years old, who tells me that the operation is nothing at all and that the benefits are extraordinary—he says he feels as though he were twenty-five again, and that it no longer tires him to walk and his mind is fresh and agile, etc., etc.—why shouldn't I do it too ? My dear, my life is my own and means the whole world to me—so why not ? I have such a fear and such a horror of old age !

My friend the poet, Pea, of Viareggio, has written to you about Shelley's Urn which they want to put up here amongst the pine-trees by the sea on the spot where his body was found. Some important London paper ought to write about it and so raise the money for this noble idea."

MILAN
February 5th, 1923

" . . . The fête for the thirtieth Anniversary of *Manon* was fantastic. At last Milan has honoured me—there were nearly 500 people at the banquet—at Cova's—and the performance was a miracle of execution and of enthusiasm—the receipts, 110,000 lire.

£200 will do for Shelley—you might send it to Enrico Pea, Viareggio.

I hear good reports of the Viennese doctor's cure—I don't believe the Kaiser has done it."

MILAN
February 12th, 1923

" *Address Poet—Pea Enrico Viareggio Italy*

Not had cigarettes yet

Manon twelfth performance still sold out

Will send thanks architect on receipt photograph theatre [1]

Lancia limousine 8 cylinders splendid

Don't know whether shall go Monte Carlo—not well to-day and nervous

Milan boring would like go away—family bores me too

Glad you are better and sciatica over

Simoni ill so Turandot *delayed*

Thanks telegram—thanks all your kindness."

VIAREGGIO
[February 1923]

" Thanks for your letter—it gives me pleasure to hear of the British *Bohème* and of the public's interest in it—

---

[1] Puccini had been appointed President of the Committee at Lucca (' *My* city ') to attend to the rebuilding of the theatre, and he had asked for the plans of the ' Gayety ' and 'Majesty ' theatres which he regarded as the most commodious in London.

although old, this opera keeps its place well.

It's nice here but . . . now I really am an old man ! And nothing interests me much— ! I work, but . . . I'm not at all pleased with that either—Germany? . . . we'll say no more about it—as you see, I am a sort of funeral—I haven't got the third act yet of the libretto !

We shall have, so they say, a good hotel here this year —will you come ? In September ? I should like to go away in August because it's too crowded—but where ? How I should like to come to London ! We'll see if it can be managed—I've heard *Lorenzino* read—it's a really good play."

VIAREGGIO
March 20th, 1923

" . . . I can't come to San Remo—I've got things to do. I've got to go to Vienna soon for *Manon*, and then Elvira is coming here for a bit—did you know that another of my sisters is dead ? [1] She was 71 and the oldest of the family—I've been very unhappy about it ; I'm not going to bore you by telling you how my moral is—black, black. I work a little or not at all—this infamous *Turandot* terrifies me and I shan't finish it, or if I finish it it will be a fiasco. I should have liked to have another subject—and nobody finds me anything—I live from day to day, like a lost soul. Enjoy the sun, since in addition to your many other enthusiasms you are always enthusiastic—for the sun.

Good-bye, dear Sybil,

Affectionate thoughts
from
your very old
GIACOMO "

---

[1] Romelde Puccini. It was she whom he had so often visited at the Convent, and who had inspired his love for *Suor Angelica*.

HOTEL BRISTOL
VIENNA
May 17th, 1923

"At last I have time to write to you—I can't tell you how much my time has been taken up here. I had your letter and one from Professor Castellani ; as soon as I get home I want to try the Insulin cure—for the time being I'm not thinking of going to the Doctor here.

Jeritza and the tenor Piccaver are singing in *Manon*—but it's not coming on before the end of the month. You who are so fond of me would be pleased to see how your Giacomo is fêted by these people here who are so hospitable and so agreeable. Vienna is a really musical city—I believe that even to-day, when it is forsaken and so different from what it used to be, it is still the leading city in the world— magnificent orchestras, concerts, amazing choirs, and a splendid Opera House of absolutely first rank.

It really is a shame that an immense city like London shouldn't have a good and permanent Opera House.

I'm here with Tonio and a friend from Viareggio and we motored here in my new Lancia. We're going back by Salzburg and the Brenner Pass as the road from Tarviz is horrible.

We're most comfortable in this hotel—it's very dear, but very *comme il faut*.

At last I've had the third act of *Turandot*. Adami came to Viareggio and in a week we finished it very well. Now the libretto is complete and very beautiful too, it's up to me to write the music ! But I shall have to work a lot to finish this blessed opera. However, now that I have a fine third act, I have more courage and desire to work."

" Still Melba ? Good—let her rake in the shekels !

Last night *Tosca* with Jeritza was *sublime* ! A *succès fou*—more than fifty calls ! A real delirium—To-night *Bohème* with the tenor Piccaver and Selma Kurz, rather too old but not yet *Melba*. I'm well—no Kaiser's doctor for me—for the present—perhaps in September. . . . ."

CHAPTER FOUR

THE LAST ACT
(June 1923–November 29th, 1924)

PUCCINI was back in his comfortable home at Viareggio. He had exactly eighteen months to live : eighteen months in which to write the last act of what he hoped would prove his masterpiece.

" Now the libretto is complete, and very beautiful too, it's up to me to write the music." For the first time for many a long weary day he was independent of his librettists ; there he was, alone with his piano, which stood invitingly open in that nice roomy study of which he was so proud. . . . But somehow the music would not come : " *Turandot* isn't progressing," he writes. " I've got absolutely no desire to work ; all music, beginning with my own, disgusts me—it's really a useless Art in this prosaic age." And a few weeks later : " I've got my work—and although I work but little it keeps me here. I've got to finish the opera for next year, and I'm very much behindhand."

In the autumn, unable to work, he set out again for Vienna, partly to seek the distractions which this kindly, music-loving city had to offer him, and partly to obtain relief from the diabetes from which he had been suffering intermittently, though never acutely, for the past twenty years.

" I'm still here. I'm having a cure for my diabetes and I'm much better.

This would be the country for you—operas, operas, nothing but operas. I've looked out for the correspondent of the *Observer,* but I haven't found him. However, I spoke to several American critics (they're nearly always *ladies*) and there are some English correspondents too—one is *The Times* correspondent—and I said it was a shame that an immense city like London shouldn't have an international Opera House of the first order—I don't know if they'll write about it but I said it to two or three of them.

Elvira and Tonio are here—to-night is the third night of *Manon,* which is really a magnificent performance. Last night *Butterfly,* the other day *Bohème,* then *Tosca* (but that wasn't so good because the absence of Jeritza, who is in America, was felt)—in other words if they want the box-office to take between two hundred and three hundred millions, it's necessary to have *Giacomino*—you know him, that now aged Maestro ! "

" It's not true that people are dying of hunger in Vienna ; one eats (though I don't, because I'm on a régime) and one eats very well, and the life here is brilliant. The theatres are full ; there's activity everywhere ; and commerce is almost on the same scale as before the War.

I've had more than enough of the Sanatorium, and I shall be very glad to get home again—amongst other reasons in order to resume my work and to get a little shooting at Torre del Lago.

Thank you for the letter-case, which I shall be glad to

have ; I really needed one, so it's come just at the right moment—thank you, dear Sybil.

Here they're giving *Manon, Bohème, Butterfly* and *Tosca*—and *Suor Angelica* and *Schicchi* will shortly be following. The house is always sold out for *Manon*—and all you have is *Old England* ! [1] What a shame ! Amongst all London's inhabitants, is there not one who contemplates the possibilities of a Lyric Opera House ? It would be good business, too."

During his stay in Vienna Puccini had been much impressed by the report that the Austrian Government were planning a special Season of Viennese opera in London—" Wagner, Strauss, Puccini—with their own orchestra, scenery and singers—including Jeritza." The Season never materialized, but on his return home Puccini hoped to be able to persuade the Fascist Government to take similar measures to encourage the spread of Italian music abroad. But the times were not very favourable ; " I don't think Mussolini is giving a thought to Italian opera at Covent Garden", he writes despondently. " Nobody even talks about it in Italy." Shortly afterwards he met the Duce for the first and only time ; but he did not succeed in making any headway. " I saw Mussolini ", he reports, " but only for a few minutes and I wasn't able to talk much—so there wasn't time to discuss Italian opera abroad." [2]

[1] The name of a General Stores to be found in many places on the Continent ; Puccini always joked about the name, and applied it indiscriminately to anything, or anybody, as a term of good-humoured contempt.

[2] It is scarcely to be wondered at that the Duce should have had other and more pressing problems to attend to at that time. But no aspect of Italian life, however insignificant, escapes his all-seeing eye for long, and the time was to come, long after Puccini's death, when the operatic stage of Italy received a tremendous new stimulus, not indeed

Meanwhile the resumption of work proved less easy than he had hoped. "I'm working a little on *Turandot*", he reports, "but very sparingly—I'll finish the opera when God wills. . . ." Early in the New Year, my mother paid him a short visit at Viareggio; she found him in fairly good health and reasonably cheerful—although he had already begun to complain of an insistent cough and a sore throat.

VIAREGGIO
February 10*th,* 1924

"I've heard of the wretched journey which you had. But by now you will be rested. . . .

The few days that you were with us were most delightful, but another time you must stay longer—I *do* hope you will.

I continue my monotonous life, working. Elvira sends you her dearest wishes—and so does

Your ever affectionate,

GIACOMO"

VIAREGGIO
February 20*th,* 1924

"What a series of disasters! Poor friend! But the worst is about Esmond—how much unhappiness and what a con-

through the financing of costly seasons abroad, but by bringing opera at home within the reach of the slenderest purse at those open-air summer performances where, for a few lire, the people can enjoy first-rate opera to their hearts' content. Only the other day I chanced in Italy on a number of the *Corriere Della Sera* (August 8th, 1937) which contained three long notices of outdoor performances given on the previous night; in the Castello at Milan *Butterfly* before an audience of 20,000; at Verona *Turandot* before a huge public of 25,000 which included Gabriele D'Annunzio; in Rome an 'extraordinary' performance of *Bohème* with Gigli as Rodolfo. And as I read of the immense enthusiasm everywhere aroused by these 'old carcasses' of his, I could not help reflecting how delighted Puccini would have been had he only lived to read these glowing accounts in the pages of his favourite, but much dreaded, newspaper.

tinuous anxiety it must mean for you ! And you were so
happy and cheerful when I saw you here—and so good and
sweet. Let us hope at least that the poor boy will soon be
well again. . . .

And in the midst of all these misfortunes you find time
to think of me and my silly little affairs and of Forzano—
oh, how good you are ! Elvira too is always talking about
you, and with the very greatest affection.

I'm continuing my work in the little room which is
all red—I hardly ever go out. I'm fairly well—perhaps
even a little better than when you were here—Touch
wood !

So much love to you and David—and try to face the
misfortunes of life bravely.

All the most affectionate thoughts

from yours

GIACOMO ''

VIAREGGIO
February 29th, 1924

" . . . Don't worry about the carpet ; if you can't
find one, leave it alone. I can make do with the one I've
got for another year—and you oughtn't always to be the
kind caterer to my caprices.

I've finished the second act completely, and now I'm
attacking the third. I read that there is going to be a
Season at Covent Garden this year but I don't expect it
will be up to much—and the Italian ballets too will be
pretty poor stuff.

It's beautifully sunny here—Spring. I'm not budging at
present ; I'm waiting for *Nerone* which it appears may be
delayed—perhaps till April.[1]

---

[1] Boito's opera, which was given for the first time in Milan at the
beginning of May.

Elvira is always on the point of going to Milan, but she never makes up her mind—I'm leading my usual life ; if it weren't for my work it would be deadly dull, but with my *travail* the time passes and I'm not bored.

My health seems good so far (touch wood !)

I'm expecting Adami, who will be here Tuesday or Wednesday to arrange the famous duet in the third act. I've got nothing else to tell you."

VIAREGGIO
March 13th, 1924

" Forgive me—I've not been at all well and I've still got a sore throat and an obstinate cough. I'm enormously, disgustingly lazy about writing letters ; I've neglected everyone—and, I confess, you too, the only person in the world who doesn't deserve such treatment—but I beg you to forgive me. It doesn't mean that you have been absent from my thoughts—very much the reverse ; but I don't know how to force myself to take pen in hand.

Adami is here to finish the libretto—the last duet, which has finally come out very well indeed. Thank you for the letter-case, which is a beauty and just the right size.

I'm not well yet, and my spirits are downcast too—I shall soon be all by myself because Elvira is going to Milan on Monday. I don't feel like facing all that confusion ; besides, I've got to work—I shall go at the last moment for *Nerone*.

Love to you and David and forgive me again for my silence. I have had, too, moments of great doubt about *Turandot*—this has worried me very much. Then serenity and faith are born again—with all these ups and downs we'll see what the reality will be."

" I leave the day after to-morrow for Milan to spend Easter there and then hear the famous *Nerone* in which I believe very little—but we'll see. My health isn't bad, but for the last two months my *throat* has been tormenting me—I'll go and see a specialist in Milan. Elvira writes to me that she is feeling well in Milan and has got her appetite back.

Thank you for your invitation—it's most attractive ! Still ! We'll see. But first of all I don't want to be a nuisance—and if I were to come to London I should like to go to the Savoy as usual. They tell me that the Colonial Exhibition is fine.[1]

I'm at work on the duet ; it's difficult, but I shall end by doing it and I hope it will give satisfaction—and then the opera (if God wills) will be finished.

At last one begins to feel the Spring here—I think of Voronoff ! I really shall end by going to see him ! Who has a better right than I ? A coal merchant, perhaps ? What a conceited remark ! "

" In a few days' time I'm going to Salsomaggiore because my throat won't get any better—Elvira is coming too. We shall stay there ten or twelve days, no longer— And how are you ? And yours ? Esmond ? And the Opera ? Heaven knows how awful the performances of the Italian opera must be ! I've done no more work ; *Turandot* lies here, unfinished. But I *will* finish it—only just at present I've got no desire to work.

The worst of it is that I am growing old—and that disgusts me ! I don't think I shall be able to come to London

[1] *I.e.* the Wembley Exhibition.

as I wanted to because of this P . . . of a *Turandot* which I still have to finish.

I haven't heard from you ; it's true that I too have been a long time answering your last dear letter—my laziness is enormous."

SALSOMAGGIORE
June 1st, 1924

" Just had your letters with the programme and the news. I'm glad that my old carcasses are still given on the stage—X will be sorry ! I go back to Viareggio on Saturday; my throat is just the same—the cure hasn't made any difference. They say that I shall be better later—we'll see.

Mrs. Angeli wrote to me too ; I'll answer her this evening. I should have liked to run away to London, but I can't make up my mind—firstly because I've still got so much work to do on *Turandot*, then because it's hot, and then because I'm not feeling very well. I'm as lazy as can be—but enough. I'll see when I'm back in Viareggio and if I can manage it I'll come. But the operatic season will be nearly over—are there any nice novelties on in the other theatres ? Dear Sybil, from now on I am an old man worth only a few shillings.

Warm regards from Elvira, who loathes being away from her own house and in the heat.

I'm smoking your Abdulla cigarettes with great enjoyment. Love to David and Vincent.

Yours most affectionately,
GIACOMO

How boring this place is !
Warmest regards,
ELVIRA "

There are no more letters.

Towards the end of August my mother spent a few

days at the villa at Viareggio. Giacomo still had a sore throat and a tiresome cough, but neither he nor anyone else paid any particular attention to it ; he had had countless ailments of a similar nature in the past which his powerful constitution had easily enabled him to overcome. Besides, his own doctor and, later, a specialist in Florence had examined his throat in turn, and had found nothing amiss . . . only my mother suspected the hideous truth—though she confided her fears to no one save Tonio.

Shortly after she left, Giacomo, who had been rendered nervous and a trifle apprehensive by the persistence of his ailment, decided to seek a second opinion himself, and paid a secret visit to another professor in Florence, who detected the presence of a small swelling in the throat below the epiglottis. Tonio, now thoroughly alarmed, hurried to Florence and begged the professor to tell him the truth. The reply was unequivocal : his father was suffering from an acute cancer of the throat, which had reached such an advanced stage that it would be hopeless to attempt to treat it ; it was a death sentence, without hope of reprieve. Tonio returned home broken-hearted, for there never was a more loving nor more devoted son ; what increased the horror of his position was that he must at all costs conceal the truth from his father and mother. At the back of his mind there remained only one hope ; doctors were no more infallible than other mortals, and it was just barely possible that the professor had been mistaken in his diagnosis. . . .

But his father's throat got no better ; he was not as yet suffering any acute pain, but the discomfort became aggravated, and at length it was decided to hold a consultation, at which Gradenigo, the noted Neapolitan specialist on this type of disease, was also present. The terrible diagnosis was confirmed, but Professor Gradenigo held out one hope to

Tonio: an operation was urgently necessary, but with the new radium treatment it was possible that Puccini's life might be saved, or at any rate prolonged for several years. He recommended that he should proceed immediately with his father to the Institut de la Couronne in Brussels, where the brilliant Doctor Ledoux was said to have rescued dozens of similar sufferers from the very jaws of death. It was only a slender hope, but—as Tonio wrote to my mother afterwards—his decision could not be in doubt; even if there was only one chance in a hundred of the operation proving successful, it was, given the horrible alternative of leaving his father to starve slowly to death in the most atrocious agony, worth trying. Tonio accepted the responsibility with a clear conscience.

Giacomo himself was only too eager to depart; for the pain in his throat had greatly increased in the past few days. And so, on November 4th, accompanied only by Tonio—for Elvira was herself far too ill to travel and had, moreover, been kept in complete ignorance of the real nature of the disease—he bade farewell to Viareggio and set forth on his last journey. Did he know the truth? It is impossible to believe that he did not at least suspect it; yet, if so, he gave no sign and comported himself with the utmost stoicism. One anxiety only appeared to obsess him: the unfinished *Turandot*. On the day before he left, he sent for Toscanini, and together they went through the all but completed score and discussed in every detail its forthcoming production, which was to take place at the earliest possible moment at La Scala; it is good to know that he was immensely cheered by the whole-hearted enthusiasm which the reading of the score had evoked in his greatest interpreter; for, since the death of Signor Giulio, there was no man whose opinion he valued more. The opera on which he had been working for nearly four years was so nearly finished ; all that remained to be done was the last duet, which was to be the *clou* of the opera, and the Finale— three weeks' work at the most, he reckoned. He had never worked before to a time-table, and he could not bear the thought that he was holding up the production : so he took with him to Brussels thirty-six pages of unfinished composition and notes ; the ' cure ' would take six weeks and there would be plenty of time to put the finishing touches, if . . .

After a preliminary examination by Doctor Ledoux, it was decided that he should go at once into the Institut de la Couronne to undergo treatment. The cure, as Tonio explained to my mother in a letter written directly after the examination, was a long and terrible one ; during the first week he would be kept under observation; during the second, there would be external applications of radium ; during the third, the radium would be applied internally in the throat by means of glass needles—but first it would be necessary to pierce a hole in the throat to enable him to breathe through a rubber tube. The growth was situated in the worst possible place, beneath the epiglottis ; nevertheless the doctor held out strong hopes that it was curable.

Giacomo and Tonio now left their comfortable hotel and moved into the Institute, where they occupied adjoining rooms. Although suffering from acute sciatica, my mother summoned up sufficient strength to go to Brussels ; there was little that she could do for her old friend, save to make a few additional arrangements for his comfort. She got him, amongst other things, a specially soft pillow (on which, at Tonio's direction, the death-mask in the Museum at Torre del Lago now reposes) and, realising that although Tonio was an angel of goodness the touch of a woman was also needed in the sick-room, wrote a very strongly worded letter to Fosca, urging her to come immediately to her stepfather. Three days later Fosca (who had only delayed her departure on account of her mother's illness) was in Brussels.

" These last two days ", wrote Tonio on the 17th, " Papa has been a little better ; yesterday we went out and lunched outside the Home. To-night he has been peaceful ; little coughing, and he was able to have a good sleep—the bleeding has practically stopped. He is so very grateful to you for your visit ; it gave him the greatest pleasure, *and has really raised his spirits.*"

It seemed indeed as though the exterior application of the radium had arrested the ill. The bleeding ceased entirely and, to his intense delight, Giacomo was even allowed to smoke a few cigarettes ; from time to time he would take those thirty-six pages of composition out of his case and gaze at them intently—perhaps after all he would win his race against time. . . .

Encouraged by these favourable symptoms, Doctor Ledoux decided that the time had come for the internal application of the radium, and on November 24th the operation took place. For three hours and a half the surgeons worked, and although only a local anaesthetic could be administered, Giacomo had still sufficient strength at the end to raise himself from the stretcher and put himself to bed unaided.

Three horrible days followed—and then it seemed as though the longed-for miracle had actually happened. The fever abated, and by the fourth day he was visibly stronger, and even able to get up for a little and read the newspapers. The doctors were delighted : *Puccini en sortira,* confidently proclaimed Doctor Ledoux. By the sick man's bedside, Fosca, now radiant with joy, sat down to send these pencilled lines to my mother.

BRUSSELS
4 P.M. *Friday*

" DEAR SYBIL,

"I couldn't answer your dear letter yesterday—all my time is spent looking after dear Papa—this letter too is written from his room where I stay day and night. Tonio and I haven't left him for an instant, and it's the greatest comfort to me to be by his side.

The letter you wrote to me to Milan grieved me more than I can say, but I understand perfectly well how you came to write it—I would have come to Brussels anyhow, because I couldn't live any more except by his side, but it was your letter which finally decided me to leave. Don't let's think of the past any more, darling—you are a *unique* friend to us all and we appreciate your affection for us more than we can possibly say. I think of you as a sister rather than as a friend, darling sweet Sybil !

Everything is going well and the doctors are more than satisfied ; our adored Papa is saved ! *Saved*—do you understand ? Certainly he has suffered a good deal, but from now on this terrible part of the cure is over, and he will only have to submit to the boredom of convalescence. There is no more physical suffering, and far less moral suffering ; it is only his nerves which have been upset, so the doctors assure us, by the radium which is at work. His throat is no longer swollen ; the radium has destroyed the tumours. I believe that on Sunday or Monday they will remove the needles and then this ghastly week will be over. It's true that he is reduced to a shadow, but the doctors assure us that he will very quickly recover ; he has a strong constitution, his heart is absolutely sound, and his diabetes has given no cause for anxiety. But how painful it is, Sybil dear, to see him with that hole in his throat, and being fed by the nose through a syringe. . . ."

Fosca's letter was never finished. It was now six o'clock, and she had gone out of the room for a minute to find my mother's address—when she was hastily summoned back by the nurse. During those few seconds of her absence Giacomo had suddenly collapsed in his arm-chair ; the radium, which had been so beneficial in destroying the tumours, had proved too much for his heart. Doctor Ledoux hastily removed the needles to relieve the pressure on the throbbing heart ; but it was too late. Giacomo was beyond human aid ; that old age which he had so dreaded he would never now know.

It was the morning of Saturday, November 29th. All through the long weary night he had fought his losing battle with Death ; early in the morning the Papal Nuncio had come to his bedside to pronounce the last benediction. And now the struggle was nearly over and he lay there, quietly dying, with Tonio and Fosca by his side ; of what was he thinking, I wonder, during those last few hours of his life ? So much had been crowded into those sixty-six years ; so many triumphs, and so few failures . . . and yet I do not fancy that it was of the past that he was thinking ; for it is said that when he had taken a silent farewell of his dear son and stepdaughter his hands began to move over the coverlet as though he were seated again at his piano, composing music. Those thirty-six pages of *Turandot*, still unfinished—was he finishing them now ? Composing music . . . it was that for which he had lived . . . " only a small thing—much too small a thing ; still—something ". . . . And so the Heavenly Father received him into Eternity, as he himself would have wished, composing music. . . .

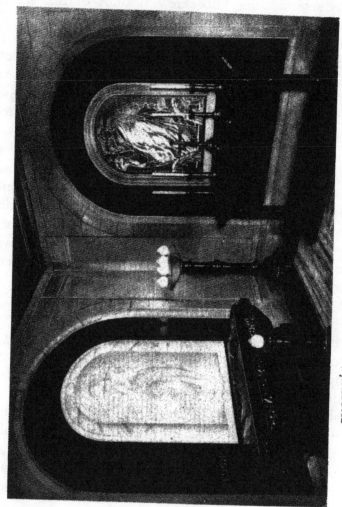

PUCCINI'S LAST RESTING-PLACE AT TORRE DEL LAGO

BIBLIOGRAPHY

APART from Puccini's letters to my mother, my chief sources have been the two works of Giuseppe Adami: "Giacomo Puccini, Epistolario" (Mondadori, Milan, 1928), which has been translated into English by Ena Makin under the title of "Letters of Giacomo Puccini" (George G. Harrap & Co., Ltd., 1931) and his more recent "Puccini" (Fratelli Treves, Milan, 1935); and Richard Specht's biography, which has been translated into English by Catherine Alison Phillips (J. M. Dent & Sons, 1933) under the title of "Giacomo Puccini. The Man, his Life, his Work". I have also consulted, and quoted from, the following works:

DRY, WAKELING. Giacomo Puccini. (John Lane, 1906.)

FRACCAROLI, ARNALDO. La vita di Giacomo Puccini. (G. Ricordi, Milan, 1925.)

LORD HOWARD OF PENRITH. Theatre of Life. (Hodder & Stoughton, 1936.)

KEY, PIERRE V. R. (in collaboration with BRUNO ZIRATO). Enrico Caruso. (Little, Brown & Co., Boston, 1922.)

KLEIN, HERMAN. The Golden Age of Opera. (Routledge, 1933.)

KOBBÉ, GUSTAV. The Complete Opera Book. (Putnam's, 1935.)

KOLODIN, IRVING. The Metropolitan Opera, 1883–1935. (Oxford University Press, New York, 1936.)

KORNGOLD, JULIUS. Die romanische Oper der Gegenwart. (Rikola Verlag, Vienna, 1922.)

MAROTTI, GUIDO (in collaboration with FERRUCCIO PAGNI). Giacomo Puccini intimo. (Vallecchi, Florence, 1926.)

MARTENS, FREDERICH H. A Thousand and One Nights of Opera. (D. Appleton-Century Company, New York, 1935.)

MELITZ, LEO. The Opera Goer's Complete Guide. (J. M. Dent & Sons, 1934.)

NEISSER, ARTHUR. Giacomo Puccini, Sein Leben und sein Werk. (Philipp Reclam Junior, Leipzig, 1927.)

NEWMAN, ERNEST. The Life of Richard Wagner, Vol. I. (Cassell, 1933.)

NORTHCOTT, RICHARD. Record of the Royal Opera, Covent Garden, 1888–1921. (The Press Printers Ltd., 1921.)

O'DONNELL, JOSEPHINE. Among the Covent Garden Stars. (Stanley Paul, 1936.)

SHAW, BERNARD. Music in London (1890–1894). Vol. III. (Constable, 1931.)

STEFAN, PAUL. Arturo Toscanini. Translated by Eden and Cedar Paul. (William Heinemann Ltd., 1936.)

TORREFRANCA, FAUSTO. Giacomo Puccini e l'opera internazionale. (Fratelli Bocca, Turin, 1912.)

TOYE, FRANCIS. Giuseppe Verdi, his Life and Works. (William Heinemann Ltd., 1931.)

WEISSMANN, ADOLF. Giacomo Puccini. (Drei Masken Verlag, Munich, 1922.)

INDEX

Abetone, Puccini's villa at, 28-9, 185
Action Française, Daudet's attack on Puccini in, 251
Adami, Giuseppe, 14, 142, 143, 198 *n.*, 228, 243 *n.*, 244, 311 ; on *Butterfly's* popularity, 59 ; his first meeting with Puccini, 214, 220-21 ; on the origin of *Two Little Wooden Shoes*, 232-3 ; entrusted with the adaptation of the *Rondine*, 255 ; makes a helpful suggestion, 255-6 ; his bad luck and good sportsmanship, 274 ; his big chance comes at last with *Turandot*, 313 *et seq.*
Adolphe, 52
Aïda (Verdi), 12, 81, 185, 190, 197 *n.*, 315 *n.*
Albert, Eugène d', 193
Alexandra, Queen, 98 *n.*, 153, 154, 189, 193, 209
Alfano, Francesco, 78 *n.*
Amato, Pasquale, creates the part of the Sheriff in the *Fanciulla*, 197
Angeli, Alfredo, 52, 101, 108, 282
Angeli, Maria, 52, 282, 284, 356
Anima Allegra (*The Cheerful Soul*), 144, 212-14, 220-23
Anna Karenina, 68
Ariadne and Blue-Beard (Ducas), 49, 135 & *n.*
At the Barn, 229 *n.*

Badini, Ernesto, as Gianni Schicchi, 305, 315
Barrie, Sir James, his uncanny gift compared with that of Puccini, 200, 201
Bassi, Amadeo, as Ramerrez in the *Fanciulla*, 208
Battistini, Mattia, is rebuked by Verdi, 111
Bedolo, Alfa, 307

Beecham, Sir Thomas, 65, 292, 297, 299, 303, 304
Belasco, David, 52, 53, 120, 201
Bellincioni, Bianca, as Manon, 240
Benjamin, Dorothy (Mrs. Charles Adams Holder), 159, 280 *n.*
Bernard, Tristan, 227-9
Bernhardt, Sarah, 41, 46
Bizet, Georges, 31, 221, 222
Blackmore, R. D., 211
Blue Bird, The (Maeterlinck), 192, 193
Bohème, La, 4, 15, 26, 48, 55, 56, 91, 106, 108, 200, 239, 262, 279, 338 ; unfortunate misunderstanding with Leoncavallo over the libretto, 31-3 ; Illica and Giacosa's share in, 33-5 ; first performance, and lukewarm reception, at the Teatro Regio, Turin, 35 ; its subsequent triumph at Palermo, 36-7 ; comes to Manchester as *The Bohemians*, 37-8 ; Melba's first appearance in, 39 ; shows remarkable powers of endurance, 40 ; Edward VII's favourite opera, 98 *n.*, 342
Bohème, La Vita di (Leoncavallo), 31, 33
Bohème, Scènes de la vie de (Murger), 31, 33
Boito, Arrigo, 34, 353 *n.*
Bonturi, Elvira. *See* Puccini, Elvira
Boosey, William, 242, 278
Buenos Aires, Puccini's visit to, 19, 67
Burke, Tom, in the *Tabarro* and *Gianni Schicchi*, 305
Burke, Thomas, his apt description of Caruso's voice, 109

Cagliostro, Count, 339
Caine, Sir Hall, 205
Caporetto, 250, 276
Capriccio Sinfonico, first brings Puccini's name into prominence in the musi-

THE END